Rewriting Wrongs

Rewriting Wrongs:
French Crime Fiction and the Palimpsest

Edited by

Angela Kimyongür and Amy Wigelsworth

CAMBRIDGE SCHOLARS

PUBLISHING

Rewriting Wrongs: French Crime Fiction and the Palimpsest,
Edited by Angela Kimyongür and Amy Wigelsworth

This book first published 2014

Cambridge Scholars Publishing

12 Back Chapman Street, Newcastle upon Tyne, NE6 2XX, UK

British Library Cataloguing in Publication Data
A catalogue record for this book is available from the British Library

ISBN (10): 1-4438-6133-2, ISBN (13): 978-1-4438-6133-5

TABLE OF CONTENTS

Part III: Imitation, Parody, Metafiction

ACKNOWLEDGEMENTS

As is often the case, a collective volume of this kind involves the participation of a number of people and organizations. This book has its origins in contacts made through the Popular Cultures Research Network based at the University of Leeds. These initial contacts led to the organization of a conference "Rewriting Wrongs: French Crime Fiction and the Palimpsest" which took place on the 14 September 2012 at Durham University. The conference was kindly supported by the Society for French Studies and brought together a group of scholars from Europe, the United States and Australia. The editors would like to thank all those who attended and participated at the conference for their contributions as well as for the discussions and debates that made the occasion such a valuable one. Thanks are also due to those who supported and encouraged in various ways, behind the scenes: Professors Diana Holmes and David Platten of the School of Modern Languages and Cultures of the University of Leeds and Dr Catherine Dousteyssier-Khoze of the Department of French at Durham University.

PREFACE

DAVID PLATTEN

Pierre Lemaître, winner of the 2013 Prix Goncourt for *Au revoir là-haut*, was previously well known as the author of *Alex*, a haunting noir thriller. In *Alex*, the eponymous protagonist, while incarcerated under some duress, makes her acquaintance with a troop of rats. This encounter is sustained over a considerable time, during which the behaviour of individual members of the troop is scrutinized as if by a zoologist. The rat is of course a totemic animal in some parts of the world but a figure of disease-bearing dread in the West. Intrepid British naturalist Sir David Attenborough shrinks at the sight of rats. He says his reaction is visceral but it is possible that his feelings are motivated culturally, conditioned by a series of negative literary representations: from the childhood warning stories of *The Pied Piper of Hamelin* and *The Tale of Samuel Whiskers*, emerging into the adult world of Orwell, Camus and now Lemaître. Despite their apparent ubiquity most people will not have an unpleasant personal encounter with rats during their lifetimes, in which case our typical aversion must well from a spring of cultural memory that Freud, in his 1925 essay "A Note Upon the 'Mystic Writing-Pad'", conceived as a palimpsest.

Derived from the Ancient Greek *palimpsestos* meaning "scraped clean and used again", the term is a sensual one, evoking the material density of parchment or the chemical magic of invisible ink. It is synonymous with the excavation of the past through the carbon dating of early Islamic manuscripts, the conservation of the famous Archimedes Palimpsest, and more recently the discovery in 2000 of the Novgorod Codex, the only known hyper-palimpsest, in which the latest imaging techniques have revealed the imprints of multiple texts on the wooden back walls of three wax tablets. In modern times the palimpsest has been used frequently as a master metaphor for learning and scholarship, reinforcing the notion that knowledge is compacted, as if in archaeological strata, rather than available through simple linear narratives. It was also developed by Gérard Genette as a tool of literary theory, allowing readers to establish precise, textual filiations but also to appreciate how meanings circulate in a wider literary universe, acquiring accretions and modifications. The magnificent culminating scene of Umberto Eco's *The Name of the Rose*, where Blind Jorge entices William of Baskerville to remove his gloves and turn the poisoned pages of the lost second volume of Aristotle's *Poetics*, is a palimpsestuous melodrama, a fusion of the material and the abstract, shooting meanings in all directions, like the flames engulfing the library where this ultimate confrontation occurs.

However, in theoretical terms the palimpsest is not a site for competing intellectual ideas or metaphysical systems; instead it is a force against entropy, helping to make connections and facilitate dialogue. In this guise, using the figure of the palimpsest as a focus for critical discussion is particularly helpful to students of crime fiction. This is because the genre has spawned different styles of writing and different, apparently incompatible reading experiences. The sealed room mystery has little in common with the blood-spattered extravagance of the serial-killer narrative, though both are categorized as "crime fiction"; one important publisher of European crime fiction in translation steers clear of excessively violent stories, as a matter of editorial policy. Most crime narratives reward the immersive reader, for whom the characters in the story are people who might even exist, or have existed, yet the genre also welcomes the calculating reader-detective interested in signs and clues and in solving puzzles, rather than in motives and emotions. But perhaps this polarization of the readers of crime fiction into the affective and the cerebral is too neat and tidy. Surely, good crime can accommodate both.

Inevitably, this leads us into a familiar cul-de-sac, of discussions about literary taste and value, of what makes a good crime novel. And this is where palimpsestic thinking comes into its own, because the palimpsest helps us to understand how texts are produced and consumed at different times and at different places and therefore how literary value can never be absolute but is contingent on many factors and will fluctuate over time. As Genette shows in his analysis of Michel Tournier's rewritings of Daniel Defoe's *Robinson Crusoe*, it can be used to illuminate the evolution of the literary canon, understood in its conventional sense. However, it can also be used to expose the steampunk tendencies of some fan fiction, or indeed the innumerable extensions of the "Sherlock Holmes" myth, some brilliant, some less so; Arthur Conan Doyle has appeared as a fictional character in at least twelve stories by eleven different writers. Moreover, the palimpsest can function as a platform, as it did one September day in 2012 at Durham University, upon which readers questing for the secret histories in the work of a writer like Didier Daeninckx, and others tracking ludic transpositions in postmodern "detective" fiction, two types of writing which would normally be mutually exclusive, intersected and found common ground.

Many of the chapters in this volume originated as papers at this one-day conference, which was conducted much in the image of its overarching theme. It might be stretching the analogy too far, but in theories of the palimpsest it is possible to glimpse an ideal, something important about research in literature and the humanities. For it presupposes the existence of what Pierre Bayard has called "la bibliothèque collective", a coming-together of minds, here students and scholars of crime literature, to discover and share knowledge without prejudice and in an environment free of hierarchy. The outcome, the book in your hands, is a true reflection of this ideal.

Introduction

Angela Kimyongür and Amy Wigelsworth

In an authoritative recent study entitled *The Palimpsest*, Sarah Dillon explains the palaeographic origins of a phenomenon traced back to the Egyptian era of the third century BC, when manuscripts were commonly reused and their original text overwritten (2007, 13). Thomas De Quincey wrote that "[a] palimpsest […] is a membrane or roll cleansed of its manuscript by reiterated successions" (1998 [1845], 139), and was not alone in emphasizing the processes of erasure and destruction. Indeed, a recent Oxford English Dictionary definition evokes:

> a parchment or other writing-material written upon twice, the original writing having been erased or rubbed out to make place for the second manuscript in which a later writing is written over an effaced earlier writing.

What these definitions neglect to acknowledge, as Dillon points out, is the inherent ambiguity of the palimpsest. In her words, the procedure had a "paradoxically preservatory power" in that "although the first writing on the vellum *seemed* to have been eradicated after treatment, it was often imperfectly erased" (2007, 12). Dillon uses the example of the Archimedes Palimpsest to illustrate her point. The document, sold at auction for two million dollars in 1998, is a Greek liturgical book, thought to date from the late twelfth or early thirteenth century. However, the remarkable value of the manuscript comes not from the surface document, but from the underlying text, paradoxically preserved for posterity: a uniquely important manuscript of Archimedes, with tremendous implications for the history of Greek mathematics and engineering (2007, 11–12).[1] The palimpsest, then, is defined by its tantalizingly incongruous marriage of the notions of destruction and suppression to those of preservation and creation. Superimposition, Dillon explains, is as much a "productive creativity" as an act of erasure (2007, 54), and the overwriting process can, in turn, engender a positive "reactivation" of the underlying layers of the palimpsest (2007, 112). Given this intriguing ambiguity, there can be little wonder that the palimpsest has been a source of ongoing fascination in many areas of cultural studies, and has developed into a fruitful metaphorical conceit used to define any cultural artefact that has been reused but still bears traces of its earlier form.[2]

Via two perceptive case studies, Dillon goes on to explore the specific resonance of the palimpsest trope in the context of crime fiction. In the first of these, she considers "classical detective fiction" (2007, 63–68), analysing Arthur Conan Doyle's "The Adventure of the Golden Pince-Nez" (1904) which, she observes, makes an explicit comparison between palimpsest reading and detective reading in the story's opening scene, where we see Holmes himself scrutinizing a palimpsest (2007, 64). Dillon explains that detective fiction contains two texts, as identified by Tzvetan Todorov in his "Typologie du roman policier" (1971 [1966]): the *fabula* (*fable*, or story), which criminal characters frequently attempt to erase or obscure, and the *sujet* (*subject*, or plot), or superimposed version of events. More recently, David Platten has evoked this arrangement in terms of a:

> dual narrative structure, in which the absent narrative of the crime gradually reappears in the pages relating the stages of the investigation, as if it had been written in invisible ink. (2011, 27)

Crucially, and perhaps inevitably, it is the story of the crime (we might also term this the subtext or urtext), rather than the story of the investigation or the superimposed version of events (the surface narrative) which is the focus of interest in the classical tradition:

> Like a palimpsest, the classical detective whodunit contains two texts: the story of the 'true' version of events which the perpetrator has erased, or attempted to erase; and the story of the ostensible version of events superimposed upon it […]. [T]he detective is involved in a process of palimpsest reading that resembles the practice of palimpsest editors in that its sole aim is the reconstruction of the underlying script - of value is that which is hidden or concealed, rather than that which is visible. […] Since the mid-nineteenth century, for palimpsest editors, to 'read' a palimpsest has meant to resurrect or uncover the underlying text; the overlying one is irrelevant. (Dillon 2007, 65)[3]

Classical detective fiction in fact exemplifies a distinction (that between *sujet* and *fabula*) common to all literary works, as Todorov himself acknowledges.[4] In much the same way, the preoccupations of "classical" and "modern" crime fictions must be seen to echo much more general perceptual shifts in interpretative criticism. In "Texte (théorie du)"

(1994 [1973b]) Roland Barthes explains how traditional interpretative criticism "cherche à démontrer que le texte possède un signifié global et secret". The text is treated "comme s'il était dépositaire d'une signification objective, et cette signification apparaît comme embaumée dans l'œuvre-produit" (1682). The structuralist view of the text as a layered palimpsest containing a hidden meaning, which the reader must retrieve and restore in order to interpret the text (Dillon 2007, 82–83) is clearly analogous to the obsession in classical detective fiction with the mysterious, underlying script. It follows that crime fiction has obvious metafictional implications, and these are a recurring theme throughout this volume.

In a subsequent case study, Dillon considers "modern detective fiction" (2007, 76–82), this time analysing Umberto Eco's *The Name of the Rose* (1984). Again, crime fiction can be seen to echo more general interpretative trends. The denouement of Eco's novel is especially significant in this respect:

> the final stage so crucial to detective palimpsest reading is frustrated: there is no revelation of an accurate correspondence between the detective's conclusions and the 'true' version of events as confirmed by their author. (Dillon 2007, 77)

The Name of the Rose thus challenges:

> the underlying assumption [of classical detective fiction] that reading can uncover the 'true' interpretation of a text, an interpretation that can then be verified by an author who retains complete control over the functioning of that text. (2007, 78)

Deduction gives way to abduction, and "detective palimpsesting" is superseded by "inventive palimpsesting", or a process of adding to the palimpsest, rather than paring it back.[5] As Dillon explains:

> ultimately, William's [William of Baskerville, the novel's detective] act of reading is a form of palimpsesting rather than palimpsest reading. He adds a further textual layer to the plot, rather than uncovering an underlying one. (2007, 79)

Eco's novel thus exemplifies his theory of the "openness" of narrative structure—"'open' works […] are characterized by the invitation to *make the work* together with the author" (Eco 1981, 63)[6]—which itself echoes the equivalence between reading and writing practices famously proposed by Barthes and his notion of the "writerly" text (1970),[7] by Iser's theory of reader response (1978), and by the endeavours of Borges's Pierre Menard (1983).

Eco's novel serves as a diegetic echo of the poststructuralist paradigm,[8] according to which the text as palimpsest is "no longer regarded as a layered phenomenon in which the hidden text is of the only significance" (Dillon 2007, 82). Rather than dissecting the palimpsest to uncover and separate the hidden text, poststructuralists seek to acknowledge "the interrelatedness of the texts on the palimpsest's surface" (Dillon 2007, 83). Dillon's description of "a surface phenomenon in which two or more texts are inextricably tangled and intertwined" (2007, 83) is reminiscent of Barthes's description of the text as "un espace polysémique, où s'entrecroisent plusieurs sens possibles" (1994 [1973b], 1682).[9] We have clearly arrived at Barthes's understanding of the text as *tissu*:

> Dans l'écriture multiple, [...] tout est à *démêler*, mais rien n'est à déchiffrer ; la structure peut être suivie, « filée » (comme on dit d'une maille de bas qui part) en toutes ses reprises et à tous ses étages, mais il n'y a pas de fond ; l'espace de l'écriture est à parcourir, il n'est pas à percer. (1994 [1968]: 147)

Barthes reiterates this new conception of the text in *Le Plaisir du texte*:

> *Texte* veut dire *Tissu* ; mais alors que jusqu'ici on a toujours pris ce tissu pour un produit, un voile tout fait, derrière lequel se tient, plus ou moins caché, le sens (la vérité), nous accentuons maintenant, dans le tissu, l'idée générative que le texte se fait, se travaille à travers un entrelacs perpétuel ; perdu dans ce tissu – cette texture – le sujet s'y défait, telle une araignée qui se dissoudrait elle-même dans les sécrétions constructives de sa toile. Si nous aimions les néologismes, nous pourrions définir la théorie du texte comme une *hyphologie* (*hyphos*, c'est le tissu et la toile d'araignée). (1973a, 85–86)[10]

Our new focus of interest is not the meaning supposedly hidden behind Barthes's "voile", but rather the veil itself, whose very texture, "dans l'entrelacs des codes, des formules, des signifiants" (1994 [1973b], 1684), is constitutive of meaning (Dillon 2007, 83). The origins of the metafictional propensity of crime fiction are, once again, laid bare: the challenges faced by the detective in relation to a given crime reproduce *en abyme* our evolving approaches to and assumptions about the text.

The conference which provided the inspiration for this volume, held at St. Chad's College at Durham University on 14 September 2012, with the support of the Society for French Studies, was conceived around the conviction that the palimpsest is a particularly fertile metaphor in the context of French crime fiction, and sought to encourage debate on the nature, function and specificity of the palimpsest in this particular context. Of obvious note in terms of the specificity of the palimpsest to French literary and cultural studies is Gérard Genette's *Palimpsestes* (1982), which is perhaps the most well-known application of the palimpsest trope to the field of literary theory. Genette uses the notion of the palimpsest to reconsider intertextuality as defined by Kristeva and Barthes, and to explore *hypertextuality*, or any relation uniting a *hypertext* to an earlier *hypotext* via processes of *transformation* or *imitation*:

> Cette duplicité d'objet, dans l'ordre des relations textuelles, peut se figurer par la vieille image du *palimpseste*, où l'on voit, sur le même parchemin, un texte se superposer à un autre qu'il ne dissimule pas tout à fait, mais qu'il laisse voir par transparence. (1982, 556)

As Genette acknowledges, hypertextuality is, in fact, universal, and this means that the study of literary palimpsests is open to interpretative excess (analogous to the "inventive palimpsesting" observed at the diegetic level):

> [...] toutes les œuvres sont hypertextuelles. Mais, comme les égaux d'Orwell, certaines le sont plus (ou plus manifestement, massivement et explicitement) que d'autres [...]. Moins l'hypertextualité d'une œuvre est massive et déclarée, plus son analyse dépend d'un jugement constitutif, voire d'une décision interprétative du lecteur. (1982, 18)[11]

As Genette suggests, reading a text with its hypertextuality in mind makes objectivity difficult, and the less obvious the hypertextuality, the greater the scope for subjective interference. Interpretation thus ends up adding a new layer to the palimpsest, rather than satisfactorily disentangling the elements already present. As Dillon puts it:

> palimpsestuous[12] reading is [...] an inventive process of creating relations where there may, or should, be none. As such, it always runs the risk of being false or fictitious. [...] palimpsestuous reading is also a process of 'imping', of extending, lengthening, enlarging and adding to the palimpsest one is writing on. [...] [I]n the process of reading the reader adds yet another text to the palimpsest's involuted surface [...] (2007: 83)

Crime fiction provides a privileged vantage point from which to observe this type of reading. As Genette explains, a palimpsestuous reading is, inevitably, a rereading, with the text read initially "pour lui-même" and then a second time "dans sa relation à son hypotexte" (Genette

1982 : 555).[13] The incongruity of such an undertaking in the context of crime fiction—which, at least in its traditional, popular form, is usually discarded after a single reading—means that palimpsestuous readings of crime fiction are acutely self-conscious.

Suspicions about the particular aptness of the palimpsest metaphor in the context of French crime fiction were also confirmed by the plethora of varied and fascinating proposals received in response to the call for papers issued for the Durham event. The organization of the resulting volume echoes the structure of the conference that inspired it: chapters are arranged into three sections that identify three broad approaches to the use of the palimpsest in French crime writing, though there is inevitably, and often productively, overlap and interchange between the three parts.

Part I, "Rewriting the Past", groups together crime novels that either rewrite episodes from the past, or whose authors evoke past lives and past identities in their writing. Claire Gorrara's "Figuring Memory as Palimpsest: Rereading Cultural Memories of Jewish Persecution in French Crime Fiction about the Second World War" begins a discussion of crime fiction and its intersections with the Second World War with what has become an iconic example of the way in which the multiple narrative layers of the crime story are particularly well suited to the uncovering of forgotten historical moments. Didier Daeninckx's *Meurtres pour mémoire* concludes with a very tangible image of the palimpsest that echoes the ways in which two sets of intersecting memories of racialized violence during the Second World War and the Algerian War of Independence are brought to light in the course of the novel. Drawing on the work of Max Silverman (2013), Michael Rothberg (2009) and Sarah Dillon (2007), Gorrara's analysis focuses on three crime novels, from three different post-war decades, in order to explore the layering of memories of the persecution of France's Jewish community during the Second World War. Silverman's model of "palimpsestic memory" is adduced to demonstrate the complexities surrounding the ways in which this difficult period of recent history is remembered and articulated in crime narratives. Sophie Watt's chapter "'Un passé qui ne passe pas'…. Un mystère sans cesse redécouvert" also invokes Max Silverman's work on "palimpsestic memory" and that of Michael Rothberg on "multidirectional memory" in order to consider the ways in which racialized violence has been depicted in contemporary texts, short stories, novels and films, that share a palimpsestuous textual structure and that range across traumatic episodes from the First and Second World Wars as well as from France's colonial past. Watt explores the ways in which these different textual forms, when read together and across each other, illuminate the echoes between past and present oppression and, in so doing, produce a critique of modern society. In "Arsène Lupin: Rewriting History" Emma Bielecki approaches Maurice Leblanc's Arsène Lupin books as novels whose intertextual practices in the early part of the twentieth century have a clear ideological dimension. Leblanc's appropriation of Conan Doyle's character Sherlock Holmes, eventually renamed Herlock Sholmès for legal reasons, is increasingly bound up with questions of French national identity; if Sholmès becomes a somewhat ridiculous figure in comparison with the quick-witted Lupin and if Paris is glamorized in comparison with a dreary London, Leblanc's intention is to bolster French national identity in the wake of historical crises such as the Franco-Prussian war, the Panama scandal and *Boulangisme*. The Lupin stories, Bielecki argues, possess a doubly palimpsestuous quality in that they purport to reveal truths hidden by layers of falsity whilst actually layering a fictional version of events over the historical record. Christine Calvet's *"Du récit à l'envers au récit de l'envers*: the Imprint of the Palimpsest in Simenon" takes as its focus another emblematic figure of francophone crime writing, Georges Simenon. Starting with the premise that Simenon's novels do not conform to classic generic expectations in that the resolution of the investigation is not their central element, Calvet examines three Simenon novels: *Les Demoiselles de Concarneau, Les Fiançailles de M. Hire* and *En Cas de malheur* to demonstrate how the investigatory narrative is overlaid by the re-emergence of past, hidden events that are not merely necessary to the framework of the detective story but are, above all, a means to understanding the characters' inner lives. The palimpsest is thus seen as a central building block of Simenon's wider literary project to write "le roman de l'homme".

Part II, "Textual Rewriting", shifts from authors and texts that use a palimpsestuous framework in order to investigate both public and private pasts to those for whom the palimpsest offers the potential for a fruitful reworking of an existing text, overlaying it with a new text through which the informed reader can spot traces of the original. Alistair Rolls's "Paris as Rewrite: Getting Away with it in Léo Malet's *XVe arrondissement*" is articulated around the argument that Malet's novel *Les Eaux troubles de Javel*, part of his series *Les Nouveaux mystères de Paris*, in which each novel is set in a different Parisian *arrondissement*, is a rewriting of his earlier work *Nestor Burma contre C.Q.F.D* which, like *Les Eaux troubles de Javel*, is set in the fifteenth *arrondissement*. Paris, or more precisely its fifteenth *arrondissement*, is posited as the palimpsest upon which the original crime was written and is now effaced by a new resolution of that crime, the space within which the original wrong is subject to a rewriting.

Andrew Watts turns to a different form of rewriting in his chapter on televisual adaptations of Balzac's *Une ténébreuse affaire*, specifically Alain Boudet's 1975 adaptation. Balzac's 1841 novel is particularly well suited to this volume's theme in that it has been described as the first French detective novel. While Watts agrees that it is not, technically speaking, a *roman policier*, it is nonetheless a work of detection, but also a palimpsest in that Balzac superimposes his own narrative over earlier texts, notably Walter Scott's *Rob Roy*, while Boudet's televisual adaptation of the novel evokes, not least through its casting, the traces of earlier television programmes that the viewer is encouraged to detect. Thus, the chapter analyses the relationship between the theme of detection and the inherently palimpsestic nature of adaptation, whereby the adapter grafts new meanings onto earlier texts. The final contribution to Part II is Adrienne Angelo's "Enigmas, Erasures and *Enquêtes*: Camille Laurens and the Palimpsest" in which the interrelationship between detective fiction and the palimpsest is seen to take a more ludic and self-conscious turn. The chapter explores Laurens's earliest writings, *Index, Romance, Les Travaux d'Hercule* and *L'Avenir*, as works that are both centred around crime, particularly crimes of passion, and marked by a porosity that enables the reappearance of characters, the multiple restaging of certain episodes, and intertextual citations. As in other texts discussed in this volume, our generic expectations of crime writing are frustrated, in this case through the subordination of the investigatory framework to a literary emphasis on the role of writing and rewriting.

The type of self-conscious and self-reflexive writing which can be seen in Laurens's work remain very much to the fore in the chapters that form Part III, "Imitation, Parody, Metafiction". The four chapters in this section explore the creative impetus behind works that deliberately set out to imitate others in order to create something new. Ellen Carter's "Taking Background Research Too Far? Caryl Férey's Cross-Cultural Borrowings" examines the cultural borrowings made by Férey, a metropolitan French writer, in order to add to the authenticity and credibility of crime works purporting to offer representations of Maori and New Zealand society from the perspective of the insider. Discussion focuses on a detailed analysis of two novels and their sources, elements of which surface in the novels as unacknowledged borrowings that Férey subsequently imported into his own work. *Utu* contains rewritten elements from Keri Hulme's *the bone people* (1985), while *Haka* borrows from the early pages of Victor Segalen's *Les Immémoriaux* (1907). Carter undertakes a detailed linguistic analysis of these borrowings and considers potential explanations for their use, as well as some of the cultural confusions resulting from Férey's choice to inform *Haka* (set in New Zealand) with borrowings from a source text set in Tahiti. Férey's choices are considered in relation to theories of Julia Kristeva, Gérard Genette, Marie Darrieussecq, Roger Little and Pierre Bayard, and Carter concludes that judgement of Férey's rewriting is made problematic because of the porosity of the borderlines between intertextuality, parody, pastiche and plagiarism, all of which have obvious connections with the palimpsest. In "*Filatures de soi*: Detectives, Disappearances and Deceit in the Crime Autofictions of Calle, Laurens and Nothomb", Elise Hugueny-Léger deploys case studies of a series of autofictional texts by Sophie Calle, Camille Laurens and Amélie Nothomb in order to explore the parallels between crime writing and autofiction. Autofiction has obvious affinities with crime writing as a genre frequently built upon a quest for identity effected through a search for clues and traces of the past. While acknowledging that the two genres are quite distinct in terms of intention, narrative devices and the use of plot or character, Hugueny-Léger examines the ways in which Calle, Laurens and Nothomb deploy, or indeed parody, traditional features of crime fiction in autofictional texts characterized by a ludic approach to the search for identity. In his study, "The Many-Layered Palimpsest: Metafiction, Genre Fiction and Georges Perec's '*53 jours*'", Simon Kemp continues the focus on the ways in which writers of self-conscious fiction, for whom the processes of writing and story construction often form the subject of their fiction, take inspiration from the structures of the detective story, particularly in its classic embodiment from which many crime writers have now departed. Kemp is at pains to emphasize the difference of Perec's "*53 jours*" from other detective metafictions that insist on distancing themselves from the genre, frequently using parody to do so. He contends instead that Perec's posthumously published novel is a "paragon of crime metafiction" in that it embraces the notion of crime fiction as a game played with the reader, celebrates it and encourages us to read it as such. Posthumous reworkings provide the critical focus of the final chapter in Amy Wigelsworth's aptly titled "Finishings Off: Murder à la Malet in Simsolo's *Les Derniers mystères de Paris*". Rather than a simple homage to Léo Malet's *Les Nouveaux mystères de Paris*, Simsolo's novel offers a continuation of Malet's unfinished series by having a serial killer provide, through the murders he commits in a number of different Parisian *arrondissements*, a palimpsestuous completion of Malet's original project. Detailed textual analysis of the novel's criminal investigation foregrounds the ways in which Simsolo resolves the tensions, implicit in Genette's definition of hypertextual continuation, between conformity to the original author's designs and the search for resolution on the one hand, and the value of innovation and open-endedness on the other. The palimpsest provides a delightfully problematic *grille de lecture* for our engagement with French crime fiction, poised *à mi-chemin* between its structuralist and poststructuralist avatars: the structuralist incarnation of the palimpsest—which, as we have seen, has notable affinities with the classical detective fiction model—often facilitates our understanding of a given crime narrative, by encouraging us to unearth an underlying text; but the poststructuralist manifestation of the palimpsest—that of a polyphonic, surface phenomenon, to which we, as readers, are invited to add our own, new layer—just as frequently problematizes our encounter with the text. Therein, we might argue, lies the ultimate appeal of the palimpsest: rather than resolving and removing the mysteries at the heart of crime fiction, and thus invalidating the genre, fictional "detective reading" and scholarly "palimpsest reading"—of which the present volume is itself an example— go beyond the confines of the structuralist project, proceeding to add new layers of complexity to both the narratives in question and the scholarly discussions they inspire, and thereby perpetuating, much to the delight of amateurs and scholars alike, this compelling and vibrant genre.

Notes

[1] See http://www.archimedespalimpsest.org/

[2] Fittingly, as Dillon points out, this new, figurative concept is itself the result of a palimpsestic process: "the concept of the palimpsest – which is at play in literary, critical and theoretical discourse subsequent to De Quincey – is a philosophical concept that has emerged from an erasure of its 'literal' or 'proper' meaning" (2007, 54).

[3] See also Russell (1867, 110–11).

[4] "[C]es définitions […] sont […] deux aspects de toute œuvre littéraire que les Formalistes russes avaient décelés, il y a quarante ans. […] : la fable, c'est ce qui s'est passé dans la vie, le sujet, la manière dont l'auteur nous le présente" (Todorov 1971 [1966], 58).

[5] Dillon observes the beginning of this shift (from deduction to abduction) in classical detective fiction—"Neither detective nor palimpsest reading […] are methods of deduction. Rather, both are practices of 'invention' – a word which means both 'to come upon', 'discover', 'find out' and 'to devise', 'contrive', 'feign' or 'make-up'" (2007, 67–68)—but notes that the element of invention involved in William's reading practice is much more explicit (77).

[6] Quoted by Dillon 2007, 79–80.

[7] '[L]e texte scriptible, c'est *nous en train d'écrire*' (Barthes 1970, 10).

[8] Genette uses the term *structuralisme ouvert*: "Car il y a, dans ce domaine, deux structuralismes, l'un de la clôture du texte et du déchiffrement des structures

internes […]. L'autre structuralisme, c'est […] celui […] où l'on voit comment un texte […] peut – si l'on veut bien l'y aider – « en lire un autre »" (1982, 557).
[9] See also Derrida's "Survivre" (2003).
[10] See also 1994 [1973b], 1683.
[11] See also Dillon 2007, 90.
[12] The adjective ("palimpsestuous") was coined by Philippe Lejeune in his Barthesian pastiche entitled "Le Roland Barthes sans peine" (1984). See Dillon 2007, 4 and Genette 1982, 557. Note the distinction made by Dillon between "palimpsestic", which "refers to the process of layering that produces a palimpsest", and "palimpsestuous", which "describes the structure that one is presented with as a result of that process" (2007: 4).
[13] Discussing Tournier's *Vendredi ou la vie sauvage*, Genette refers to a "lecteur imprévu et sans doute importun [qui] vient alors se superposer au destinataire recherché, et cette double « réception », par elle-même, dessine ce qu'on pourrait décrire comme un palimpseste de lecture" (1982, 523).

Works cited

"The Archimedes Palimpsest" <http://www.archimedespalimpsest.org/> [accessed 21 February 2014].

Barthes, Roland. 1994 [1968]. "La mort de l'auteur." In *Œuvres complètes Tome II 1966–1973*, 491–95. Paris: Seuil.

—. 1970. *S/Z*. Paris: Seuil.

—. 1973a. *Le Plaisir du texte*. Paris: Seuil.

—. 1994 [1973b]. "Texte (théorie du)." In *Œuvres complètes Tome II 1966–1973*, 1677–89. Paris: Seuil.

Borges, Jorge Luis. 1983. "Pierre Menard, auteur de *Don Quichotte*." In *Fictions*. Paris: Gallimard.

De Quincey, Thomas. 1998 [1845]. "*Suspiria de Profundis*." In *Thomas De Quincey: Confessions of an English Opium Eater and other writings*, edited by Grevel Lindop, 87–181. Oxford: Oxford University Press.

Derrida, Jacques. 2003. "Survivre." In *Parages*, 110–203. Paris: Galilée.

Dillon, Sarah. 2007. *The Palimpsest*. London: Continuum.

Doyle, Sir Arthur Conan. 2001. *The Penguin Complete Sherlock Holmes*. London: Penguin.

Eco, Umberto. 1981. *The Role of the Reader: Explorations in the semiotics of texts*. London: Hutchinson.

—. 1984. *The Name of the Rose*. Translated by William Weaver. London: Picador.

Genette, Gérard. 1982. *Palimpsestes : la littérature au second degré*. Paris: Seuil.

Iser, Wolfgang. 1978. *The Act of Reading: a theory of aesthetic response*. London: Routledge & Kegan Paul.

Lejeune, Philippe. 1984. "Le Roland Barthes sans peine." *Textuel*, vol. 15: 11–19.

Platten, David. 2011. *The Pleasures of Crime: Reading Modern French Crime Fiction*. Amsterdam – New York: Rodopi.

Rothberg, Michael. 2009. *Multidirectional Memory: Remembering the Holocaust in the Age of Decolonization*. Palo Alto CA.: Stanford University Press.

Russell, Charles William. 1867. "Palimpsest literature, and its editor, Cardinal Angelo Mai." In *The Afternoon Lectures on Literature and Art*, 96–132. London: Bell and Daldy.

Silverman, Max. 2013. *Palimpsestic Memory: The Holocaust and Colonialism in French and Francophone Fiction and Film*. New York and Oxford: Berghahn Books.

Simpson, J.A., and E.S.C. Weiner, eds. 1989. *The Oxford English Dictionary* (2nd edn), 20 vols. Oxford: Clarendon Press.

Todorov, Tzvetan. 1971 [1966]. "Typologie du roman policier." In *Poétique de la prose*, 55–65. Paris: Seuil, Collection Poétique.

PART I:

REWRITING THE PAST

CHAPTER ONE

FIGURING MEMORY AS PALIMPSEST: REREADING CULTURAL MEMORIES OF JEWISH PERSECUTION IN FRENCH CRIME FICTION ABOUT THE SECOND WORLD WAR

CLAIRE GORRARA

The figure of the palimpsest and memories of the Second World War have particular traction in the case of French crime fiction. The unsettling sense that widely circulating stories of wartime bravery and sacrifice cover over more troubling stories of guilt, shame and loss is common currency in French crime fiction about the Second World War.[1] Indeed, the palimpsest as a metaphor for intersecting war memories is given concrete form in Didier Daeninckx's critically acclaimed novel *Meurtres pour mémoire* (1984). As the novel draws to its end, Inspector Cadin and historian Claudine Chenet enter Bonne Nouvelle metro station whilst it is undergoing renovation. As they watch, an Algerian worker scrapes away at decades of posters on advertising hoardings:

> Claudine s'arrêta devant un coin de mur. Elle me montra un carré de céramique à demi recouvert de lambeaux de papier jauni qui résistaient aux efforts d'un travailleur algérien. On ne distingua qu'une partie du texte mais le sens ne s'en trouvait pas affecté: « … est interdite en France… coupable à être condamn… cour martia ... lemande … personne qui porte … sortissants jui … peine allant jusqu'à la mo… éléments irrespon … à soutenir les ennemis de l'Allemagne.....met en garde .... coupables eux-mêmes et la population des territoires occupés. (Daeninckx 1984, 215–16)

Peeling away the successive layers of advertisements reveals the German occupier's edict announcing the penalties should French men and women be discovered to have harboured Jews evading capture.[2] It is this "hidden" text of the persecution of the Jewish population in occupied

France that the novel intermeshes with stories of racialized violence
perpetrated against demonstrators on 17 October 1961 in Paris at the
height of the Algerian War. In the novel, these two histories are brought
into contact via the character of the perpetrator André Veillut, a scarcely
veiled reference to the real-life figure of Maurice Papon, wartime civil
servant and Paris police prefect during the Algerian War. As this final
scene of a palimpsestic layering of texts and histories in the novel makes
explicit, Daeninckx is invoking a model of memory predicated on
transversal connections—both transnational (France and Algeria) and
transhistorical (Second World War and the Algerian War). The fragmented
and elliptical form of the military notice in the metro station suggests that
the story of the wartime persecution of the Jewish population is one that is
difficult to decipher after so many years but can—and should—be read in
relation to other instances of State-sanctioned violence. The project of the
novel is to resurrect these histories, to make the "lost" voices of the past
speak, and to do so via a textual layering that sets memories of the
wartime past in relation to other apparently distinct events in twentieth-
century French history.

  In this chapter, the modelling of memory as palimpsest will be
explored in three French crime novels that represent the apparent loss and
recuperation of Jewish memories of the Second World War: Léo Malet's
Du rébecca rue des Rosiers (1958), Jean Mazarin's *Collabo-Song* (1981)
and Murielle Szac's *Un lourd silence* (1999). In each of these three novels,
spanning a fifty-year period, the focus of inquiry will be upon the
transversal connections that bring into contact different group memories of
the Second World War at a given historical juncture. Such "knotted
histories" (Rothberg 2011) of memory traces and intersections allow for a
layering of French war memories that brings to light often startling and
unexpected reconfigurations of the past. To this end, this chapter will itself
be a layered and composite investigation, as it will read these three crime
narratives across and through post-war French memory debates, as well as
through the work of literary and cultural critics, Sarah Dillon and Max
Silverman. Their work provides a departure point for reflecting on notions
of memory as palimpsest and for demonstrating how such a concept can be
mobilized to better understand cultural remappings of French
memories over the post-war period.

Figuring the Palimpsest

The work of Sarah Dillon on the palimpsest in literature, criticism and theory provides rich material for reflecting upon how the palimpsest as literary trope might intersect with the genre of crime fiction and with memory transmission (Dillon 2007). Firstly, Dillon highlights the metaphorical potential of the palimpsest as a means of approaching the multiple inscriptions of the past in textual practice. In her observations on the palimpsestic recovery of "lost texts",[3] she contends that the figure of the palimpsest connotes both literary erasure, an original text erased by an overlaid inscription, but also, paradoxically, preservation, as fragments of the original inscription are resurrected by the work of new reading practices. Secondly, Dillon makes a compelling argument for the connections between what she terms "palimpsest reading" and "detective reading". For Dillon, as with the structure of a palimpsest, the narrative economy of the classical detective story is predicated upon the recovery of a hidden text (the "true" story of the crime) which seeps through and eventually supersedes the surface text (the story of the investigation).

This modelling of detective fiction via the trope of textual layering is a productive methodology for rereading French wartime memories, above all those associated with the Jewish community. Such stories are often figured as rescued from beneath (or read through) the accretion of other wartime inscriptions. These other memories, be they those of resistance or collaboration, do not compete with Jewish memories but rather intersect and cross-fertilize with them. Indeed, the transversal reading practice generated by the French crime novels in this chapter is commensurate with Dillon's coupling of postmodern detective fiction—in this case Umberto Eco's *The Name of the Rose*—and a "palimpsestuous reading". This Dillon defines as "a process of reading that attempts to negotiate and do justice to the interrelatedness of the texts on the palimpsest's surface" (2007, 83). Such a reading practice is one that is attentive to the entanglement of textual layers (and memories), not their separation and arbitrary disassociation, promising connections that configure the text (and the past) in new ways.

Dillon's dual imagining of the palimpsest as a figure of simultaneous loss and recovery and her focus on the interrelatedness of palimpsestuous layers is a model of literary-critical practice that bears comparison with the work of scholars of French cultural history. In *Palimpsestic Memory: The Holocaust and Colonialism in French and Francophone Fiction and Film* (2013), Max Silverman invokes the figure of the palimpsest in order to capture the multiple connections across time and space of different histories

of violence within a francophone context.[4] Firstly, Silverman mobilizes
the figure of the palimpsest to demonstrate how, in the work of cultural
memory, the present is shadowed or haunted by the past. In Silverman's
formulation, this is a past which is not immediately visible but one which
comes progressively into view, setting up a relationship between past and
present:

> [in] the form of a superimposition and interaction of different temporal
> traces to constitute a sort of composite structure, like a palimpsest, so that
> one layer of traces can be seen through, and is transformed by, another.
> (Silverman 2013, 3)

As with Dillon's literary-critical model, Silverman's conception of
French cultural memory constructs the palimpsest as a privileged figure of
interconnectedness or entanglement, richly evident in literary and filmic
narratives. Secondly, Silverman contends that such a "palimpsestic
memory" is not simply a combination of two distinct moments in time but
the result of a cluster of apparently disparate spaces and times which,
combined, "create a different spatio-temporal configuration" (Silverman
2013, 3). This gives rise to textual inscriptions of memory that refuse a
linear history of past events in favour of a patterning of past and present
alive to the interplay of similarity and difference. For Silverman, as for
other cultural critics of "multidirectional memory" (Rothberg 2009), this
palimpsestic memory brings into view hybrid and overlapping histories. In
the cases of colonialism and the Holocaust, such a reconfiguration of
memory opens up a critical space for imagining what Silverman terms a
"cosmopolitical memory" (2013, 179), a form of cultural memory
sensitive to new solidarities that challenge conventional boundaries and
histories of nation and race.

Silverman's model of palimpsestic memory is an exciting one when
applied to post-war cultural production and the Second World War in
France. Firstly, it captures a sense of the superimpositions and productive
interactions of different inscriptions of the past over time. Cultural memories
of war are constructed as fluid, contingent and open to future transformations
that are powerfully engaged in creative acts of remembrance. Secondly, it
refutes a progressive teleological model of the evolution of war memories
that we might associate with now canonical studies of French war
memories, such as Henry Rousso's *Le Syndrome de Vichy* (1987). In
Rousso's psycho-social model of memory, dominant post-war memories
of national resistance in the 1950s and 1960s give way to darker memories
of collaboration in the early 1970s. These are superseded by resurgent
memories of Jewish persecution in the 1980s, heralding an era of

"obsession" with France's wartime past that persists into the present day. Cultural memory as palimpsest clearly challenges the notion that layers of memory sit in opposition to each other as discrete elements—resisters versus collaborators versus Jews. It generates instead a model of interconnectedness and emphasizes the extent to which each group memory is seen through, and transformed by, its relationship with other wartime memories circulating in the public arena at a given moment. Thirdly, palimpsestic memory draws attention to the ambiguities informing the many textual and memorial inscriptions of the past. These have the potential to interrupt each other; are inhabited by each other; only have meaning in relation to each other. There may be memory contest and conflict or memory consensus and convergence but there is never a definitive essence of the past. In short, palimpsestic memory highlights the complexities involved in attempting to understand why, how and what emerges when memory traces overlap, intersect and transform each other in relation to the charged context of war.

Layering Cultural Memories of Jewish Persecution in Post-War French Crime Fiction

Inscriptions of Jewish experiences of the Second World War in French crime fiction are many, varied and diffusely located over the post-war period. For whilst it has become something of a commonplace to herald the coming to awareness of a Jewish memory of the Holocaust in the 1980s, it is equally true that such cultural memories were never hidden from view and have, since the end of hostilities, been visible in popular cultural production, such as French crime fiction. The figure of the persecuted Jew, the exile, the collaborator, as well as the Jewish concentration camp survivor, are recurrent features of French crime fictions from the 1950s and 1960s, such as André Héléna's *Les Clients du Central Hôtel* (1959) or Hubert Monteilhet's *Le Retour des cendres* (1961), as well as from more recent decades.[5] However, these inscriptions have mutated in response to the cultural context of their production and in relation to other more dominant inscriptions of the past. In a palimpsestic modelling of memory, it is the tensions between these contextually dependent and superimposed layers of war memory that allow a contemporary reader to conjecture on the politics and poetics of French war memories. This chapter will now proceed to offer three sets of case notes for understanding shifts and transformations in cultural memories of Jewish persecution in French crime fiction, drawn from the 1950s, 1980s and 1990s. Each set of case notes will highlight a different cultural matrix for understanding the place of Jewish wartime experiences in broader French cultural memories of the Second World War: from displacement to entanglement and, finally, intersection. These successive textual and historical layers provide illuminating material for considering the agility and responsiveness of the palimpsest as a model of cultural memory.[6]

Case Notes 1: Displacing Jewish Memories

Léo Malet's *Du rébecca rue des Rosiers* (1958) forms part of the series *Les Nouveaux mystères de Paris*, published between 1954 and 1958. Each of the fifteen novels in the series is set in a different *arrondissement* of Paris with Malet using the city space as a palimpsestuous site on which to depict multi-layered histories where past and present intersect. In these novels, city space is no mere backdrop for action but an imaginative landscape onto which individual psychology and social history are projected. The history of the Second World War and the wars of decolonization are a recurrent reference in the narratives as their legacies trigger crime and disorder. In *Du rébecca rue des Rosiers*, the crime intrigue centres on a secret wartime history of Jewish persecution that re-emerges into the textual present of the late 1950s. Narrated from the first-person perspective of private detective Nestor Burma, the novel lends itself to a palimpsestic reading of different textual layerings of Jewish wartime experiences filtered through the generic conventions of crime fiction. For it is via Burma's equivocal narration, both sensitive to the horrors of wartime persecution but tainted with anti-Semitic stereotypes, that stories of Jewish perpetration, victimization and heroic agency are simultaneously disclosed and displaced onto the city space.

Du rébecca rue des Rosiers begins with the discovery of a woman's body in the apartment of Fred Baget, an acquaintance of Burma's and a well-known artist. This picture is complicated by the Jewish identity of the woman, Rachel Blum, and the collaborationist past of Baget who is fearful that the murder and subsequent investigation will lessen his chances of being awarded the *Légion d'honneur* to which he aspires. The murder weapon, an SS dagger with the German inscription "my honour is my loyalty" raises the spectre of continuing French anti-Semitism. This is reinforced by the language and reductive racial stereotypes of the novel, such as the derogatory terms Baget uses to label Rachel Blum ("youpine"), the casual racism of the police and the repeated reference to secondary characters and their supposed Semitic physiognomy and vices. Burma's investigation eventually converges on the figure of Saul Bramovici, a Jewish collaborator and Gestapo informant who denounced fellow Jews for profit and self-advancement.[7] He escaped at the Liberation and fled to London to run a crime syndicate. Now returned to Paris, Bramovici is living under an assumed name and is hiding in the wartime refuge of a Jewish family, all of whom, bar the son Samuel Aaronovicz, perished in the extermination camps. Assuming the identity of this Jewish survivor of the camps, whom he subsequently kills, Bramovici, the Jewish collaborator, masquerades as a victim of the Holocaust, hiding in the cellar where the Aaronovicz family sought refuge during the war years before their denunciation.

In the novel, the evocation of two particular city spaces complicates the ostensibly anti-Semitic discourse of the novel (the Jew as collaborator and murderer not victim). These locations function as palimpsestuous *lieux de mémoire*, haunting presences of the tensions surrounding Jewish wartime experiences in the France of the 1950s. The first location is Bramovici's hiding place, an abandoned house where the Aaronovicz family evaded their persecutors. It exudes an air of loss and desolation in the twilight rain as Burma attempts to make it yield up its wartime secrets:

> La maison en question est vraiment sinistre, vénéneuse au possible, surtout à cette heure crépusculaire et sous méchant crachin qui tombe. Sa façade s'écaille … Un des battants du monumental portail de bois est couvert d'affiches, la plupart en hébreu, et d'inscriptions à la craie. Sur l'autre est fixé un avertissement émaillé: DANGER. (Malet 2006, 225)

The graffiti, the Hebrew inscriptions and the warnings of danger are partial but visible memory traces of the house's past as a sanctuary for Jewish families. This is confirmed for Burma when he discovers the cellar used by the Aaronovicz family, a dark, damp crypt-like cellar suggestive of a burial chamber. Due for demolition, the house captures the horror of the war years and the temptation to erase Jewish wartime memories of persecution under layers of more valorous inscriptions of French resistance bravery, prevalent during the 1950s.

The second privileged location in the novel is the *Mémorial du martyr juif inconnu*, opened in 1956 in Paris to commemorate the Jewish victims of the Holocaust. This is a visible site of remembrance in sharp contrast to the hidden Aaronovicz refuge. It is here that Bramovici is stoned to death by Jewish families once his crimes are revealed, his body left for the police to collect at the memorial gates. The ritualistic nature of the punishment and its location at the *Mémorial juif* indicate a very different layering of Jewish wartime experience projected onto the urban fabric of Paris. Here, a wartime story of Jewish agency, rather than the "abyss" of Jewish persecution and denunciation linked with the abandoned house, ends on an image of the recovery of Jewish collective identity on a site which commemorates the victims of the extermination camps in the fourth *arrondissement* at the symbolic heart of Paris.

What might we make of this complex layering of Jewish war experiences as palimpsestic memory? Firstly, *Du rébecca rue des Rosiers* enables the reader to gauge the fractured and contradictory inscriptions of Jewish wartime experience circulating in wartime France in the early post-war decades. Like other French crime novels of the 1950s and 1960s, there is the disturbing recourse to the figure of the Jewish collaborator who denounces other Jewish characters to the authorities and expresses no remorse or guilt. On one level, this figuration can be said to confirm continuing post-war anti-Semitism in its stereotypical depiction of Jewish greed, avarice and betrayal from within the Jewish community itself. Such a figure could also be read as reflecting the memory politics of the late 1950s and early 1960s, transitional years in many respects—from one Republic to another; and from one war to another—and in which war stories of French heroism were in the ascendancy. French characters and France as a nation assume no guilt in Malet's novel, for guilt is displaced onto the Jewish community. Rather, *Du rébecca rue des Rosiers* sets up a particularist interpretation of war crimes in which crimes against Jews are committed by Jews and punished by the Jewish community. However, this is also a novel which reveals deep-seated tensions about what is and how to figure a Jewish experience of the Second World War. A palimpsestic reading of the novel would highlight the entanglement of multiple Jewish wartime experiences: the Jew figured as perpetrator and victim but also as an avenging agent of justice. Such a composite figure of memory could be said to stand in for a far broader meditation on French national guilt, responsibility and war crimes in the late 1950s: who was the hero, the victim and the perpetrator? Can a community and people be all three simultaneously? In a decade often linked with a dominant resistance epic, this novel reveals the "lost" stories that could still be read beneath and through such overlaid inscriptions.

Case Notes 2: Entangled Jewish Memories

Jean Mazarin's *Collabo-Song* (1981) provides a very different fictional iteration of Jewish wartime experiences. Unlike Malet's novel of the late 1950s, which confines Jewish wartime memories to the Jewish community itself (Jews as collaborators, victims and agents of justice), Mazarin's novel filters cultural memories of Jewish wartime experience through memories of collaboration, transforming them both in the process.

Collabo-Song follows the Occupation itinerary of a young Parisian housewife, Laure Santenac, and the circulation of post-war myths surrounding her sudden disappearance in the spring of 1943. It begins with a present-day investigation into her life history by an anonymous extra-diegetic narrator and then moves back in time to reconstruct her individual spiral downwards and her choice of collaboration. She moves from passive observer of the politics of Vichy to implication in the worst excesses of collaboration as the lover of a leading light of the French Gestapo involved in the torture of Jews and resisters. One of the innovations of the novel is to figure the lead protagonist as female and to focus upon agency, choice and responsibility. For in the narrative economy of the novel, Laure is not seduced or coerced into collaboration by the lies and falsehoods of male protagonists, but willingly accepts and benefits from the power and prestige that collaboration brings her in occupied Paris. This choice—personal and political—is intermeshed with a narrative of anti-Semitism and it is this layering of collaboration and anti-Semitism as war stories that constitutes a fictional instance of palimpsestic memory.

From its very first pages, *Collabo-Song* makes clear the banality of anti-Semitism in occupied France as Laure's husband, Edouard, is able to continue his career as a surgeon due to the support of a leading consultant known for his anti-Semitic views. Indeed, Laure's first act of collaboration comes in her denunciation of her new maid, Mireille, whom she supposes to be Jewish, having found tracts in her room warning Jews of impending round-ups. This act of denunciation is the tipping point for Laure, the first in a series of connected events that will see her denounce her own husband as Gaullist resister and then choose to align herself with supporters of Vichy and, eventually, Bernard de Monsoult, a French Gestapist. Yet, in the layering of fictionalized war memories, any polarized reading of collaborator and Jew is resolutely undermined as each group memory is read through and transformed by the other. For Laure's opposite in the novel, the betrayed Mireille, is in fact a German informant, placed in the Santenac household to spy on Edouard who, it later transpires, is the leader of a nascent Gaullist network. Yet, the figure of Mireille is herself a substitute having replaced the first "Mireille", Rosette Goldenberg, a Jewish student and resister, who is arrested and, the reader assumes, murdered in events preceding the novel. It is her German substitute who takes her place in the resistance network and her post in the Santenac household. Post-war, with only fragments of information available to the narrator, Rosette Goldenberg is assumed to have betrayed the resistance network when it is decimated and is condemned as a double agent, playing to the cultural stereotype of the collaborating Jew, so evident in Malet's fiction.

Yet, as the palimpsestic layering of collaboration and Jewish persecution multiplies in the novel, Laure, the collaborator, ends her life as a Jew, in an ironic twist of fate. With the tide of war turning, Laure takes up the suggestion of her Gestapist lover, Bernard, to escape with her considerable wealth by posing as a Jew and making use of a clandestine escape network. Visiting the unassuming Dr Eugène as Laura Goldenberg, drawing on the identity of the murdered Jewish resister Rosette Goldenberg,[8] her fate is sealed. The reader learns, in the novel's epilogue, that Laure disappeared in 1943, one of the 65 victims, mostly Jewish, whom the infamous Dr Petiot murdered in his apartment following the promise of escape from occupied France. *Collabo-Song* problematizes a clear differentiation of collaborator and Jew. Laure, the wife of a Gaullist hero, the denouncer of Jews and the mistress of a Gestapo torturer, ends her life as the Jewish victim of Dr Petiot, while Rosette Goldenberg, Jewish resister and victim, becomes the incarnation of the traitor whose name is taboo, even for her close relatives, as the extra-diegetic narrator discovers. Indeed, it is this female-to-female connection that accentuates how far memory traces of the past are imbricated in each other. As present-day witnesses deny knowledge of Laure's collaborationist past and Rosette's resistance credentials, one witness laments the difficulty of ever disentangling such narrative skeins: "tout n'a peut-être été si blanc ou si noir" (Mazarin 1998, 12).

As palimpsestic memory, *Collabo-Song* offers much to consider for the twenty-first century reader. Firstly, it signals how, from the 1970s, Jewish memories of the Occupation were being closely connected with other group memories, such as those of collaboration, and no longer perceived as a separate and marginal area of fictional and historical representation. This shift has to do with the pioneering work of French and American historians of the period who highlighted the systemic nature of collaboration in France and the extent to which Vichy had mobilized indigenous anti-Semitism to further its political ends (Paxton 1972; Ory 1976; Gordon 1980). Secondly, the novel highlights how far the interpenetration of collaboration and persecution would lead to a reassessment of both. As Silverman's model of palimpsestic memory demonstrates, such a modelling of memory helps us to understand the effects of the "superimposition and interaction of different temporal traces to constitute a sort of composite structure" (Silverman 2013, 3). In *Collabo-Song*, collaboration contaminates the legacy of Jewish resistance and Jewish persecution becomes the moral barometer with which to judge the crimes of collaboration.[9] In the final section of this chapter, focusing on novels from the late 1990s, the effects of these intersecting traces are made visible through and to a third generation of fictional protagonists.

Case Notes 3: Intersecting Jewish Memories

Murielle Szac's *Un lourd silence* (1999) is a crime novel aimed at adolescent readers and therefore offers a very different publishing context for considering palimpsestic memory and French crime fiction. As with other crime fiction marketed at younger readers, it has an implicit pedagogical purpose and makes use of a teenage protagonist to help readers identify with the dilemmas and debates of "storying war" in fiction.[10] This concern to understand the layering of the past in the present is made explicit in the novel's preface, entitled "Pourquoi j'ai écrit ce roman". Szac asserts:

> J'ai écrit ce roman parce que je suis convaincue d'une chose: chacun d'entre nous a besoin de savoir d'où il vient. Pas de liberté ni d'avenir sans mémoire de son passé, sans l'histoire de ses racines. (Szac 2009, 6)

Here the novel alerts the younger reader to questions of history and identity and the need to challenge which war stories have been transmitted and how.

Set in present-day Lyon, *Un lourd silence* affirms the complex layering of three interrelated cultural memories of war: collaboration, resistance and Jewish persecution. The teenage first-person narrator, Vincent, aged seventeen, begins the narrative intent on learning more about his maternal grandfather, Anatole Morel, who died in September 1944 but whose life and death are shrouded in mystery, apart from oblique references to his wartime bravery and sacrifice. Vincent has interpreted this as the resistance epic but, as he discovers more about this shadowy family figure, his grandfather is revealed as a member of the Lyon militia. As he attempts to untangle fiction from reality, Vincent develops a friendship with a wartime neighbour of his grandparents, Hanna, a Polish Jew who was denounced to the authorities by his grandfather, and whose daughter, Myrha, died in Auschwitz, aged six. Resistance, collaboration and persecution are intertwined as key figures in the main protagonist's entourage bring together a troubling nexus of guilt, responsibility and shame.

It is via the third generation and its filtering of the past that a palimpsestic memory emerges. Vincent's unveiling of his family's fantasy of wartime honour sets the scene for a full-scale reconstruction of French war memory as elements of the most valorous aspects of France's war, such as the Resistance, are tested and found wanting. Lyon, famously remembered as the capital of the Resistance, is the setting for Vincent's troubling role as an agent of memory, forced to pierce through the family myth in order to make visible stories of collaboration and persecution. The first of these, collaboration, literally rises to the surface in the form of a black notebook—a "hidden" text—which charts the last months of Anatole Morel's life from 23 October 1943 to 2 September 1944. It is to Szac's credit that the fictionalized entries build the portrait not of a monster but rather of an individual seduced by the authoritarian values of the Vichy regime. Devotion to family, a desire for stability, a belief in the rule of law and a limited intellect all offer some explanation for Anatole Morel's choices, which end in suicide.

In sharp contrast, no such complete picture of Jewish persecution emerges. As in Malet's and Mazarin's novels, the story of Jewish persecution is told in fragments since the underlying text of wartime horror is hard to decipher for the teenage narrator. On three occasions, he is given different but complementary visions of Jewish persecution: firstly, via the ageing and idiosyncratic Hanna; secondly, via the viewpoint of a member of a Christian organization in Lyon which attempted to save the Jewish children rounded up in Lyon in August 1942; and, thirdly, via an older friend whose knowledge comes from historical studies and research. Each version of the story of Jewish persecution condemns the French authorities as actively engaged in anti-Semitic persecution.

The effects of these intersecting war memories on the teenage narrator are twofold: firstly, they force a reflection on the ethical responsibility of post-war generations to remember such events and to attempt some form of emotional reparation. For Vincent, this begins as a rejection of his family's past, and his flight from Lyon to become homeless for a period. This gives the third-generation protagonist literal and metaphorical distance from his family and allows him to make the choice not to adopt the same "lourd silence" with regard to the past. Demonstrating his solidarity with others beyond the family, Vincent ends the novel reunited with Hanna, the Holocaust survivor, who absolves him of his guilt for the crime of denunciation committed by his grandfather. Secondly, the novel proposes a multidirectional model of memory in the spirit of Silverman's conception of memory as palimpsest by bringing together different voices, sites and times with the prospect of creating new solidarities and a "cosmopolitical memory". While Vincent works as a youth worker in an ethnically mixed suburb of Lyon, he comes into contact with other war stories of persecution but this time told from the perspective of the children of forced migrants. In one scene, the novel makes explicit links between the wartime persecution of Jewish families in France and present-day atrocities as young Farid mimics the distress and fear of his mother as a displaced person (Szac 2009, 90). Through this episode, *Un lourd silence* underscores how a rediscovered past of Jewish persecution can act as a catalyst for reflection on other global events, creating identification with displaced children as one of the most vulnerable groups in such situations.

Reading *Un lourd silence* as palimpsestic memory enables the reader to understand the extent to which Jewish memories of the Second World War are transforming in the twenty-first century. The separatist narratives of Jews versus "French" in Malet's text have disappeared, to be replaced by a far greater appreciation of how different war memories interrupt, reconfigure and inhabit each other. The layering of war memories in Szac's fiction enables transversal connections to be made with experiences and histories beyond France's borders. This posits the importance of generational transmission as a key facet of contemporary memory culture. Layers of past and present intersect and illuminate each other, whilst the transcultural figure of the "lost" child gives affective impact to the tropes of memory transmission. The reasons for this shift in the understanding and figuration of wartime Jewish persecution in France in the 1990s can be attributed to a number of factors: firstly, French State recognition of the role of the Vichy regime in the rounding up and persecution of Jews in wartime France, a recognition famously acknowledged by Jacques Chirac in 1995 on the fifty-third anniversary of the *rafle du Vélodrome d'Hiver*; secondly, the changing pedagogical framing of the Second World War in French classrooms, now studied within the context of a human rights discourse and a more internationalist appreciation of the war's prosecution and legacies. As *Un lourd silence* and other French crime novels of the last two decades make evident, rereading the wartime past through such layers of memory allows new configurations to emerge, as well as potential points of solidarity.[11]

Conclusion

This chapter has shown the extent to which a model of palimpsestic memory allows a different cultural mapping of war memories to emerge. This is a mapping that goes beyond the generic conventions of crime fiction and implicates far broader circuits of French cultural memory. It is a model of memory that looks for depth and relation rather than sequence and difference; this is not "my memory as opposed to your memory" but rather "my memory read *through* your memory". What such a layered reading of French war memories makes visible is the ever dynamic relationship between different memory texts, media and audiences. Supposedly repressed wartime memories, such as those surrounding Jewish persecution, can be recuperated, for, while not dominant at a given moment, they persist in traces that some texts make visible in surprising fashion as this chapter has demonstrated. Such a palimpsestic model of memory also allows twenty-first century readers to conjecture on memory formulations to come, as new inscriptions overlay older inscriptions, both national and transnational. Indeed, a palimpsestic model of memory poses the question of how the Second World War might be read across and through not only France's wars of decolonization but more recent events, such as the Rwandan genocide or the wars in Iraq and Afghanistan. As a mobile trope of memory, the palimpsest offers a powerful cultural tool for investigating our layered pasts and presents.

Notes

[1] This narrative patterning of the Second World War as a "secret history" is evident in more recent crime fiction which figures second- and third-generation protagonists who attempt to learn more of their parental heritage. Examples here include Thierry Jonquet's *Les Orpailleurs* (1993), Claude Amoz's *L'Ancien Crime* (1999) or Alain Wagneur's *Homicide à bon marché* (1996).
[2] In the epilogue, Daeninckx makes reference to advertisements for different brands of mineral water. The cultural connotations of Vichy and Evian mineral waters, for example, creates a circuit of fluid associations that gesture at the intersecting histories of the Second World War (Vichy) and the Algerian War (the Evian accords).
[3] Dillon also uses the evocative expression "murdered texts" in order to convey a sense of the violence perpetrated upon texts of former ages in the palimpsestic process of erasure (Dillon 2002, 13). This clearly resonates with both the historical and genre concerns of this chapter.
[4] I am indebted to Max Silverman for sharing a pre-publication draft of the introduction to his monograph for the preparation of this chapter.
[5] For a fuller study of the image of the Jew in French crime fiction, see Rozenberg Akoun 2004.
[6] The following case notes draw upon textual interpretations developed for my 2012 monograph devoted to French crime fiction and cultural memories of the Second World War. I thank Manchester University Press for their kind permission to make use of such analyses here.
[7] This is a clear reference to Joseph Joanovici, a well known Jewish collaborator who trafficked goods with the German authorities.
[8] The doubling (and substitution) of names and wartime itineraries in the novel is an effective marker of the "entanglement" of wartime group memories and identities as Mazarin constructs them.

[9] Margaret-Anne Hutton examines *Collabo-Song* as part of a broader corpus of texts that interrogate constructions of crime, criminals and the forces of law and order in her study of French crime fiction and literary representations of the Second World War (Hutton 2013).

[10] This term is taken from Mitzi Myers's informative essay concerned with fictional representations of war aimed at younger readers (2008).

[11] See Angela Kimyongür 2011, 371–81, for a study of contemporary French crime writer Maurice Gouiran and war memories. Kimyongür offers a stimulating reading of four of Gouiran's novels from the 2000s and focuses upon their representation of "lost" memories of war and the imperative to learn from such occluded episodes in French and francophone history.

Works cited

Amoz, Claude. 1999. *L'Ancien Crime*. Paris: Payot et Rivages.

Daeninckx, Didier. 1984. *Meurtres pour mémoire*. Paris: Gallimard.

—. 1991. *Murder in Memoriam*. Translated by Liz Heron. London: Serpent's Tail.

Dillon, Sarah. 2007. *The Palimpsest: Literature, Criticism, Theory*. London: Continuum.

Gordon, Bertram. 1980. *Collaborationism in France during the Second World War*. Ithaca: Cornell University Press.

Gorrara, Claire. 2012. *French Crime Fiction and the Second World War: Past Crimes, Present Memories*. Manchester: Manchester University Press.

Héléna, André. 2000 [1958]. *Les Clients du Central Hôtel*. Paris: Éditions E-Dite.

Hutton, Margaret-Anne. 2013. *French Crime Fiction 1945–2005: Investigating World War II*. Farnham: Ashgate.

Jonquet, Thierry. 2000 [1993]. *Les Orpailleurs*. Paris: Gallimard.

Kimyongür, Angela. 2011. "'The Beast Never Dies': Maurice Gouiran and the Uses of War Memory." *Journal of War and Culture Studies* 4.3: 371–81.

Malet, Léo. 2006 [1958]. *Du rébecca rue des Rosiers*. Paris: Robert Laffont.

Mazarin, Jean. 1998 [1981]. *Collabo-Song*. Cadeilhan: Zulma.

Monteilhet, Hubert. 2008 [1961]. *Le Retour des cendres* in *Hubert Monteilhet, Omnibus*. Paris: Éditions de Fallois.

Myers, Mitzi. 2008. "Storying War: an Overview." In *Under Fire: Childhood in the Shadow of War*, edited by Elizabeth Goodenough and Andrea Immel, 19–27. Detroit, MI: Wayne State University Press.

Ory, Pascal. 1976. *Les Collaborateurs 1940–1945*. Paris: Éditions du Seuil.

Paxton, Robert. 1972. *Vichy France: Old Guard, New Order 1940–44*. New York: Columbia University Press.

Rothberg, Michael. 2009. *Multidirectional Memory: Remembering the Holocaust in the Age of Decolonization*. Palo Alto CA.: Stanford University Press.

—. 2010. "Introduction: Between Memory and Memory, from *lieux de mémoire* to *nœuds de mémoire*." *Yale French Studies* 118–19: 3–12.

Rousso, Henry. 1990 [1987]. *Le Syndrome de Vichy: de 1944 à nos jours*. Paris: Éditions du Seuil.

Rozenberg Akoun, Nadine. 2004. "L'image du juif dans le roman policier français au XXème siècle: évolution et permanence." PhD diss., Université Paris VIII.

Silverman, Max. 2013. *Palimpsestic Memory: The Holocaust and Colonialism in French and Francophone Fiction and Film*. New York and Oxford: Berghahn Books.

Szac, Murielle. 2009 [1999]. *Un lourd silence*. Paris: Gallimard.

Wagneur, Alain. 1996. *Homicide à bon marché*. Paris: Gallimard.

CHAPTER TWO

« UN PASSÉ QUI NE PASSE PAS »[1]…
UN MYSTÈRE SANS CESSE REDÉCOUVERT

SOPHIE WATT

Je n'ai pas envie mais besoin de savoir ce que l'on a fait en mon nom.
(Daeninckx 2008, 17)

In "'Direction les oubliettes de l'histoire': Witnessing the past in the contemporary French polar", Charles Forsdick (2001) analyses the *travail de mémoire* of the "roman historico-policier" by visiting areas of history that have been ignored or simply forgotten. Numerous scholars have discussed the importance of the cultural, social and political history disclosed in French crime fiction, noting close links between the mechanisms of the *travail de mémoire* and those of detective stories. Through an examination of a number of Didier Daeninckx's detective stories and other fictions that follow a detective narrative line, this chapter will pay particular attention to the ways in which processes of remembrance and associated rewriting techniques in crime fiction are embedded within a critique of modern society. I argue that these texts not only generate the writing of an alternative historiography, but also anchor present-day neocolonial violence in an ongoing history of abuses.

A comparative study of Daeninckx's *Cités perdues* (2005) and two novels by Philippe Claudel, *La petite fille de Monsieur Linh* (2005) and *Le Rapport de Brodeck* (2007), highlights this phenomenon, whereby the process of remembrance brings together several traumatic periods of French history, while producing a critique of modern society. The multidirectional nature of the memory of traumatic events allows for these events to be read and understood as part of a wider historical narrative of nation-building. While the historical connections between particular traumatic moments in history, such as the Holocaust and colonization, have already been established by thinkers such as Hannah Arendt and Frantz Fanon, their resonance within French cultural production has been examined only recently by scholars such as Max Silverman (2013) and Michael Rothberg (2009; 2010). Drawing on Silverman's "palimpsestic memory" and Rothberg's concept of "multidirectional memory", I suggest that the *travail de mémoire* of *polar* history[2] and other detective-like narratives takes place via a multidirectional form of memory rooted within a palimpsestuous textual structure which eventually produces the writing of a continuing history of violence.

On the one hand, these novels rebuild and connect historical links through the palimpsestuous nature of the textual structure, but they also create a web of intertextual and cultural references which bring together a universal sense of suffering while keeping intact the uniqueness of each traumatic event. In order to show the ways in which this web of intertextual and cultural references functions, a second corpus of texts will be examined, looking at the ways in which the merging of traumatic histories is often cemented by an overflowing cultural intertextuality that brings together different narrative forms: photography and cinema. To exemplify this point I will examine the links between Daeninckx's *La Route du Rom* (2003) and two works by French-Algerian film director Tony Gatlif, *Latcho Drom* (1993) and *Liberté* (2010), which deal with the history of the persecution of the gypsy community. The cultural and discursive links between these three texts exemplify what Gérard Genette (1997) labels "paratextuality", which intersects in some cases with "metatextuality", engaging the reader/viewer in a critical reading of contemporary France. Finally, reading these texts together sheds light on the way in which the continuing history of racialized violence they reveal is inscribed within characters and within places. This phenomenon adds a further layer of meaning and reveals the depth and the ongoing sense of history rooted simultaneously within the corporal identity and collective topography underlying each traumatic moment.

Narratives as "multidirectional" memory

In her study of crime fiction as war narrative, Claire Gorrara argues that:

> memories of the Second World War can allow authors to make cross-cultural and transhistorical connections which generate reflection on present-day social violence and exile. (2012, 127)

This is particularly true of the authors studied in this section: Daeninckx and Claudel. Both demonstrate a sense of duty to the *devoir de mémoire* in the ways they revisit traumatic moments in one individual's history that parallel a traumatic moment in French history. Both portray episodes of persecution of and crimes against minorities. Perhaps more importantly, the varying sources of racialized violence overlap within the narration, creating what Rothberg calls a "nœud de mémoire", according to which:

> "Knotted" in all places and acts of memory are rhizomatic networks of temporality and cultural reference that exceed attempts at territorialisation (whether at the local or national level) and identitarian reduction. (2010, 7)

Daeninckx and Claudel explore the different directions memory takes when dealing with trauma, Rothberg's "multidirectional memory". This form of "knotted memory":

> considers a series of interventions through which social actors bring multiple traumatic pasts into a heterogeneous and changing post-World War II present. (Rothberg 2009, 4)

Daeninckx's and Claudel's fiction ultimately unearths the roots of an oppressive present.

In Daeninckx, this type of interconnection finds clear ramifications in contemporary forms of oppression. *Cités perdues,* a collection of six short stories, roots neocolonial and global racialized violence within French colonialism and the history of the First and Second World Wars, by revisiting the historical intersections of the two wars, French colonialism and neocolonialism. The juncture between the Holocaust in France and French colonialism also has narrative implications in the present-day working and living conditions of migrant workers and their marginalization within French society, as well as in neocolonial practices rooted in the global economy. The opening story, "Cités perdues", unveils new forms of neocolonial culture and practices anchored within the economic and political fabric of contemporary France. It sets the tone for the stories that follow. Commissaire Drovic investigates the murder of Ludovic Hakcha, an employee of the *Cormoran* travel agency, who has been found dead amongst the ruins of a housing estate building soon to be demolished. Early in the investigation, Ludovic is identified in the press as a Muslim fundamentalist merely because his father was Algerian and because his death is linked to the discovery that the travel agency is in fact an illegal private security firm (Daeninckx 2005, 55). Daeninckx uses the ongoing neocolonial context and prejudices to weave the narrative together and to challenge normalized assumptions about race and religion.

Such companies act as a front for modern mercenary armies—commonly called Private Military Companies (PMCs), lucrative businesses currently used by all Western governments. Illegal in France, they use different façades. The *Cormoran* travel agency provides private paramilitary forces to Western powers involved in Bosnia, Chechnya, Transnistria, Iraq and Afghanistan. *Cormoran* forms a parallel with the *Titania*, a company involved in the Abu Ghraib interrogations (87), that figures in the third story, "Dead day in Deauville". This story chronicles the life of a man responsible for the sacrifice of resistance fighters during the Second World War and who is now CEO of a PMC. In the global economy, wars represent a very profitable business, in which corporations such as Black Water USA and other PMCs have a vested interest (Scahill 2007). Daeninckx takes the reader into realms of corporate imperialism, where the privatization of violence is a form of oppression that has gradually grown out of and been learned from both the genocidal project that led to the death camps and from the colonial structure.

The historical links formed within and between the narratives of the different short stories herald a transition between the realms of memory and the writing of contemporary history. This process connects historical narratives together where they are usually read separately. The narratives push the reader towards a metatextual form of reading, allowing for a more critical interpretation of media stories which are habitually reified and isolated from their historical context. For Genette, "*metatextuality*" discloses "the *critical* relationship par excellence" (1997, 4). Daeninckx uses fiction to provoke a critical response from the reader. He explores an ongoing intertextuality between different narratives, constantly hopping between fiction and historical facts and events which bind them together.

Indeed, the use of a historically factual yet apparently insignificant event and/or place as a setting is a key component of Daeninckx's narrative technique. In the first short story, "Cités perdues", the event is the destruction of the housing estate *La Cité des 4000* in La Courneuve (Seine-Saint-Denis). This estate was completed in 1964 to house immigrants from North Africa, particularly Algerians. An attempt to renovate what had become a social and ethnic ghetto was undertaken in 1986, only to lead to its final destruction between 2000 and 2004. The demolition of its last building was the largest operation of this kind in France and took only 22 seconds.[3] The murder of Ludovic is echoed in the destruction of the ghetto. The need to silence the traces of oppression prevails and triggers the narration, not only of this story, but of the entire book, which can be read as a kaleidoscope through which the reader discovers and glimpses the past of those who were housed in the French suburbs following the wars of decolonization. The main thread can be followed from one short story to the next via a metonymic chain of violence.

In the second story, "Les chiens et les lions", the colonial troops used during the Second World War (in particular, the 25th regiment, the *Tirailleurs Sénégalais*, who fought and were killed by the Germans in Montluzin near Lyon in June 1940) represent the imagined past of the ancestors of the second and third generations of immigrants living on the margins of French urban centres and French society as described in "Cités perdues". The fate of the *Tirailleurs Sénégalais* in "Les chiens et les lions" is simultaneously reminiscent of the massacre of colonial troops during the First World War. This more distant past is explored in the fourth story, "Tu ne doubleras pas", with the massacre of those who stayed in the colony to build the first road in Senegal, and with their exploitation on the plantation:

> Si la France a besoin de nos jambes en Champagne, sur la Somme, au bord de la Marne, nos bras lui aussi sont nécessaires pour construire la première portion de route qui reliera les forêts de cocotiers au rivage.
> (Daeninckx 2005, 99)

The intertwining of the colonial troops' history in "Les chiens et les lions", and that of Préfet Jean Moulin's first arrest and torture for refusing to accuse these troops of looting and rape, resonates with the torture and killing of a resistance group framed for revealing the wrong information to the Germans in, "Dead day in Deauville". The sacrifice of these colonial troops is echoed further in the fifth story, "Rubrique sports", with the massacre of the Manouchian group.[4] The sacrifice of all these people, who have in common their foreign origins, is linked throughout to a betrayal and a sense of impunity that is finally countered by the detective-story framework that proposes a solution to the crimes of which they are victims.

The narrators of each story—like the reader—have the space in which to reflect on these intersections and to ponder some of the connections, which suggest that the narrators have an existence "between" the stories and shed light on the hidden roots of the societal order. The final story, "Initiales BB", is crucial to understanding the oppressive order. The narrative weaves together the history of the First and Second World Wars, the history of French colonialism and the ongoing history of neocolonial practices. The reader is confronted with a shift from the realm of remembrance to that of present-day oppression. It is with this shift that we see the emergence of a new structure of power articulated around a global form of control. New forms of memory appear as a result of this new structure of power and can be seen as acts of dissent.

The link between the neo-liberal order inscribed within colonial violence, the trauma of the Second World War and the wars of decolonization can be found in Claudel's two novels, *Le Rapport de Brodeck* and *La petite fille de Monsieur Linh*. The novels uncover a complex structure articulated around the trauma suffered by the protagonists. In both, the nature of the trauma is revealed gradually in the course of an investigation and is echoed within each text as they describe the nature and impact of racialized violence on the individual. Monsieur Linh, a Vietnamese refugee who has left behind a dead son and daughter-in-law, has emigrated to France out of necessity in order to care for his baby granddaughter. He meets a widower, Monsieur Bark, and they build a strong and intimate friendship. *Le Rapport de Brodeck* is the story of several investigations into the murder of *De Anderer* (*l'autre*), Brodeck's survival in the death camps, the tragedy of his wife Emelia's treatment at the hands of the soldiers and the villagers, and the hidden past and shameful present of the villagers. These narratives intersect around the violence of the trauma experienced by each character. Some of the villagers who have murdered *De Anderer* ask Brodeck to write a report. The writing of the report is split between the fiction of what Brodeck is expected to write and the reality of what happened. Brodeck decides to comply with what is required of him because he knows that *De Anderer*'s murderers will kill him otherwise. But he also decides to write the truth about the event which ultimately will survive in his memory and which brings him to write about the past of the village, that of the inhabitants and his own past. This second *rapport* represents a *mise en abyme* of the fiction and parallels the intellectual exercise of reading between the lines of any official history, because in this novel, the official history, *le rapport*, is a fictional version of the facts, while the truth is disclosed progressively in a parallel narrative.

As with Daeninckx's short stories, both narratives create a dialogue in the sense that Brodeck's trauma is reminiscent of that of Monsieur Linh. The multiple layers of history are exposed as the narrative develops. A network of secrets within each narrative creates and reinforces a dialogue between the two stories. Both protagonists are the product of resistance to an extreme form of violence. For both, life is their death sentence: "Moi, j'ai choisi de vivre ma punition, c'est ma vie," says Brodeck (Claudel 2007, 355). When Monsieur Linh survives a car accident, the narrator comments on Monsieur Bark's reaction using free indirect speech: "Son ami est vivant. Vivant! Ainsi songe-t-il, ce peut être aussi cela

l'existence!" (183). They are also closely linked by the *devou* .
"Le vieil homme se nomme Monsieur Linh. Il est seul à savou .
s'appelle ainsi car tous ceux qui le savaient sont morts autour de lui" (9).
In *Le Rapport de Brodeck*, the intimate link between memory and identity
is woven into the first lines of narrative by the need to write and tell: "Je
m'appelle Brodeck et je n'y suis pour rien. Je tiens à le dire. Il faut que
tout le monde le sache" (11), and again into the final lines after Brodeck
has decided to leave the village: "Je m'appelle Brodeck, et je n'y suis pour
rien. Je m'appelle Brodeck, c'est mon nom. Brodeck. De grâce, souvenez-
vous. Brodeck" (416).

Unlike those in Daeninckx's stories, Claudel's narrators are never
explicit enough to reveal exactly the source and site of extreme violence.
In fact, Claudel's novels retain a purposefully vague sense of history. It is
down to the reader to match up the narratives with the history. Yet both
Claudel and Daeninckx achieve a similar result, either with the precision
of a historian about the source of the violence or through the elliptical
nature of the trauma. They both reach a universal sense of suffering that
has been normalized and accepted by official history. In Claudel's novels,
the elliptical narrative technique, which nonetheless provides a very
specific vocabulary of suffering, gives both texts a universal dimension. In
La petite fille de Monsieur Linh, the level of violence strikes the reader
retrospectively when Linh's granddaughter, who has been the object of all
his attention and his reason for living, is revealed to be nothing more than
a plastic doll. The first description of the little girl that accompanies the
evocation of the death of her parents re-emerges in the memory of the
reader who then realizes that that she had been decapitated:

> Il y avait le corps de son fils, celui de sa femme, et plus loin la petite, les
> yeux grands ouverts, emmaillotée, indemne, et à côté de la petite une
> poupée, sa poupée, aussi grosse qu'elle, à laquelle un éclat de bombe avait
> arraché la tête. (Claudel 2005, 13)

The violence of the trauma is revealed through the narrative tools of
the prolepsis and the analepsis with which the novel begins and ends. It is
thus only when the reader reaches the end of the story that he realizes the
truth; that what we believed to be a doll is actually the baby girl. The
horror of the reality of the war shocks the reader *a posteriori*. This mental
image reveals the nature and intensity of Monsieur Linh's trauma.

Brodeck's first mention of his time in the camps comes after he recalls
meeting Fédorine, "au début d'une autre guerre", when as a child he was
the only survivor in his village: "Regarde bien petit Brodeck, tu viens de là
et tu n'y retourneras plus car il ne restera plus rien de lui bientôt" (Claudel

2007, 29). His memory of this tragic moment merges, within a few lines, with his memory of the camp: "les gardes ne m'appelaient plus Brodeck mais *Chien Brodeck*" (30). In both novels the title is indicative of this indirect way of portraying the identity of the protagonists. *Le rapport*, and the process of writing it, reveal a great deal about Brodeck's need to tell: "Je tiens à le dire" (11); "tu sais écrire, tu sais les mots, et comment on les utilise et comment ils peuvent dire les choses" (11); "Tu diras le wagon, tu diras, tu raconteras, tu diras tout" (78). Yet Brodeck constantly reasserts the impossiblity of telling and his enduring desire to forget: "J'aurais aimé ne jamais en parler" (11); "Je le redis, moi, j'aurais pu me taire, mais ils m'ont demandé de raconter [...]" (14). The narrative is structured as a constant deferral of the truth. While Brodeck is reluctant to reveal and name it, the truth unfolds: *De Anderer*'s death and Brodeck's social death are revealed by the use of preterition as a way of distancing himself from the narrative: "the paradoxical figure of affirmation and denial, of saying and not saying [...]".[5] Yet, what is at the core of Brodeck's narrative is his own crime. The recounting of how, in the train taking them to the camp, Brodeck steals the last drops of water from a woman and her baby, is triggered by the absurdity of the crime against *De Anderer*'s animals when the villagers decide to let his horse and donkey drown. Brodeck himself is revealed as a murderer and becomes "*Chien Brodeck*" (355). Brodeck finds himself in Primo Levi's moral "Grey Zone": "Now nobody can know for how long and under what trials his soul can resist before yielding or breaking" (60). Both Brodeck and Monsieur Linh have had their life spared but have been robbed of their humanity and sanity; Brodeck goes on to commit a crime while Monsieur Linh loses his mind. Brodeck's wife, Emilia, gang-raped by the soldiers and some villagers while attempting to save three foreign girls, is the only one of the women to survive, but, like Monsieur Linh, loses her sanity and can no longer function in everyday life. In all cases, trauma radically changes the victim's personality.

The content of both Claudel's narratives is sensational and yet heavily marked by a sense of commonality. On the one hand, the reader is constantly reminded of the banality of the perceived event and of the protagonist. Yet the events at the core of the narration demonstrate an extraordinary level of violence. The juxtaposition of both the banal and the sensational can almost be read as a hiatus that forces the reader beyond the individual history. In *Le Rapport de Brodeck*, Brodeck says of himself "Je ne suis rien" (24). This common experience of trauma can also be seen in Monsieur Linh:

Ils sont des centaines, comme eux. Vieux, jeunes, attendant docilement, leurs maigres effets à côté, attendant sous un froid tel qu'ils n'en ont jamais connu qu'on leur dise où aller. Aucun ne se parle. Ce sont de frêles statues aux visages tristes, et qui grelottent dans le plus grand des silences. (2005, 12)

This description of the refugees with whom Monsieur Linh arrives breaches the specific and personal history and could be applied to other sufferers. It can be read as a description of prisoners in a death camp. In the apportioning of violence there is a form of universality that reminds the reader that the victim could indeed be anyone. The uniqueness of the trauma is never questioned, but the universal condition of suffering is reinforced:

Nous étions devenus des ombres pareilles les unes aux autres. On pouvait nous confondre, on pouvait en éliminer quelques-unes chaque jour, parce qu'on pouvait en ajouter quelques autres tout aussitôt, et cela ne se voyait pas. Les mêmes silhouettes et les mêmes visages osseux occupaient toujours le camp. Nous n'étions plus nous-mêmes. Nous ne nous appartenions plus. Nous n'étions plus des hommes. Nous n'étions qu'une espèce. (2007, 90)

In *La petite fille de Monsieur Linh*, the dedication speaks for itself: "*A tous les Monsieur Linh de la terre et à leurs petites filles*". Each traumatic story is personal to Brodeck, Emilia and Monsieur Linh, and yet resonates for all individuals persecuted and uprooted during any war. The contrast with the level of violence is often implicit and suggested without historical precision and links both personal stories to the universal trauma of violence. As Rothberg observes, "when the productive, intercultural dynamic of multidirectional memory is explicitly claimed [...], it has the potential to create new forms of solidarity and new visions of justice" (2009, 5). The sense of universality transmitted by the merging of historical narratives and traumas is also often disclosed by some form of cultural intertextuality.

Overflowing cultural intertextuality: from narrative to photography, cinema and topography

The merging of traumatic histories is in a few cases not limited to text but reaches other types of cultural production, creating an echo effect around the same traumatic event. One of Claudel's narrative techniques in *Le Rapport de Brodeck* is to borrow sentences from other texts such as *Le*

Défi de la molécule by Primo Levi. Brodeck feels the need to tell *De Anderer* about Emilia's rape and upon asking forgiveness for confiding in him, Brodeck receives the following answer from *De Anderer*: "Ne vous excusez pas, dit-il d'une voix aussi imperceptible qu'un souffle, je sais que raconter est un remède sûr" (2007, 300). Unlike Primo Levi, whose experience in Auschwitz was recounted, Brodeck's report is destroyed despite his survival. At the novel's conclusion, he is no longer *le chien Brodeck* from the camps but *Brodeck*, which is the final word of the novel. The recollection of his name is highly symbolic since the journey of writing the report has allowed him to claim back his name: "raconter est un remède sûr".

The name is also at the core of another Daeninckx novel: *La Route du Rom* (2003). The name and story of Antonio Cuevas, sterilized during the war because of his gypsy origins, is inscribed on the walls of the camp where he was imprisoned. His fate is echoed in the name of his nephew Jesús, a musician who appears in Tony Gatlif's 2000 film *Vengo*, and who is killed in the cellar of the school which was once the camp where Antonio was imprisoned, and where he discovers the name of his uncle on the walls. Gabriel Lecouvreur, aka Le Poulpe, investigates the murder of Jesús and eventually uncovers the tragic story of his uncle. This detective structure unveils the dark side of the fate of gypsies during the war and resonates with the images and sounds of other texts. This merging is cemented by an overflowing cultural intertextuality which brings together different narrative forms: photography and cinema. It creates a web of meanings implying that culture is "a *site of struggle*".[6] In *La Route du Rom*, the ways in which the narrative is anchored within contemporary cultural production in France becomes clearer as the narrative unfolds. There was a concentration camp (although not used just for Tziganes) located in a school in the centre of Valognes.[7] Daeninckx used the memoirs of one soldier, G K Roessler, in order to recreate this real-life camp in a fictional town "Corneville" (Strainchamps 2010).

The history of the reality behind the concentration camps used in occupied France for the internment of gypsies was unveiled by photographer Mathieu Pernot in his book, *Un Camp pour les bohémiens* (2001). His illustrations, which originate from archival sources of *passeports anthropométriques* that the gypsies were required to have signed by an employee at the town council of each town to which they travelled, evoke the ID image on the cover of Daeninckx's book.[8] After reading the story of Antonio Cuevas, which begins with "ils m'ont confisqué mon carnet anthropométrique" (Daeninckx 2003, 21), one cannot ignore the importance of the image as part of the process of identifying, stigmatizing and persecuting. The intertextuality is extended further into the cultural sphere with Daeninckx's epigraph "Au Vengo de Tony Gatlif" and is pursued within his narrative through the characters Jesús and Gabriel, who meet on the set of *Vengo*. This metatextuality is plural, multidirectional and active. Another level of intertextuality is indicated in the fate of the gypsies who were sent to Auschwitz, which, although never named, is clearly evoked:

> Mon grand-père, Manuel Cuevas dit le Hongroyeur, habitait ici, dans cette région. Il a disparu en compagnie d'un demi-million de Roms. Parti en fumée comme les bûches de ta cheminée. (2003, 191)

The reference is unmistakeable and is underlined by the fact that Andrés, Jesús's friend, talks to the same doctor who sterilized Jesús's uncle at the camp in Valognes. This intertextuality, with Gatlif's films on the one side, and the underlying history of the fate of the gypsies in Auschwitz on the other, is reinforced for those familiar with another of Gatlif's films, *Latcho Drom*[9] (1993) in which one scene directly refers to the atrocities endured by the gypsy community in Auschwitz. It opens with a close-up shot of barbed wire next to train tracks and a travelling shot takes the viewer to the footprints of a woman accompanied by what begins as an extra-diegetic song about the suffering of the gypsies in Auschwitz, and ends with a diegetic song sung by the same woman. A series of close-ups on her face, and hands holding a cigarette, follow the smoke drifting up through the barbed wire. The sequence ends with a close-up of her arm, revealing her tattooed matriculation number, followed by a travelling shot along the small river and the melting ice.

The racialized violence endured by all these protagonists is often inscribed within their body, creating concrete links between memory and identity. Marked, mutilated or amputated, the image of an atrophied body becomes the materialization of suffering. This is without doubt the strongest narrative link that brings these texts together. Triggered by a "crime", and the discovery of a dead body, these texts are also unified by the fact that other protagonists bear the stigma of the crime committed against the individual and of crimes against humanity. These crimes are metonymically inscribed within the bodies of the protagonists. In *La Route du Rom*, the secret resides in the body of Antonio, sterilized as a young man and unable to recover from physical torture. He has left the family with whom he was living and the woman he loved to lead a sedentary life running a cinema because of the shame of being unable to have a family. Monsieur Linh's mental health is the secret in Claudel's novel. His granddaughter, rescued from the Vietnam War, is in fact a plastic doll that

Monsieur Linh holds onto as if it were a vital part of his identity. Yet his real granddaughter, as the reader realizes towards the narrative's close, has been decapitated. Brodeck is often described as physically and mentally damaged by what happened to him in the camp. His physical description echoes his mental state and difficulties of engaging with the world around him. He often insists on the description of his body during his stay at the camps: "J'avais pourtant le corps d'un mort" (Claudel 2007, 81) and shortly after: "Je ne savais plus sourire" (91). His wife Emilia has been affected mentally by the collective rape to which she was subjected and can no longer function: "son âme errait quelque part, je ne savais où, mais je me suis juré d'aller l'y reprendre [...]" (298). In the fourth story of *Cités perdues,* "Tu ne doubleras pas", the Senegalese boy loses his arm while fighting in France. In the other short stories the practice of torture is a constant reference. The metonymic chain of violence has its ramifications in the physical and mental state of all these characters. They bear the physical traces of the violence to which they have been subjected, just as the places where the violence occurred still retain traces of racialized violence despite the passage of time.

The reading of these narratives, inscribed and anchored within geography, forces us to realize the extent to which the places described are semantically linked. French urban (and rural) spaces bear the traces of the racialized violence unveiled by their representation in the narratives. In *La Route du Rom*, Daeninckx reveals a shameful side of French history. Seven concentration camps were created specifically for gypsies.[10] The concentration camp in Valognes is now a private school, whose website makes no mention of the building's history. In Daeninckx's narrative, Antonio's story is inscribed on the walls of the school's cellar (which is also where Jesús, his nephew, is shot). In *Cités perdues*, the *cité* and the destruction of the buildings is the site for the discovery of Ludovic's body. This *cité* is in the same geographical area as Drancy, the location of the transit camp where Jews were held before being sent to Auschwitz. In *Cités perdues*'s last short story, "Initiales BB", the notion of lost spaces and lost histories is reinforced by the continuing colonization of spaces in the post-industrial era that discloses the need to erase chapters of history, while in Claudel's novels, the geographical references are very allusive, which reinforces the fact that the locations could be anywhere.

The intertextual dialogue going back and forth between Daeninckx and Gatlif continues in *Liberté*, Gatlif's 2010 film dedicated to the deportation of a gypsy family to the camp of Malines in Belgium and eventually to Auschwitz in convoy Z on 15 January 1944. The opening scene of the film is a close-up of the barbed wire of a camp, a close-up very reminiscent of the scene in *Latcho Drom* where the camp survivor is singing. The barbed wire of the opening shot in *Liberté* vibrates at the sound of the extra-diegetic piano music as if the wires were the strings of an instrument. These multiple layers of signification are reminiscent of a palimpsestic form of writing and memory-building, as analysed by Silverman. Rooted in Rothberg's *nœud de mémoire*, Silverman argues that these interconnections take the shape of condensed spatio-temporal traces (2013, 25–26). For Silverman, these layers of meaning are connected via different narrative techniques that allow for different moments of racialized violence to echo each other within the cultural memory of the French nation. As Rothberg notes, it is within this process of "inscription and reinscription, coding and recoding" (2010, 7) that multidirectional memory incorporates the direction of the present and gradually fuses with history as it happens. The narrative becomes, then, a text of reference in which historical data and archival documents can be located and reused.

The need for the authors discussed here to borrow fragments of forgotten and/or repressed history, as well as to evoke places marked by the violence of trauma and that have subsequently been asepticized and/or destroyed, discloses a project of rewriting wrongs. These works were published between 2003 and 2007 and share the same pattern of a mystery being constantly rediscovered. Bringing together the same traumatic moments in French history, while weaving them within the hermeneutics of crime fiction, serves to help understand present and ongoing forms of oppression. The narrative structure of a crime story allows a form of metatextuality to take place. Daeninckx's text critically addresses Gatlif's films on the subject. Brodeck comments on the links between his personal history and History:

> Je songeais à l'Histoire, la grande, et à la mienne d'histoire à la nôtre, ceux qui écrivent la première connaissent-ils la seconde? […] vivre et continuer à vivre, c'est peut-être décider que le réel ne l'est pas tout à fait. (Claudel 2007, 360)

These works contribute to the writing of an alternative historiography, but most importantly, they train the reader to engage in a metatextual form of reading.

Intertextuality and, specifically, metatextuality are at the core of the rewriting process and create a palimpsestuous sense of memory. This multi-textual layer of information allows the reader to reflect on society and to make connections with the past. What is striking in these works is that this multi-textual layer of information is also firmly rooted within a landscape of violence, which anchors the present in the past.

Conclusion

For Michel de Certeau, the writing of history is the systematic organization of a social writing, the way in which society organizes itself as a text, as a technocratic system.[11] Using the example of May '68, de Certeau argues that he understands the event as the oral expression that made possible the eruption of a challenge to the system of social representation. The texts that disclose a multidirectional form of memory and produce an alternative historiography are the product of a form of dissent. They contest the system by which society is represented and offer an alternative paradigm.

The detective narrative structure reinforces the quest for a critical understanding of the present. The progressive weaving of multiple narratives, the cultural and historical intertextuality of the First and Second World Wars, the history of French colonialism and the enduring history of neocolonial practices together, finally discloses a shift from the realms of remembrance to the realms of present-day and ongoing oppression. This shift gives way to the process of writing history, which reveals a palimpsestuous sense of identity in the protagonists as well as in the reader and viewer.

Notes

[1] This expression is borrowed from Henry Rousso and Eric Conan's *Vichy, un passé qui ne passe pas* (1994).
[2] For Kristin Ross, *polar* history's principal characteristic is the writing of an alternative historiography (2010).
[3]   http://fresques.ina.fr/jalons/fiche-media/InaEdu01839/la-destruction-de-deux-barres-d-immeubles-a-la-cite-des-4000-de-la-courneuve.html
[4] The *groupe Manouchian* was formed during the Occupation and was a resistance group led by Missak Manouchian and involved with the FTP-MOI (*Francs-tireurs et partisans – Main-d'œuvre immigrée*) in Paris. The group was ambushed and arrested in November 1943 and its members executed in February 1944. Didier Daeninckx has written another four books and comics about Missak Manouchian and the group: *Viva la liberté, 1939–1945* la Résistance (tome III) (2004), *Carton jaune!* (2004), *Missak, l'enfant de l'affiche rouge* (2009), *Avec le groupe Manouchian: Les immigrés dans la résistance* (2010). In 2009, Robert Guédiguian directed the film *L'armée du crime* as an act of homage to the Manouchian group.
[5] This is reminiscent of Susan Suleiman's analysis (2006).
[6] Gorrara uses John Storey's analysis to remind the reader of one of the pillars of analysis within the Marxist tradition: that culture is a *site of struggle* for meaning (2012, 11).

[7] Founded in 1904, the school was a girls' school, the *Institution Sainte Marie*. From 1940 to 1944, the building was occupied by the Germans and the school had to move to a Benedictine convent.

[8] These *passeports* have nowadays been replaced by the *carnet de circulation*. In February 2011 the National Assembly rejected a bill to put an end to discriminatory measures against the gypsy community.

[9] In Romany, *Latcho Drom* means "bonne route".

[10] Linas-Montlhéry, Jargeau, Goudrecieux, Moisdon-la Rivière, Montreuil-Bellay, Angoulême, Saliers.

[11] Radio interview with Michel de Certeau (1976).

Works cited

Certeau, Michel de. 1976. Entretien. <https://mediaserver.unige.ch/play/66105> [accessed 20 April 2014].

Claudel, Philippe. 2005. *La petite fille de Monsieur Linh*. Paris: Éditions Stock.

—. 2007. *Le Rapport de Brodeck.*Paris: Éditions Stock.

Daeninckx, Didier. 2003. *La Route du Rom*, Paris: Le Seuil.

—. 2005. *Cités perdues*. Paris:Verdier.

—. 2008. *Petit éloge des faits divers*. Paris: Gallimard.

Forsdick, Charles. 2001. "'Direction les oubliettes de l'histoire': Witnessing the past in the contemporary French polar", *French Cultural Studies,* 12.3, 333–50.

Gatlif, Tony. 1993. *Latcho Drom*.

—. 2010. *Liberté*.

Genette, Gérard. *Palimpsests: Literature in the Second Degree*. Translated by Channa Newman and Claude Doubinsky. Lincoln: University of Nebraska Press, 1997.

Gorrara, Claire. 2012. *French Crime Fiction and the Second World War. Past Crimes, Present Memories*. Manchester : Manchester University Press.

Jalons pour l'histoire du temps present. 2004. "La destruction de deux barres d'immeubles à la Cité des 4000 de La Courneuve." <http://fresques.ina.fr/jalons/fiche-media/InaEdu01839/la-destruction-de-deux-barres-d-immeubles-a-la-cite-des-4000-de-la-courneuve.html> [accessed 20 April 2014].

Levi, Primo. 1986. *The Drowned and the Saved*. New York: Vintage International Random House.

Pernot, Mathieu. 2001. *Un Camp pour les bohémiens, Mémoires du camp d'internement pour nomades de Saliers*. Arles : Actes Sud.

Ross, Kristin. 2010. "Parisian Noir", *New Literary History,* 41.1, 95–109.

Rothberg, Michael 2009. *Multidirectional Memory*: *Remembering the Holocaust in the Age of Decolonization*. Stanford: Stanford University Press.

Rothberg, Michael, Debarati Sanyal, and Max Silverman, eds. 2010. *Yale French Studies*, 118/119.

Scahill, Jeremy. 2007. *Black Water: The Rise of the World's Most Powerful Mercenary Army*. New York: Nation Books.

Silverman, Max. 2013. *Palimpsestic Memory: The Holocaust and Colonialism in French and Francophone Fiction and Film*. New York: Berghahn.

Strainchamps, Bernard. 2010. "Le roman est un chantier". Interview of [*sic*] Didier Daeninckx. <http://www.feedbooks/com/interview/11/le-roman-est-un-chantier> [accessed 20 April 2014].

Suleiman, Susan Rubin. 2006. *Crises of Memory and the Second World War* Cambridge, MA: Harvard University Press.

CHAPTER THREE

ARSÈNE LUPIN:
REWRITING HISTORY

EMMA BIELECKI

In 1905, the magazine *Je Sais Tout* published a short story by Maurice Leblanc, an obscure writer who up until that point had toiled earnestly in the field of realism. This story introduced to the French reading public a new hero: Arsène Lupin, gentleman thief. Part Casanova, part Robin Hood, dandy, connoisseur, and cat burglar, a character who, in the tradition of Vidocq, operates on both sides of the law, Lupin quickly became established in the pantheon of fictional heroes, and his exploits continue to interest readers to this day. In addition to the twenty Lupin books authored by Leblanc between 1905 and 1939, all of which are still in print, there have been countless pastiches, parodies, radio dramas, TV serials and films based on his adventures. A variety of French authors have used the character since Boileau-Narcejac first brought him back to life in the 1970s in a series of five authorized sequels, from the French medievalist Michel Zink, an academic historian who is also the author of *Arsène Lupin et le mystère d'Arsonval* (2004), to the contemporary crime writer Michel Bussi, whose first novel *Code Lupin* (2006) was, as the strapline on the cover puts it, "un *Da Vinci Code* normand". A simple IMDb (Internet Movie Database) search for the name "Arsène Lupin" yields 104 results, ranging from a 1910 German short, *Arsène Lupin contra Sherlock Holmes*, to the most recent French adaptation, released in 2004, directed by Jean-Paul Salomé and starring Romain Duris in the title role, via a 1918 Russian adaptation listed as *Posledeniye priklyucheniya Arsena Lyupena*, the 1932 Hollywood version starring John and Lionel Barrymore, Alexandre Astruc's 1980 TV series, *Arsène Lupin joue et perd*, a Canadian children's cartoon series of the mid-1990s, *Night Hood*, a video game called *Sherlock Holmes: Nemesis*, and an Italian adult film from 2000 directed by the pornographer Luca Damiano. His popularity is certainly not confined to Europe and North America. In Japan a manga series by Monkey Punch, *Lupin III*, has become a significant media franchise in its own right, spawning further hypertexts, such as the 2007 Philippine TV series, *Lupin*.

That Leblanc's stories should have proved so susceptible to what Genette would term hypertextual transformation is unsurprising.[1] They themselves engage in a variety of intertextual practices. This chapter will explore two examples of such practices, examining the use of the figure of Sherlock Holmes as an antagonist in some of the earlier stories, and the function of the frequent allusions to the historical fictions of Alexandre Dumas throughout the corpus. As we shall see, the ideological dimension of the texts is never more apparent than when they are at their most floridly, most flamboyantly fictive. This is just one of the many paradoxes that structure the Lupinian universe, and contribute to its appeal.

Transformation and Disguise

The palimpsestic quality of Leblanc's writing—its extensive use of intertextual allusion—is closely linked in the Lupin saga to a thematics of transformation. At the level of representational content, the stories are obsessed with ideas of disguise and misidentification, as Lupin bewilders the police and his victims by adopting a seemingly endless series of alternative identities. But readers too are often the victims of an imposture; the question which structures the Lupin stories is never so much "Whodunit?" as "Who is it?", as the entertainment value of many of the stories is at least partially generated by the reader's uncertainty as to the identity of the eponymous hero. The importance of disguise is foregrounded at the very beginning of the Lupin saga, when, in the first story, "L'Arrestation d'Arsène Lupin", the protagonist is introduced as: "l'homme aux mille déguisements: tour à tour chauffeur, ténor, bookmaker, fils de famille, adolescent, vieillard, commis-voyageur marseillais, médecin russe, torero espagnol" (Leblanc 1961–69 (1), 281). The list here stresses the range and diversity of Lupin's disguises; he can be any age, any class, any nationality. But it also offers the reader two clues as to the nature of the diegetic universe that Lupin inhabits. The reference to the "chauffeur" stresses its contemporaneity. The world Lupin inhabits is a resolutely modern one,[2] filled with cars, telephones and electric lights, and he himself is often associated with newfangled gadgetry. As he explains to the detective Isidore Beautrelet in *L'Aiguille Creuse*, his ability to control the international arts and antiques market would be unthinkable without the use of a telephone (Leblanc 1961–69 (2), 446). Indeed, in the second Lupin story, "Arsène Lupin en prison", in which he masterminds the audacious burglary of a chateau from a cell in the Santé, his antagonist, Inspecteur Ganimard, pondering how Lupin could have entered the house, instructs his underlings: "qu'on ne cherche pas de souterrain, de pierres tournant sur un pivot, et autres balivernes de ce calibre. Notre individu n'emploie pas des procédés aussi vieux jeu. Il est d'aujourd'hui, ou plutôt de demain" (Leblanc 1961–69 (1), 310). These words echo ironically throughout the saga, for Lupin has recourse many times to "[des] balivernes de ce calibre", frequently uncovering long-forgotten tunnels and secret passages. Indeed, one of the narrative threads that run through the corpus as a whole, and act as a device to tie together a number of disparate elements, is the conceit that Lupin solves four riddles engraved on a mirror belonging to Cagliostro—the famous eighteenth-century confidence trickster who, as we shall see, plays an important role in the text—but which the latter was never able to decipher.

Lupin is, therefore, frequently "vieux jeu". Indeed, the list of his disguises announces this aspect of the stories when it includes a reference to a "torero espagnol", a figure straight out of central casting. This ushers into the text an exotic, romantic, but hokey note, and immediately establishes that the arena in which Lupin acts is in fact that of the cultural imaginary. His world is ostentatiously fictional. The master metaphor of the stories is a theatrical one: Lupin is consistently presented as both actor and impresario, staging an extravaganza for the amusement of a grateful public. The show he puts on is constructed out of some rather antiquated plot devices—secret passages, hidden treasure, long-lost relatives—and relies heavily on all the tropes and topoi of nineteenth-century popular fiction. Disguise is precisely one of those topoi. In her monograph, *La Naissance du roman policier français*, Elsa de Lavergne adduces a historical reason for the frequency with which depictions of criminality in the nineteenth-century popular novel engage with the idea of disguise: following the abolition of branding in 1832, the question of how to identify recidivists was one with which the authorities struggled (2009, 125–26). By the end of the nineteenth century, however, the development of reliable technologies of identification (forensic anthropometrics and fingerprinting) had gone some way to solving this problem. Of this development Lavergne writes:

> Ce tournant décisif dans l'identification judiciaire ne sonne pourtant pas le glas des pratiques carnavalesques propres au roman populaire. Les personnages continuent de s'y inventer sans cesse de nouvelles identités et de se grimer à outrance pour échapper aux policiers. [...] Les romanciers soulignent alors ces pratiques d'un autre temps avec une distance ironique marquée. (2009, 126–27)

Thus Lavergne suggests that by the early twentieth century the idea of disguise, which had been linked to a serious social anxiety for much of the nineteenth century, subsisted as a purely literary device, one that novelists deployed in a knowingly ironic fashion, part and parcel of a broader tendency for this corpus of writing to resort to the hoariest of plot devices with all the glee of a child raiding a dressing-up box. In the case of the Lupin texts, a strongly marked metafictional dimension is created not only through the use of stock plot devices and conventions, but also through frequent intertextual allusions in a parodic or ludic register. Perhaps the most extended intertextual engagement in the texts involves the appearance in three early stories of an English detective, a Mr. Herlock Sholmès, and his phlegmatic assistant, Dr Wilson, of 219 Parker Street.

From Sherlock Holmes to Herlock Sholmès

In fact, when the celebrated English detective first appeared in the Lupin universe, it was under his original name, in the story "Sherlock Holmes arrive trop tard", published in *Je Sais Tout* in June 1906. In this story, Leblanc appropriates Conan Doyle's creation in a fairly straightforward fashion, introducing the master detective as a foil to Lupin's arch-criminal, pairing the two figures in a way that is typical of *Belle Époque* crime fiction where every Holmes has his Moriarty, every Fantômas his Juve. Leblanc's texts present the French police as relentlessly inept, as explained by the narrator of "La Dame Blonde", who adumbrates from within the diegesis an explanation for the success of the Lupin stories in the following terms:

Ce qui nous réjouit dans ce qu'on pourrait appeler les spectacles Arsène Lupin, c'est le rôle éminemment comique de la police. Tout se passe en dehors d'elle. (Leblanc 1961–69 (2), 15–16)

Certainly the appeal of the *Aventures Extraordinaires* lies at least partially in their vaguely anarchist dimension, a general anti-authoritarian tendency, a contempt for any claims the State makes which place limitations on the individual. But the absence of a convincing antagonist risks emptying out the stories of all drama and tension. It is precisely, and explicitly, to play the role of worthy adversary that Sherlock Holmes is introduced. Thus when Lupin and Holmes briefly encounter each other in "Sherlock Holmes arrive trop tard", the moment is charged with tension as the narrator exclaims:

Et, si quelqu'un avait pu les surprendre à cet instant, c'eût été un spectacle émouvant que la première rencontre de ces deux hommes, si étranges, si puissamment armés, tous deux vraiment supérieurs, et destinés fatalement par leurs aptitudes spéciales à se heurter comme deux forces égales que l'ordre des choses pousse l'une contre l'autre à travers l'espace.
(Leblanc 1961–69 (1), 475)

In the end, and as the title of the story suggests, Holmes does not play a decisive role in the unfolding of the narrative. In this first story he is ultimately little more than another witness to Lupin's genius. The final lines of the story serve to set up the next instalment in the saga, as Holmes promises himself that one day he will avenge his humiliation by apprehending the famous thief:

J'ai l'idée, voyez-vous, qu'Arsène Lupin et Sherlock Holmes se rencontreront de nouveau un jour ou l'autre... Oui, le monde est trop petit pour qu'ils ne se rencontrent pas... et ce jour-là...
(Leblanc 1961–69 (1), 485)

If Holmes's use of the third person here to refer to himself, combined with the liberal use of suspension points to mark the cliffhanger ending, teeters on the brink of parody, it never quite crosses over into it. Sherlock Holmes is used in this story to fulfil a clear narrative need for a worthy opponent, to generate suspense and tension, and he is used in an essentially serious way.

This short story was subsequently republished in 1907 in the collection *Arsène Lupin: Gentleman-Cambrioleur*, but legal wrangles at that point forced Leblanc to change the name of the character to Herlock Sholmès. This phonetic modification might have been a legal necessity, but it is also symptomatic of the way in which in the next two stories Leblanc wrote used the figure of the English detective. "La Dame Blonde" and "La Lampe Juive", subsequently published together as the second instalment in the *Aventures Extraordinaires* under the title, *Arsène Lupin contre Herlock Sholmès*, are far more parodic, and subject the English detective to a series of transformations, all of which tend to ridicule him. They also signal the introduction of a more chauvinist dimension into the stories. If the opening instalment in the Lupin saga, which unfolded on board a transatlantic liner during a crossing to New York, presented Lupin as essentially a man in transit, a cosmopolitan figure, able to embody with equal ease a Russian doctor or a Spanish matador, over the course of the saga he is increasingly identified as a quintessential Frenchman, and his destiny, as we shall see, becomes tied to that of the *patrie*.

From the start, the battle between Lupin and Sholmès is cast in terms of a battle between France and England, so that when Lupin, described in both "Sherlock Holmes arrive trop tard" and "La Dame Blonde" as "notre voleur national" (Leblanc 1961–69 (1), 459; (2), 10), contemplates pitting his wits against those of Sholmès, he exclaims: "Enfin, Trafalgar sera vengé!" (Leblanc 1961-69 (2), 67). Through these two characters, a sharp contrast is drawn between England and France, between London and Paris. London is presented as the acme of dreariness:

> La triste rue s'étendait entre les façades mornes des maisons, sous un ciel noir d'où tombait une pluie méchante et rageuse. Un cab passa, un autre cab. (Leblanc 1961–69 (2), 173)

Paris, on the other hand, is consistently presented through all the Lupin stories as a glittering, fabulous space. The keynotes of the representation of Paris in the stories are resumed in the opening sentence of *La Demoiselle aux yeux verts*:

> Raoul de Limézy flânait sur les boulevards, allégrement, ainsi qu'un homme heureux qui n'a qu'à regarder pour jouir de la vie, de ces spectacles charmants, et de la gaiété légère qu'offre Paris en certains jours lumineux d'avril. (Leblanc 1967, 5)

This opening sentence, with incredible economy, conjures up a certain image of Paris, the Paris of the boulevards, of the *grands cafés*, the Paris of luxury, where a young man of leisure can saunter aimlessly, and the gaiety of the city is reflected in the vivacity of its citizenry. Just as Lupin, in his ebullience, is the perfect representative of Gay Paris, so Sholmès, indistinguishable from any "honnête citoyen de Londres" (Leblanc 1961–69 (2): 70) is a drab figure, and drab not only compared to Lupin, but to Conan Doyle's Holmes. All the dandiacal, *fin de siècle* characteristics that Sherlock Holmes possesses—his drug addiction, his aestheticism, his cultivation of sensation, his desire to burn always with that hard gem-like flame—are entirely absent from representations of Sholmès, because they have been hived off into Lupin. At the start of "La Dame Blonde", Sholmès is described as:

> une sorte de phénomène d'intuition, d'observation, de clairvoyance et d'ingéniosité. On croirait que la nature s'est amusée à prendre les deux types de policier les plus extraordinaires que l'imagination ait produits, le Dupin d'Edgar Poe, et le Lecoq de Gaboriau, pour en construire un à sa manière, plus extraordinaire encore et plus irréel. Et l'on se demande vraiment, quand on entend le récit de ces exploits qui l'ont rendu célèbre

dans l'univers entier, on se demande si lui-même, ce Herlock Sholmès, n'est pas un personnage légendaire, un héros sorti vivant du cerveau d'un grand romancier, d'un Conan Doyle, par exemple. (Leblanc 1961–69 (2), 70)

Here Leblanc pays homage to Conan Doyle in an exuberantly metafictional fashion, and acknowledges his influence, but over the course of the two stories it becomes clear that this influence is visible in the characterization of Lupin, rather than the depiction of Sholmès, for this thumbnail sketch is in fact much more apt to describe the French thief than Leblanc's English detective. Sholmès relies heavily on a painstaking process of gathering physical evidence to build his cases, in sharp contrast to Lupin, whose detective work is characterized by ingenuity and intuition. In his book, *The Pleasures of Crime*, David Platten draws attention to the contrast between an early French tradition of detection represented by Poe and Gaboriau, which is characterized by a disregard for or even suspicion of physical evidence, and an English tradition, exemplified by Conan Doyle, which is much more positivist (2011, 27–33). He suggests that this reflects the differing philosophical traditions of Britain and France. Certainly in Leblanc's texts a contrast in crime-solving styles is part and parcel of a broader concern with national differences, where English phlegm is set against French verve. And the parodic nature of Leblanc's texts exemplifies one of the qualities that the stories identify as typically French, which is a capacity for playfulness and for an imaginative transformation of the world.

Between History, Fiction, and Myth: Lupin and National Identity

Leblanc's texts therefore use the figure of Sherlock Holmes to construct a certain image of Englishness, which is negatively coded, and placed in opposition to a glamorous idea of Frenchness. This concern with national identity is a salient feature of the Lupin saga as a whole. In his autobiography *Les Mots*, Jean-Paul Sartre, recalling his childhood love for stories of heroism and derring-do, writes that in the early years of the twentieth century:

la France fourmillait de héros imaginaires dont les exploits pansaient son amour-propre. […] J'adorais […] Arsène Lupin, sans savoir qu'il devait sa force herculéenne, son courage narquois, son intelligence bien française à notre déculottée de 1870. (Sartre 2010, 64)

Here Sartre, qua materialist literary critic, identifies the Lupin texts as
performing a specific ideological role in consolidating a sense of French
national identity, compensating on the imaginative plane for humiliations
suffered on the historical one. Although, as we saw earlier, the State and
its apparatuses are regarded with suspicion within the Lupin stories, which
present the police and judiciary as hapless and the Parliamentary regime as
venal and corrupt,[3] the nation is of vital importance. The character of
Lupin himself is a Barresian combination of egoist anarchism and
nationalist sentiment. On the one hand he is a man who calls himself into
being—Arsène Lupin after all is a self-chosen pseudonym—and therefore
represents a fantasy of self-creation. But, at the same time, he is a man
who chooses to link his destiny to that of France. The key moment in this
trajectory is at the end of *813*, where Lupin inadvertently kills his lover
after discovering that she is in fact a deeply disturbed murderer, and then
decides to kill himself. At the last moment, however, he eschews suicide
in favour of joining the Foreign Legion, a decision which points both to
his marginality and his essential Frenchness. The final words of the story,
spoken by Lupin, are as follows:

> Puisque la mer n'a pas voulu de moi, ou plutôt puisque, au dernier
> moment, je n'ai pas voulu de la mer, nous allons voir si les balles des
> Marocains sont plus compatissantes. Et puis, tout de même, ce sera plus
> chic… Face à l'ennemi, Lupin, et pour la France!
> (Leblanc 1961–69 (3), 427)

There is here a familiar constellation of Lupinian motifs. He asserts the
pre-eminence of his own will in refusing suicide and demonstrates his
sangfroid through witticizing at a moment of despair. He combines the
frivolous and the serious in the fashion of the dandy, insisting on the
importance of a chic death. His motivation for joining the Foreign Legion
is not primarily ideological but driven by a death wish. And yet in the very
final words of the text Lupin consecrates himself to the service of his
homeland.

But beyond Lupin's own strong attachment to France, the texts
themselves can be considered a *lieu de mémoire*, in which a certain image
of Frenchness is produced through a configuration of aspects of French
history. Indeed, one of the ways that the Lupin saga could be described as
having a palimpsestuous quality is precisely through the way in which it
takes certain events from history and transforms them, purporting to offer
the reader access to a kind of secret history. The idea of the palimpsest
here operates in two different ways. The stories themselves insist on the
idea that they are revealing a truth that has been obscured by a layer of

false speculation, rumour and misinformation. Some of the stories use an intra-diegetic narrator, who is rather in the tradition of Watson, although he is never a fully realized character, but an individual who for some reason is taken into the confidence of the protagonist, granted special access to his life, and allowed to chronicle it. This intra-diegetic narrator is not consistently used; many of the stories have an extra-diegetic, third-person narrator. Where this intra-diegetic narrator is used, however, he often prefaces the story with a claim such as the following, from "La Dame Blonde":

> Chaque fois que j'entreprends de raconter quelqu'une des innombrables aventures dont se compose la vie d'Arsène Lupin, j'éprouve une véritable confusion, tellement il me semble que la plus banale de ces aventures est connue de tous ceux qui vont me lire. [...] Mon excuse, c'est que j'apporte du nouveau: j'apporte le mot de l'énigme. [...] Je reproduis des articles lus et relus, je recopie d'anciennes interviews: mais tout cela je le coordonne, je le classe, et je le soumets à l'exacte vérité. (Leblanc 1961–69 (2), 10)

The narrator here presents himself as performing an editorial role that involves a work of collection, compilation and classification, in order to bring to light a hitherto obscure truth. This applies equally to the discourse that surrounds history in the stories, where it is suggested that they are revealing a secret version of history.[4] Of course, though, what they are actually doing is the opposite; the Lupin stories have a palimpsestuous quality in so far as they superimpose on the historical record a fictive version of events.

This fictive version of events sometimes functions fairly transparently in the way in which Sartre describes, soothing wounded French vanity. In the novels the Franco-Prussian War, the Panama scandal, and the debacle of *Boulangisme*—in fact "tous les événements funestes à notre pays" (Leblanc 1961–69 (1), 29)—are the fault of a woman called Joséphine Balsamo, the Countess of Cagliostro, a descendant of the eighteenth-century adventurer, Cagliostro. As mentioned above, Cagliostro is an important point of reference in the text. There are two aspects of the use of the figure of Cagliostro that I wish to highlight. First, the link with Cagliostro qua historical figure is one of the many ways that Lupin is consistently linked with the *Ancien Régime*. On numerous occasions Lupin's power is tied to his ability to recover knowledge lost during the Revolution, most strikingly in *L'Aiguille Creuse*, where he enters into possession of a State secret that Marie-Antoinette was thought to have taken to the grave with her, and thus becomes "le dernier héritier des rois de France" (Leblanc 1961–69 (2), 380). But if Lupin is sometimes associated with the Bourbons, he is also often compared to Bonaparte. In "La Dame Blonde", for example, Lupin says that only Napoleon had "une destinée comparable à la mienne, mieux remplie, plus intense" (Leblanc 1961–69 (2), 64). The use of the figure of Bonaparte in the text seems to be part and parcel of that dimension of the texts identified by Sartre, their function as a vehicle for a specific idea of Frenchness. In his study of the Napoleon cult in nineteenth-century France, the historian Sudhir Hazareesingh has suggested that at the end of the nineteenth century, the legend of Napoleon underwent a change in France. It ceased to be associated with a specific political project, as it had been from Waterloo through to the collapse of the Second Empire, and became instead a more nebulous expression of "romantic nostalgia":

> a longing for an era of adventure which was understood to have ended, at least in its 'classical' sense; for some, it was also becoming the privileged expression of an individualistic, nationalist cult of transcendental heroism. It was in this spirit that the writer Maurice Barrès celebrated Napoleon as a 'professor of energy' in his novel *Les Déracinés*. (2004, 261)

The Lupin novels, in their use of the idea of Napoleon, seem to draw on the discourse that surrounds the Emperor in Barrès's work, where, as Hazareesingh suggests, there is a striking combination of individualism and nationalism. In *Les Déracinés* (first published in 1897), Barrès had written that: "le tombeau de l'Empereur [...] est le carrefour de toutes les énergies qu'on nomme audace, volonté, appétit' (1967, 228–229). These energies are all embodied in the figure of Lupin. But Lupin is comparable to Napoleon in another sense as well, not simply because of the personal qualities that are ascribed to him, but in terms of how he functions as a figure who is able to contain contradiction and tension. In *Les Déracinés*, in the scene in which a group of young Frenchmen gather at the Invalides to commit their lives to the service of their nation, the body of the Emperor is described as: "un des plus beaux parchemins à déchiffrer. A ses rides, se vérifieraient tant d'images de Napoléon accumulées dans les musées, dans les bibliothèques, dans la légende" (Barrès 1967, 230). Here the text figures Bonaparte's body as something rather like a palimpsest, on which a number of different texts are superimposed. The Napoleon legend, as described in Barrès's text, has many different strata. It is precisely this that enables Bonaparte to emerge as such a totemic figure in the text. The Emperor is multiplex, a man for all seasons; his legend is inclusive enough to hold within it many different values. This capaciousness is a quality that Lupin also possesses. Like Napoleon he is a figure who can contain contradictions. He is both Bourbon and Bonaparte, legitimate king and usurper, outlaw and *justicier*, egoist anarchist and patriotic conservative. In the figure of Lupin, therefore, some of the contradictions and competing forces in French history meet and can be held in a precarious balance.

The second point I want to make regarding Cagliostro concerns the fact that he is as much a literary as a historical figure, the hero of one of Dumas's sprawling historical novels, *Joseph Balsamo*. In invoking Cagliostro, Leblanc plugs his stories into a pre-existing fictional historiography. To consider the tendencies of that historiography, the nature of its vision of French history, is beyond the scope of this chapter. What I shall focus on here is the effect of the fact that here again fiction slides into metafiction, in a way that, counter-intuitively perhaps, in fact consolidates the ideological work the texts are doing in their representation of Frenchness. As we have seen, the Lupin texts very much insist that they belong in a specific literary tradition. A particularly striking assertion of this tradition is at the beginning of *Les Dents du tigre*, which was the first Lupin novel written and published after the First World War. The First World War inflected the stories in various ways, the most striking of which is the marginalization of the figure of Lupin himself. Thus in *Le Triangle d'or* the protagonist is an invalided soldier called Patrice Belval, and in *L'Éclat d'obus* a young army officer named Paul Delroze, neither of whom features anywhere else in the Lupin canon. This shift away from the figure of Lupin points to a certain tension. On the one hand, through concentrating on characters other than Lupin, the novels suggest that the war enables other men to emerge as champions of French values, that any ordinary French soldier is potentially a heroic figure, worthy of writing about (although Lupin does feature in the texts as a *deus ex machina*). At the same time the marginalization of Lupin, one suspects, is designed to avoid exposing the fragility of the superman fantasy as described by Sartre, which might be difficult to sustain in the face of the reality of trench warfare. In any case, it is with *Les Dents du tigre*, published in 1920, that Lupin takes centre stage once more. The opening chapter is entitled "D'Artagnan, Porthos, et Monte Cristo", a reference to a conversation between two ancillary characters which serves to introduce the main character, Don Luis Perenna (one of Lupin's anagrammatic pseudonyms), described as a man: "que ses chefs appelaient tout court: le héros, celui dont nous disions qu'il était brave comme d'Artagnan, fort comme Porthos… −Et mystérieux comme Monte Cristo" (Leblanc, 1961–69 (7), 20). By referencing Dumas here, the text inscribes itself in a specific tradition, asserting a basic continuity between past and present, at a moment in the saga where such an assertion is particularly weighted with significance, given the pressures of history. After the First World War,

Lupin re-emerges and reassures the reader that there has been no irreparable loss, no radical rupture. Enjoyment for the reader is a curious compound of our delight in disguise and mystery, and the pleasures of recognition.

In his study of Lupin fansites on the Internet, Marc Lits has said that for new avatars of Lupin to be acceptable, they must:

> garantir le plaisir de retrouver celui-ci 'tel qu'en Lui-même enfin l'éternité le change.' 'Je te reconnais, dit le lecteur devant une nouvelle version des aventures lupiniennes […]. Tu me prouves qu'au fond rien ne change, et que si le temps passe, toi et moi continuons à rester les mêmes'. (2011, 66)

This attempt to escape from the order of time entirely is already inscribed in Leblanc's original stories, in which Lupin was born trailing his own legend. In the first story, following the very first mention of Lupin in a telegram informing the passengers on the transatlantic liner that the famous thief is among them, the narrator exclaims: "Arsène Lupin parmi nous! l'insaisissable cambrioleur dont on racontait les prouesses dans tous les journaux depuis des mois!" (Leblanc 1961–69 (1), 281). This opening establishes Lupin as a character belonging to the realm of myth, in the sense described by Umberto Eco in "The Myth of Superman". Eco explains the structure of myth thus:

> The traditional figure of religion was a character of human or divine origin, whose image had immutable characteristics and an irreversible destiny. It was possible that a story, as well as a number of traits, backed up the character; but the story followed a line of development already established, and it filled in the character's features in a gradual, but definitive manner.
>
> In other words, a Greek statue could represent Hercules or a scene of Hercules' labors; in both cases, but more so in the latter, Hercules would be seen as someone who has a story, and this story would characterize his divine features. The story has taken place and can no longer be denied. (1984, 107)

Eco goes on to contrast this mythical structure with that of the modern novel, in which, "the event has not happened *before* the story; it happens *while* it is being told, and usually even the author does not know what will take place" (1984, 109). Leblanc's stories attempt a fusion of these two structures. On the one hand, the experience they offer the reader is one of surprise; the narrative twists and turns are unpredictable and the stories often confound the reader's expectations. At the same time, the stories frequently posit a putative reader who is entirely familiar with Lupin's exploits, who already knows how the story unfolds. There is an odd insistence in many of the stories that these versions are a retelling of stories that are already in circulation, as in the section quoted above from *La Dame Blonde*, in which the narrator presents himself as an editor engaged in a work of collation, producing the definitive version of a story that nonetheless, in its broad outlines, is already well known to the public. These sorts of narrative interjections present Lupin as a character belonging to the realm of myth, not history, a character who is not caught in the irreversible forward movement of time. The simple expedient of not writing the stories in chronological order further ensures that Lupin need not age. He is the master of disguise, and of transformation, but from the changes that time effects he is exempt.[5]

Conclusion: Lupin as Trickster

As should by now be evident, it is impossible to talk about Lupin without talking about contradiction. Paradoxicality is the essence of Lupin, who is first and foremost a trickster figure. In an article on Hermes, William G. Doty explores six characteristics that define the Greek god in his role as trickster: he practises deception and theft; he is skilled in interpretation, the founder, indeed, of hermeneutics, the science that bears his name; he is the divine connector, active in the sphere of the erotic, broadly conceived as referring to the many ways in which people are drawn to each other; he is associated with laughter and comedy; he is multiplex, and finally he is a creator, restorer, and healer. Using Doty's inventory, we can read Lupin as a modern avatar of Hermes, his caduceus the cane that he carries (and which is itself a paradoxical object, both a sign of his status as a sophisticated man about town, but also potentially a weapon).[6] Like Hermes, Lupin is a thief and a confidence man, but he is also a detective, skilled in interpreting clues and solving riddles. He is himself a prince of romance, but also sometimes acts as a matchmaker, bringing couples together. He is essentially a comic creation in a ludic universe. He has lived many lives and, lastly, he is a basically beneficent character. In his analysis of Hermes as a creator, restorer, and healer, Doty acknowledges that: "Trickster analysts have argued whether tricksters are prosocial benefactors and creators or merely negative characters indicating a deity opposed to or in tension with a 'high god' creator" (1993, 54). He goes on to advocate the former position:

> Typically the trickster helps humans adjust by stipulating social boundaries, even if he does so by metonymically transgressing them. He brings symbolic organization to the personal universe [...]. Likewise Hermes organizes the social cosmos, working out interconnections among

people, boundaries between nations and realignments of military or political power. (1993, 54–56)

Lupin functions in just such a fashion as a "prosocial benefactor": he solves mysteries, restores order, reunites lovers and rights wrongs. Often he is presented as operating at a geopolitical level. He purges the French administration of a corrupt deputy in *Le Bouchon de cristal*, saves France from disaster in *L'Éclat d'obus*, and personally conquers Mauritania but generously offers his fiefdom to France in *Les Dents du tigre*. His transgressions are committed in the name of establishing a new and more perfect order. He disrupts fixed patterns of identity, but at the same time he insists on the survival of older cultural forms. Just as the palimpsest is defined by an interplay of effacement and presence, so the Lupin corpus is defined by an interplay of disguise and recognition, its hero everchanging but always the same.

Notes

[1] See Genette 1982, 11–14 for a definition of hypertextuality.

[2] In fact Lupin would always remain a creature of the *Belle Époque*. Those stories published after the First World War were often set in the pre-war era and characterized by a sense of nostalgia, with only cursory references to cocktails and jazz to acknowledge the advent of *les années folles*.

[3] *Le Bouchon de cristal*, for example, uses the Panama Affair as a background on which to embroider the rather dark story of a miscarriage of justice, blackmail and government corruption.

[4] The fact that the texts present themselves as offering a secret history doubtless explains the fact that a surprisingly large corpus of work has built up around the idea that the Lupin cycle is a repository of arcane knowledge, a code which, if cracked, will reveal an extraordinary secret. This is the premise of Michel Busi's novel, *Code Lupin* (2006), but some readers of Leblanc have taken this idea seriously. Patrick Ferté, for example (1992), has claimed that Leblanc's stories are a gloss on the Rennes-le-Château saga, a favourite topic for those interested in French esoterica. The fact that Leblanc's stories are something of a magnet for such readers is doubtless a function of their own engagement with esoteric discourse, principally through the inclusion of the figure of Cagliostro.

[5] This aspect of the Lupin novels, the fact that he is never diminished by age, is gently ironized by Boileau-Narcejac in their authorized sequels. In *Le Secret d'Eunerville*, there are numerous references to the age of the characters. Lupin, ever the lothario, at one point makes a pass at a young woman, which is presented as rather age-inappropriate and seedy. As he himself says: "Tu n'as plus 20 ans, mon petit" (Boileau-Narcejac 1973, 30).

[6] Léo Fontan's illustrations established the iconography of Lupin, canonically depicted in evening dress with a monocle and a cane.

Works cited

Barrès, Maurice. 1967. *Les Déracinés*. Paris: Plon.

Boileau-Narcejac. 1973. *Le Secret d'Eunerville*. Paris: Des Champs Elysées.

Doty, William G. 1993. "A Lifetime of Trouble-Making: Hermes as Trickster." In *Mythical Trickster Figures*, edited by William J.Hynes and William G. Doty, 46–65. Tuscaloosa: University of Alabama Press.

Eco, Umberto. 1984. *The Role of the Reader: Explorations in the Semiotics of Texts*. Bloomington: Indiana University Press.

Ferté, Patrick. 1992. *Arsène Lupin, supérieur inconnu: la clé de l'œuvre codée de Maurice Leblanc*. Paris: Guy Trédaniel.

Genette, Gérard. 1982. *Palimpsestes: la littérature au second degré*. Paris: Seuil.

Hazareesingh, Sudhir. 2004. *The Legend of Napoleon*. London: Granta.

Lavergne, Elsa de. 2009. *La Naissance du roman policier français: du Second Empire à la Première Guerre mondiale*. Paris: Éditions Classiques Garnier.

Leblanc, Maurice. 1961–69. *Les Aventures d'Arsène Lupin, gentleman-cambrioleur*, 8 vols. Paris: Hachette/Gallimard.

—. 1967. *La Demoiselle aux yeux verts*. Paris: Le Livre de Poche.

Lits, Marc. 2011. *Le genre policier dans tous ses états: d'Arsène Lupin à Navarro*. Limoges: Presses Universitaires de Limoges.

Platten, David. 2011. *The Pleasures of Crime: Reading Modern French Crime Fiction*. Amsterdam: Rodopi.

Sartre, Jean-Paul. 2010. *Les Mots et autres écrits autobiographiques*. Edited by Jean-François Louette, Gilles Philippe, and Juliette Simont. Bibliothèque de la Pléiade. Paris: Gallimard.

CHAPTER FOUR

DU RÉCIT À L'ENVERS AU RÉCIT DE L'ENVERS: THE IMPRINT OF THE PALIMPSEST IN SIMENON

CHRISTINE CALVET[1]

Georges Simenon's detective stories tend not to conform to what we expect of the genre. In both the novels featuring the mythical figure of Maigret, and in the many more that do not, the outcome of the investigation is not central. Even though it provides the main material for the development of the plot—the search for the culprit, for his alibi and modus operandi, for clues and for proof; the depiction of various figures and mechanisms of the judiciary system—, it mainly serves to bring to light the multiple "stories", whether superficial or intimate, at work in a given character's life. The developments of the main plot result in the re-emergence of a whole framework of past events, which soon prove themselves vital to the narrative. The story of the crime lends a new resonance to past situations which have changed characters' lives. Catastrophe is triggered, inevitably, by guilt, be it that of Jules in *Les Demoiselles de Concarneau,* M. Hire in *Les Fiançailles de M. Hire*, or M. Gobillot in *En Cas de malheur.* This chapter aims to investigate the resurgence and the intricacy of "stories" in Simenon's works. The rewriting of life proves futile without the recapture of the past. Though often underestimated, the poetic dimension of the novels hinges on the ways in which characters' inner lives are brought to light through an investigation of the remnants of past lives and of the superimposed images of their destinies.

Introduction

Traditionally conceived in terms of intertextuality and hypertextuality, to borrow the terminology of Barthes (1973), Genette (1982), and Kristeva (1969), the palimpsest will be considered here in its original sense, that of a material reused in such a way that an underlying text is seen to resurface. The corpus for this chapter is composed of three novels which Simenon himself described as "romans durs" or "de la destinée".[2]

Jules Guérec, the main character of *Les Demoiselles de Concarneau* (1936),[3] is an unmarried head-fisherman, who kills someone accidentally. *Les Fiançailles de M. Hire* (1933) focuses on a solitary man, M. Hire, who is wrongly suspected of murder. In *En Cas de malheur* (1956), lawyer Lucien Gobillot writes a diary in which he confesses having been seduced by a dubious female client who will go on to be murdered. Accidental killing, murder, rape, characters living on the periphery of society: all provide the staples of the detective story, even though an attentive reader may note in the arrangement of the plots that the novel does not entirely respect the constraints of this supposedly well-defined genre.

The development of the main plot, based on the successive layers of a given character's previous lives, announces the key narrative principle of superimposition. This chapter will examine how the palimpsest and the effects it has on the narrative reveal what Simenon calls "l'homme nu". I will contend that the characters try in vain to rewrite lives ruled by the forces of destiny, the various facets of which constitute the palimpsest of the plot.

1. Superimposition: character and plot

A careful study of the construction of Simenon's novels shows their relative similarities. Tables 1–3 at the end of this chapter summarize the plot standards at work in the various narratives. In each novel, the reader is offered an episode of a life which will soon be thrown into turmoil. The stories begin *in media res*. In *Les Demoiselles de Concarneau*, the reader witnesses the crime, whereas in the other two novels he knows from the start of the narrative that a crime has already been committed. In all three cases, the main character is depicted in his daily environment, as shown in the incipit of *Les Fiançailles de M. Hire*:

La concierge toussota avant de frapper, articula en regardant le catalogue de la Belle Jardinière qu'elle tenait à la main :
- C'est une lettre pour vous M. Hire.
Et elle serra son châle sur sa poitrine. On bougea derrière la porte brune. C'était tantôt à gauche, tantôt à droite, tantôt des pas, tantôt un froissement mou de tissu ou un heurt de faïences, et les yeux gris de la concierge semblaient, à travers le panneau, suivre à la piste le bruit invisible. Celui-ci se rapprocha enfin. La clef tourna. Un rectangle de lumière apparut, une tapisserie à fleurs jaunes, le marbre d'un lavabo. Un

homme tendit la main, mais la concierge ne le vit pas, ou le vit mal, en tout
cas, n'y prit garde parce que son regard fureteur s'était accroché à un autre
objet : une serviette imbibée de sang dont le rouge sombre tranchait sur le
froid du marbre. (2003 [1933], 175)

When his concierge provides an incriminating witness statement
(despite not actually being sure she has seen him), M. Hire finds himself
under suspicion, and harassed by the police, who take the blood stains
from a simple razor cut to be an indication of his guilt. This false trail will
culminate in M. Hire's death. The explicit reference to "La Belle
jardinière" produces an *effet de réel*, as does the implicit allusion to the
œuvre of Ponson du Terrail.[4] With little preparation for the revelation to
come, the plot gives direct access to the character's intimate thoughts, by
means of internal focalization. From the very beginning, then, a number of
clues or implicit elements set the stage for the development of the narrative.

The *in media res* device enables Simenon to introduce the characters
not chronologically, but through a variety of narrative ellipses, prolepses
and analepses. The relative tranquility of a daily routine is disrupted by an
incident, which triggers, in turn, a disruption in the narrative, and an
apparently inexorable conflation of past and present events. Simenon
declared: "Je ne sais rien des événements avant de commencer un roman"
(1968, 314). In other words, he had no specific design when he began a
novel, instead simply living his characters' lives and following his instinct.
He added: "Le roman commence et, au fur et à mesure, tous les jours, mes
personnages avancent sans que je sache ce qui leur arrivera…" (Roger
1989 [1963], 161). The narrative is only disorganized in appearance, of
course, and in fact corresponds to a precise design: the process of
disruption enables the author to bring to light the character's hidden past,
the importance of which will be confirmed time and again, as in the case
of the character of Jules in *Les Demoiselles de Concarneau*.

Jules is dominated by his sisters and family. A "vieille histoire"
involving a pregnant girl bubbles in the background, resurfacing at the
slightest hint of tension, as exemplified in the following outburst by
Céline:

> - Et toi ? Tu crois que je suis tranquille quand je te vois comme ça ? Je ne
> tiens pas à recommencer la vieille histoire …
> Le mot était lâché. La *vieille histoire* revenait sur le tapis ! Une histoire
> lamentable qui, deux ou trois fois par an, au cours d'une dispute, remontait
> soudain à la surface.
> Et pourtant, maintenant, il y avait près de quatorze ans de cela ! Jules
> Guérec n'avait pas trente ans. (2002–04 [1936], 834)

The recurrence of the noun phrase "vieille histoire" (italicized in the text) is to be interpreted not as a leitmotiv, but rather as the symptom of an incurable disease. After an encounter with a prostitute one night, Jules drives home and accidentally kills a child. The money offered to the child's mother to buy her silence is, of course, reminiscent of the money given to the pregnant girl's family fourteen years before. The resurfacing of past situations inevitably entails similar behaviours which, while being of no use to the investigation, emphasize Céline's pragmatic and authoritative nature.

The principle of one story that discloses another is part of the very essence of the detective plot, in which the story of the investigation and the story of the crime often go hand in hand. In the given corpus, the story of the investigation, *mise en abyme*, becomes mixed up with a series of mistakes or false leads, or is obscured by the resurfacing of past stories, as in *En Cas de malheur*, in which the narrative is no longer aimed at solving a mystery or punishing the culprit. The stories simply accumulate, emphasizing the various dissonant echoes of the past. The rhetoric of interrogation means that the reader comes to be directly involved in family situations:

> Est-ce que seulement quelqu'un aurait encore pu dire comment c'était arrivé ? A cause de Marie Papin ? A cause de l'accident ? A cause des coups donnés par Guérec à sa sœur ?
> A cause de tout cela, oui… Mais sans doute y avait-il d'autres causes qui remontaient plus loin. Ils en étaient arrivés sans le savoir à un point où un rien avait suffi à détruire une harmonie en apparence éternelle.
> (2002–04 [1936], 884)

Jules tries hard to keep up appearances by denying the accidental killing and attempting to remove traces of it. Yet the palimpsest revealed by the plot shows the impossibility of erasing the past and proves that the truth of the present cannot be written or rewritten on the same material.

M. Hire goes through a similar experience when his childhood resurfaces in the course of the narrative, and with it the painful memory of his rejection by others:

> Le rire nerveux, Alice ne pouvait s'empêcher de comparer la photographie à M. Hire.
> - Quel âge aviez-vous ?
> - Onze ans.

Onze ans ! Et ce n'était pas un gamin ! Ce n'était pas un homme non plus ! Sur la photographie, on le distinguait des autres du premier coup d'œil.

Il n'était pas plus grand qu'eux, mais il était si gras qu'il n'avait rien d'enfantin. Ses mollets nus étaient énormes, un peu de travers, les genoux noyés de graisse. Il avait un double menton et les yeux, dans ce visage empâté, restaient fixes et tristes.

Il était impossible qu'il jouât avec les gamins dans la cour ou dans le préau, impossible qu'il eût des rapports quelconques avec eux, car c'était déjà un vieux bonhomme, grave et poussif. (2003 [1933], 228)

M. Hire is, always has been, and always will be, incapable of wooing Alice. As a simple narrative alibi, the photograph cannot help to solve the mystery, and yet it stands out as a piece of evidence which displays the contrasting facets of the past and brings the character's present life to light. The plot takes on the form of a palimpsest, where the present leaves its imprint on the immutable inscriptions of the past.

The distortion of the present accounts for the duality of both the plots and of the characters' behaviour. Guilt engenders unease. Simenon examines the reactions of M. Hire. A desperate fight against time takes place, driving the character "au bout de lui-même".[5] The same process occurs for Jules Guérec, faced with the nightmare of hearing that he may be sent to jail for the accidental killing:

On peut dire que c'est dès ce moment que tout commença. Tout quoi ? Tout rien ! Une autre vie ! Quelque chose comme un cauchemar confus, un brouillard d'où n'émergeaient que des détails saugrenus. (2002–04 [1936], 821)

This tangled temporality is at its most pronounced in *En Cas de malheur*. The only linear—and yet artificial—element is the chronological indication provided by the dates "dimanche 6 novembre au lundi 2 décembre", from which the year is missing. The past resurfaces in the diary only in snatches, with no real coherence, the past life merging insistently with the present of the writing itself, an effect enhanced by the *mise en abyme* of the palimpsest created by the overlay of the diary and the narrative. The interspersed narration engenders repetitions, omissions—both deliberate and involuntary—, prolepses and analepses, all of which defy the supposed chronology of events. The plot, far from helping to resolve the investigation, paves the way for a new crime, when the lawyer's client is assassinated by Mazetti, the jealous fiancé. The narrative gives no details of the arrest and condemnation of this new culprit, with the novelist giving precedence to other information, as suggested from the very beginning:

Dimanche 6 novembre

Il y a deux heures à peine, après le déjeuner, dans le salon où nous venions de passer pour prendre le café, je me tenais debout devant la fenêtre, assez près de la vitre pour en sentir l'humidité froide, quand j'ai entendu derrière moi ma femme prononcer :
- Tu comptes sortir cet après-midi ?
Et ces mots si simples, si ordinaires, m'ont paru lourds de sens, comme s'ils cachaient entre leurs syllabes des pensées que ni Viviane ni moi n'osions exprimer. Je n'ai pas répondu tout de suite, non parce que j'hésitais sur mes intentions, mais parce que je suis resté un moment en suspens dans cet univers un peu angoissant, plus réel, au fond, que le monde de tous les jours, qui donne l'impression de découvrir l'envers de la vie. (2002–04 [1956], 409)

The syntactical arrangement of the last sentence gives rise to an important narrative ambiguity. The relative clause which closes the paragraph—"qui donne l'impression de découvrir l'envers de la vie"—characterizes both "l'univers un peu angoissant" and "le monde de tous les jours". The narrative is, therefore, clearly aimed at bringing to light that which "se cache entre les syllabes". The narrative rests both on the temporality of the character's diary and on the internal reactions that the writing process is supposed to trigger. Standing by the window—symbolically blurred by the mist—, the lawyer is eager to feel the damp pane in order to differentiate between the real and the imaginary. The progress of the plot is assured by alternate fragments of past events and present emotions, as when Yvette and Mazetti remind the lawyer of his own marriage, urging him to describe his wife:

Elle était la femme de mon patron, d'un homme que j'admirais et qui était célèbre. Elle vivait dans un monde bien fait pour éblouir l'étudiant pauvre et fruste que j'étais la veille. Elle était belle et j'étais laid. De la voir me céder, c'était un miracle qui me gonflait tout à coup de confiance en moi-même et en mon destin. (2002–04 [1956], 471)

There is a constant oscillation between the recent past experiences reported in the diary and snatches of a more remote past: "Je regrette à présent, d'être remonté si loin dans ma vie," Gobillot says, "car ce n'est pas du passé, mais du présent, que je m'étais promis de m'occuper dans ce dossier. On prétend que l'un explique l'autre et j'hésite à le croire" (2002–

04 [1956], 448). And yet, the lawyer's previous lives are brought to the surface in order to shed light, or rather cast a shadow, on reality. Ultimately, the investigation amounts to a literary alibi enabling an introspective narrative. The narrator invites the reader to understand the various trajectories of the characters and to decipher a palimpsest composed of multiple layers of the past and the re-enactment of these layers, as part of an ineluctable determinism.

2. The palimpsest and the destiny of "l'homme nu"

Sans doute est-ce une erreur que de voir dans l'intrigue, dans la recherche du criminel l'essentiel du roman policier [...]. Limitée à elle-même, l'intrigue serait de l'ordre du jeu d'échec – artistiquement nulle. Son importance vient de ce qu'elle est le moyen le plus efficace de traduire un fait éthique ou poétique dans toute son intensité. Elle ne vaut que par ce qu'elle multiplie. (Malraux 1933)

These words, written by André Malraux in his preface to William Faulkner's *Sanctuary*, ring true for most of Simenon's novels. The plot, with its multiple superimpositions, is a true palimpsest, and acts as a sort of negative which reveals the very essence of the characters. The novelist's work thus becomes a sort of two-way mirror, whose intermingling reflections repeatedly evoke the image of "l'homme nu", so that both novelist and reader are made to cross the mirror. In terms of the realist or naturalist aesthetics which were, formerly, Simenon's main source of inspiration, the writer steps into his characters' intimate world to experience episodes of their lives and scrutinize them just as a fine art student studies the human *écorché*. The reader is invited to share this investigation into human nature. It would perhaps be more relevant, however, to speak about "tropisms".[6]

Disruption and crisis are central not only to the substance of the plot, in bringing the weight of the past to bear in the present, but also to the characters' awareness of the ineluctable resonance of tragedies they had believed confined to the past. However desperately they may resist, they are unable to escape their destinies. The impulses of male characters, for example, reappear in the narrative present, hampering the unravelling of the plot, as illustrated by the "histoire" of Jules Guérec:

A trois heures, la réunion était finie. Jules Guérec aurait pu rentrer à Concarneau avant la nuit, mais il savait bien que c'était à peu près impossible. Chaque fois qu'il venait à Quimper, c'était le même drame. Il savait vers quelle rue il se dirigerait, coûte que coûte, une rue où, à n'importe quelle heure, deux ou trois femmes de Paris se promenaient lentement en se retournant sur les hommes. (2002–04 [1936], 808)

Such modalizers as "A peu près impossible", "chaque fois", "même", and "coûte que coûte" prepare the ground for the events to follow. Jules's inability to do what he "could" or "should" is the source of his ever present feeling of guilt. He is always late, unable to make up for his faults, and writes to the mother of the deceased child as follows:

Ma chère Marie, maintenant vous savez tout et vous devez imaginer mon désespoir… Moi qui espérais tant effacer mon crime involontaire en vous rendant heureuse… (2002–04 [1936], 878)

The resurfacing of the truth makes for an inextricable situation, summed up by Céline as follows:

Fais-en l'expérience… Dis-lui : j'ai tué votre enfant avec mon auto, mais je vous ai apporté du chocolat, des jouets, j'ai donné quinze francs par jour à votre frère et maintenant je ne demande qu'à vous épouser… (2002–04 [1936], 868)

In *Les Fiançailles de M. Hire*, the protagonist's ambiguous identity, his visits to brothels, his past thefts, and his voyeuristic tendencies all constitute fragmented yet interconnected elements of the narrative. The character becomes decidedly three-dimensional: at once victim, culprit, and investigator. Governed by his instincts and urges, he is both a subject and an object of manipulation. The same is true of Lucien Gobillot, whose wife tolerates his extra-marital affairs.

Whatever life has in store for them, Simenon's characters are first and foremost preoccupied with keeping up social appearances. Yet the palimpsest formed by the plots is designed to lay bare the truth, detective fiction being characterized by a distinct social environment, as is obvious in the following description from *En Cas de malheur*:

Il est le fils d'un maçon et d'une laveuse de vaisselle, a été élevé avec ses frères et sœurs dans un quartier pauvre et a entendu parler des patrons comme d'êtres inaccessibles. Pour lui, à partir d'un certain niveau social, les hommes sont faits d'une autre pâte que la sienne. J'ai presque connu ça, moi aussi, à mes débuts boulevard Malesherbes, et pourtant je n'avais pas un si lourd héritage d'humilité. (2002–04 [1956], 484)

Mazetti's identity is recalled, superimposed, we might say, onto the career of the lawyer who, giving free rein to his thoughts, writes:

Du jour au lendemain, sans raison dont je me souvienne, cette période-là a été révolue et une autre a commencé, nous avons fait partie, successivement, de plusieurs coteries avant d'aboutir à notre milieu actuel. Il m'est arrivé d'envier ceux qui restent dans un même milieu toute leur vie. (2002–04 [1956], 450)

Simenon takes advantage of the diary form to transcribe his characters' train of thought and to see through the surface to the internal divisions which define the human condition. This "déshabillage" leaves characters otherwise typical of the genre devoid of the boundaries which hitherto allowed us to categorize them. Improvised investigators get the better of official ones: in *Les Demoiselles de Concarneau*, it is Céline who understands everything and solves the problems in her own way; similarly, M. Hire identifies the culprit before the police; Maître Gobillot resorts to dubious devices and acquaintances, and even changes his plea, in order to absolve his mistress. With questionable elements of their past brought into the present, victims thus morph into villains. Feeling no remorse, Gobillot admits coldly:

Ces deux-là ne comprendront jamais ce qui leur est arrivé, ni pourquoi je me suis acharné avec tant de cruauté à détruire l'image qu'ils avaient d'eux-mêmes. A l'heure qu'il est, je suis persuadé qu'ils n'en sont pas remis, qu'ils ne se sentiront jamais comme avant. (2002–04 [1956], 432)

The palimpsest takes shape through the overlay of the character's various attempts at writing and rewriting his own story under the narrator's control. The narrative combines the layers of falsified writing with the very admission of this falsification.

Whether they fight to escape their fate or to take advantage of the situations with which they are confronted, the characters ultimately find themselves caught in the plot threads woven by their deviant behaviours. By delving into their past, Simenon only brings them back to their essential being, a process that Maître Gobillot's words seem to sum up as follows:

Me suis-je trompé sur mon compte dès le début de mon existence ? Mon père a-t-il connu ces angoisses-là et a-t-il regretté de ne pas être un mari et un père de famille comme les autres ?

Comme quels autres ? J'ai pu me convaincre, par l'expérience, que les « familles comme les autres » n'existent pas, qu'il suffit de gratter la surface et d'aller au fond des choses pour retrouver les mêmes hommes, les mêmes femmes, les mêmes tentations et les mêmes défaillances. Seule la

façade change, le plus ou moins de franchise ou de discrétion – ou
d'illusions ? (2002–04 [1956], 486–487)

The palimpsest reveals social beings stripped back to their former
selves, and who shy away from any confrontation with their own image:

> Dans son bureau en sous-sol, rue Saint-Maur, il y avait un morceau de
> miroir et M. Hire se regarda, sous la lampe, avec la peur de découvrir en
> lui quelque chose d'anormal. Mais non ! Il avait les cheveux très bruns,
> presque bleus, de sa mère. Ses moustaches étaient finement roulées au fer,
> ses lèvres bien dessinées et d'un rose ardent. Il était un peu gras mais cela
> ne l'empêchait pas de rester souple et d'être le plus fort du club de
> bowling. (2003 [1933], 226–227)

Though reassured for a while by the image of himself he sees in the
splintered mirror, M. Hire will not escape his fate. The images seen in the
mirror are soon shattered by reality. A threatening mood pervades the
narrative, as shown by the clues which prove unreliable and unhelpful for
the investigation. Yet even more important are elements of the plot that
serve as presages of impending situations, such as the character's
disappearance in *Les Fiançailles de M. Hire*:

> Il ne marquait aucun étonnement à la vue de M. Hire qui le fixait, les yeux
> ronds. Il remua. Ce fut pour lever le bras, retirer la pipe de sa bouche et
> lancer un nuage de fumée qui, amassée contre la vitre, effaça un instant le
> visage comme l'eût fait une gomme. (2003 [1933], 319)

The smoke symbolically erases the suspect's face, which means not
only that the investigator will not manage to solve the mystery but also
that M. Hire will meet a definitive end, falling to his death from a roof
while being chased. By eroding the surface of a mirror which reflects not
only the characters' daily lives, but also their destinies, the palimpsest-plot
discloses unexpected clues. After being hidden away in darkness, the
inexorable truth makes a reappearance so dramatic that the characters, like
Jules Guérec and his sisters, are themselves taken aback: "Ils avaient vécu
plus de la moitié de leur vie," the narrator says, "avec l'idée que le reste
s'écoulerait de la même façon et voilà qu'en quelques jours, moins d'une
semaine, tout était balayé, transformé au point qu'ils ne s'y
reconnaissaient pas" (2002–04 [1936], 882).

Fate strikes constantly: the narrative is interspersed with suggestions of
abnormality and the character gradually traverses a crisis which will
eventually prove fatal. His attempt at rewriting his own situation will not
change what the powers of destiny have already prescribed for him. M.

Hire's heavy breathing—while he tries to concentrate on a film at the cinema before meeting his fiancée, Alice—foreshadows what will come next:

> [...] maintenant il se calmait. Il regardait l'écran. Il faisait même un effort pour comprendre le film.
> Malgré tout, il eut encore un soupir, un gros soupir gavé et impatient tout ensemble, car il y a des moments où cela fait mal d'attendre de la sorte au point que, les doigts crispés comme par une crampe, les genoux trépidants, on a à la fois envie de rire et de gémir. (2003 [1933], 237)

The sigh, both of joy and of suffering, adumbrates the final breath of M. Hire. The narrative closes with the last convulsive stages of his erratic existence, and lends the novel's title its ironic dimension. M. Hire and Alice will never come together, and the heart of the former, along with his longed-for engagement, will be broken.

Conclusion

Simenon's characters are ruled by a principle that makes them act in spite of themselves, leading to dramatic situations and tragic endings. The investigatory element of the plots is minimal, and its outcome has more to do with chaos than with the expected return to order. In Simenon's novels, the specific narrative structure of the detective story enables the author to compose "une sorte de chœur antique qui relie les personnages entre eux et ficelle l'intrigue".[7] The function assumed by fate in the narrative is to be understood not only in terms of the general narrative organization, but also in terms of the poetic dimension introduced by the resurfacing narratives.

The superimposition of the plots and the overprint effect produced play an important part in the vision of man as "naked". From the very first obstacle, crisis is a means of revealing truth, soon followed by the penalty which causes suffering, pain and unease, without the cathartic purification traditionally associated with tragic drama. In one of his speeches Simenon said: "Je me rapprochais de l'homme, de l'homme tout nu, de l'homme en tête à tête avec son destin qui est, je pense, le ressort suprême du roman" (1968, 295). The writer's purpose is to unroll his characters' parchment scrolls and, more generally, to expose the desires and innermost wishes of man when he is confronted with reality and falls prey to the determinism of his life and instincts. This is exemplified by the story of Jules and his sisters who, after leaving Concarneau, are "condamnés à vivre ensemble" (2002–04 [1936], 885); and by Lucien Gobillot, who has to resign himself to the death of his mistress, and states:

Je n'ai jamais pris la vie au tragique. Je me défends encore. Je cherche à rester objectif, à me juger et à juger les autres froidement. Je cherche surtout à comprendre. (2002–04 [1956], 462)

This echoes Simenon's *ex libris*, "comprendre et ne pas juger", which is in itself another form of palimpsest: both the palimpsest narrative and the novelist's stance relate to a single life which, though it cannot be relived, is reconfigured by a given medium or attitude. In the end, there are always culprits other than the culprit himself, with family background and relatives, social origins, and uncontrolled impulses just some of a variety of extenuating circumstances. In Simenon's work, the palimpsest is necessary to the narrative on many levels, and the novelist's literary approach dictated by a single ambition: "écrire un grand roman", "le roman de l'homme", to which all his novels contribute. As part of this project, his characters will perhaps never find "the innocent sleep, Sleep that knits up the ravell'd sleeve of care" (Shakespeare 2008, 2.2 35–36, 127).

Notes

[1] This paper has been translated from French to English by Nathalie Vincent-Arnaud, Professor at the Department of English at the University of Toulouse-Le Mirail and Amy Wigelsworth, co-editor of this volume.

[2] "Romans durs", "romans de la destinée" or "romans-romans" (to use another of Simenon's terms for such works) can be defined as novels in which Maigret does not feature.

[3] *Les Demoiselles de Concarneau* was first published in instalments in *La Revue de France*, from 15 December 1935 to 1 February 1936, under the title *Les Trois demoiselles de Concarneau*, before its publication as a book in 1936 (Paris: Gallimard).

[4] The title of one of the chapters of *Le Dernier mot de Rocambole* (1867) is "La Belle jardinière".

[5] Simenon uses this expression to refer to the situations of his main characters in the course of the different novels.

[6] I refer to "tropisms" in the sense given to them by Nathalie Sarraute in her preface to *L'Ere du Soupçon* (Sarraute 1956). The *Dictionnaire alphabétique et analogique de la langue française* (6 volumes, Le Robert 1969) describes a tropism as "[une] [r]éaction élémentaire à une cause extérieure ; acte réflexe très simple".

[7] See *Des entretiens exemplaires*, avec André Parinaud, 1965.

Works cited

Barthes, Roland. 1973. *Théorie du texte*. Paris: Encyclopoedia Universalis.

Genette, Gérard. 1982. *Palimpsestes, La littérature au second degré*. Paris: Seuil.

Kristeva, Julia. 1969. *Sèmèiôtikè. Recherche pour une sémanalyse*. Paris: Seuil.

Malraux, André. Préface à *Sanctuaire* de William Faulkner. Paris: Gallimard.

Ponson du Terrail. 1867. *Le Dernier mot de Rocambole*, IV: La Belle jardinière. Paris: E. Dentu.

Roger, Stéphane. 1989 [RTF, J. Taillandier, diffusion de l'interview: novembre et décembre 1963]. *Portrait souvenir de Georges Simenon, Entretien*. Paris: Quai Voltaire.

Sarraute, Nathalie. 1956. *L'Ere du Soupçon*, Paris : Gallimard.

Shakespeare, William. 2008. *The Tragedy of Macbeth*. Edited by Nicholas Brooke. Oxford: OUP (The Oxford Shakespeare).

Simenon Georges. 2003 [Fayard, 1933]. *Les Fiançailles de M. Hire*. Paris: Omnibus. *Tout Simenon*, tome 18/27, 2003, 173–259.

—. 2003 [Gallimard, 1936]. *Les Demoiselles de Concarneau*. Paris: Omnibus. *Tout Simenon*, tome 19/27, 807–888.

—. 2002 [Presses de la Cité, 1956]. *En Cas de malheur*. Paris: Omnibus. *Tout Simenon*, tome 8/27, 2002, 406–514.

—. 1968. *Le Romancier*, Lausanne: éditions Rencontre. *Œuvres complètes*, tome 17/72, 273–303.

—. 2001. *Mes apprentissages. Reportages 1931–1946*. Edited by Francis Lacassin. Paris: Omnibus.

—. 2003. *Georges Simenon, Des entretiens exemplaires (1955-1968-1975)*, Paris: Harmonia mundi, Les grandes heures INA/Radio France, 2 CD.

Todorov, Tzvetan, 1971. "*Typologie du roman policier*". In *Poétique de la prose*, 55–65. Paris: Seuil.

Table 1: Plot summary of *Les Fiançailles de M. Hire*

Title (Year of publication)	Main characters	Plot triggers (events/ incipit)	Evolution of plot	Multiplications of plot	Plots/Resurfacing stories	End of narrative (excipit)
Les Fiançailles de M. Hire (1933)	M. Hire, lives in Villejuif	Savage murder of a prostitute (prior to narrative)	Concierge's statement	Alice seeks to lay the blame on M. Hire	Sad memories of M. Hire's childhood	Death of M. Hire
	Alice, companion of Emile, the culprit		Interrogation of M. Hire	M. Hire tries to escape in order to marry Alice	M. Hire's criminal record: indecent exposure	Miscarriage of justice
			Tailing of M. Hire by police	M. Hire writes a letter to the prosecutor to expose the culprit		Forthcoming sentence of the culprit (posterior to narrative)
	Emile, companion of Alice		Resolution of crime by M. Hire: Emile is the culprit			

Table 2: Plot summary of *Les Demoiselles de Concarneau*

Title (Year of publication)	Main characters	Plot triggers (events/ incipit)	Evolution of plot	Multiplications of plot	Plots/ Resurfacing stories	End of narrative (excipit)
Les Demoiselles de Concarneau (1936)	Jules Guérec, head-fisherman	Car crash: accidental killing of child	Death of child	Resolution of mystery by Céline	The "vieille histoire" (Germaine, the girl made pregnant by Jules)	Investigation fails
	Céline, Jules's sister	Hit-and-run offence (Jules)	The culprit conceals the crime	Céline buys the mother's silence		Culprit remains unpunished
			Miscarriage in investigation (car number plate)	Jules and his sisters keep moving on	Céline buys Germaine's silence	Uprooting of the Guérec family
	Marie Papin, mother of dead child				Humiliating hunting episode	

Table 3: Plot summary of *En Cas de malheur*

Title (Year of publication)	Main characters	Plot triggers (events/ incipit)	Evolution of plot	Multiplications of plot	Plots/ Resurfacing stories	End of narrative (excipit)
En Cas de malheur (1956)	Lucien Gobillot, lawyer	Armed robbery and assault (prior to narrative)	Culprit absolved thanks to Gobillot	Gobillot's affair with Yvette	Gobillot writes his diary: childhood, studies, first dubious plea, first meeting with his wife	Death of Yvette
	Yvette Maudet, client then mistress of Gobillot			Rape and assassination of Yvette by Mazetti		Mazetti is caught (sentence posterior to narrative)
	Léonard Mazetti, Yvette's lover				Backgrounds of Yvette's victims exposed	

PART II:

TEXTUAL REWRITING

CHAPTER FIVE

PARIS AS REWRITE:
GETTING AWAY WITH IT IN LÉO MALET'S
XVE ARRONDISSEMENT

ALISTAIR ROLLS

In his "Work-in-Progress" study of the Bastille, Keith Reader notes Walter Benjamin's "fragmentary and citational mode of writing" in *The Arcades Project*, which he explains is "often compared to a collage or palimpsest" (2010, 56). If Reader stops short of declaring Paris itself a palimpsest ("Paris abides and changes," he writes on page 63), the inference is nonetheless there. Indeed, for a scholar like Ross Chambers (1999), writing the city and walking the city are one and the same act, performed in a double space: steps taken on the city streets as they unfold before us in real, present time recall steps (re-)inscribed (remembered, re-presented) in historical, or mythological, time. To this extent, Paris is a double city—both itself and exemplary of its (own) otherness, but also both particularly modern while at the same time paradigmatic of the great cities of modernity[1]—and as such it recalls the Paris of Charles Baudelaire's prose poetry. Indeed, like the prose poem, Paris "n'a ni queue ni tête, puisque tout, au contraire, y est à la fois tête et queue, alternativement et réciproquement".[2] We should note the irony of the concluding prose poem, or "Épilogue", in which the Satanic pull of poetry into the Parisian streets is complete—with Paris described as a brothel, jail or hell on earth, the victory of prose over poetry is total—but which is the only poem to present itself, and its Satanic prose, in verse form, and thus as pure poetry.

Of course, in Baudelaire's crowning, and quasi-overarching, (non-prose) prose poem, Paris fuels a naming exercise but is itself only named metonymically, as the capital, in this case of France but also of prose poetry, if not of critical Modernity itself. And as Michel Covin has shown,[3] Paris's necessary metonymic presence in the prose poems is such that the poems can unfold inside the city's streets, in real time; the outside, the timeless context, is always already given. Thus, the prose poems serve as an urtext in both time and space. In spatial terms, Paris is double; it is always itself and *anywhere out of the world*, always itself *and* a metaphor for the modern metropolis. Temporally, Paris stands for that typically Baudelairean intersection of the existential moment in time and the infinity of abstract, poetic values. In this second sense in particular, Baudelaire's prose poetics is of fundamental importance for another important intersection, this time of desire and knowledge, which will inform the present reading of Léo Malet's own rewriting of Paris: fetishism.[4]

As a form of disavowal, or partial repression,[5] fetishism allows the Freudian subject to have his cake and eat it: the young boy who believes his mother to be phallic does not have to stop believing in this even when he knows it to be untrue; instead, by reverting his gaze to an object glimpsed immediately before the revelation of the truth, he is able to erect a screen memory that will allow reality (the existential truth of the situation) to coincide with desire (for mother to be phallic, which now becomes the capitalized Truth of myth), hence the intersection of two incompatible world views and the construction of a particularly useful double space.[6] The mythical phallic mother is therefore both just that, a myth, but also present, in the world. In this sense, she recalls Baudelaire's paradoxical Venus, both impossible, or necessarily absent to the world, and there in the street.[7] For Baudelaire, disavowal is a response to the trauma brought about by the Haussmannization of his city, which remains Paris and in fact becomes itself more fully in the myth (of a lost self) that the poet founds and subsequently bequeaths to his poetic successors, among the most notable of whom were the surrealists, while at the same time it morphs into an unrecognizable Other.

According to Michelle Emanuel, it is just such a change in the Parisian cityscape that caused Léo Malet to abandon his *Nouveaux mystères de Paris* after completing stories set in only fifteen of the twenty *arrondissements* (2006, 123). While not wishing to argue against such a position, based as it is on the author's own reported comments on his praxis, I should suggest that this same trauma (Emanuel describes it, less inspiringly, as a form of depression) is precisely the driving force of the prose poetics and *flâneur*-detection that are common to the works of Malet and Baudelaire. It is therefore the ever changing face of Paris, which is nevertheless periodically rendered more starkly dramatic (in the decades of the mid-century in both the nineteenth and twentieth centuries) in what might be referred to as overdetermined moments in history,[8] that produces rather than terminates Malet's series. For, as Emanuel notes, Malet considered himself a "fétichiste moyen et obsédé sexuel total" (2006, 77).[9] Thus, it would appear that Malet's evident interest in women's underwear is keener when the garments are adorning women's bodies than when they are standing in lieu of them, in the perversely auto-antonymic role of the Freudian screen. And yet, once again, this admission on Malet's part seems, appropriately enough, to be itself only partial, and it is precisely on the image chosen by Emanuel to illustrate the half-heartedness of Malet's fetishism that I shall predicate my argument for a much more profoundly fetishistic drive at the basis of Malet's enterprise. Indeed, the underwear in question ("une culotte bleue à volants"), which is hanging on a clothes line at the very beginning of *Les Eaux troubles de Javel* (set in the XVe *arrondissement*), does far more than define (or delimit) its owner Jeanne Marigny; rather, it liberates the metonymic association, acting as a kind of deconstructionist hospitality ("knickers as host", perhaps, to fetishize J. Hillis Miller) and screening—both pointing to and veiling—other virtual wearers, and, as will be seen, one other woman in particular.

My aim here, therefore, is to expose another, rather romantic side to Malet's novels, one that emphasizes the fetishism at the expense of a purely sexual obsession; I shall at the same time take issue with Emanuel's statement that, "[i]n *Les Nouveaux mystères de Paris*, the guilty are punished" (2006, 85). For, if, as I suggest, *Les Eaux troubles de Javel* (1957) is a rewrite of *Nestor Burma contre C.Q.F.D.* (1945), it is so precisely in order that the beloved woman may recommit the same crime *and be allowed to get away with it*.[10] Implicit, finally, in my analysis of Malet's novel as rewrite are its reflection of Paris as palimpsest and a Bayardian re-solution of the case.[11]

The site of our entry into *Les Eaux troubles de Javel*, rue de la Saïda, is depressing to the point of bolstering Emanuel's claim that urban modernization may have driven Malet from his Parisian project. On the other hand, this bleak backdrop with its "infecte brouillasse" (Malet 2006 [1957], 5) does more than simply refer back to the *brouillard* that hung over the pont de Tolbiac just a year earlier;[12] rather, it frames the novel within the intertext of mythologization predicated on Baudelaire's new poetics of modernity. Thus, when Nestor Burma's gaze has been arrested by these liminal blue knickers, with their frills fluttering on the clothes line, the reader is already primed for a woman to pass by.[13] And when she does, her air of familiarity owes a debt to a woman passing by more recently than Baudelaire's archetype:

Nous parvenions au premier, lorsqu'un grand barouf se produisit au-dessus de nous. Quelqu'un descendit l'escalier à toute vitesse, au risque de s'abîmer le portrait, claquant des talons sur les marches sonores. [...]

C'était une jeune fille de dix-huit, vingt ans, avec des cheveux châtains emprisonnés sous un foulard noué au menton. Elle portait [...] une de ces jupes pincées au-dessous du genou et plissées à partir de là que le moindre mouvement fait tourbillonner. Elle avait une certaine élégance, de jolies jambes gainées de bas assez fins, une jolie frimousse maquillée sans excès et des souliers à hauts talons. (2006 [1957], 8)

Indeed, the similarity to the following scene, from *Nestor Burma contre C.Q.F.D.*, is striking:

Elle surgissait du couloir à soixante centimètres duquel je me tenais immobile. J'étais trop contre le mur pour que semblable mésaventure ne m'arrivât pas si quelqu'un faisait précipitamment irruption de l'immeuble. Or, la jeune fille en était sortie littéralement en trombe. Je n'avais jamais vu quelqu'un d'aussi pressé ! Elle allait rapidement, au rythme souple de ses jambes fines et élégantes, merveilleusement gainées d'une soie rare pour l'époque. Ses souliers à hauts talons ne faisaient aucun bruit. Elle portait un tailleur bleu par-dessous une veste de fourrure. Ses cheveux auburn se confondaient avec la couleur du mouton doré. J'avais seulement entr'aperçu son visage. Il ne m'avait pas paru vilain du tout.
(1985 [1945], 126)

This textual reference can usefully be interpreted through the lens of the cinematic image. The stock fetish elements—the fur, stockings and high heels—point to what I consider to be Malet's more profound fetishism. Laura Mulvey's comments are thus apposite here:

The image of a woman on a screen achieves a particular spectacular intensity partly as a result [...] of a homology of structure. Just as an elaborate and highly artificial, dressed-up, made-up appearance envelops the movie star in 'surface', so does her surface supply a glossy front for the cinema, holding the eye in fascinated distraction away from its mechanics of production. (1996, 13)

Jeanne's passing-by in the first quotation above is appropriately staged: it operates fetishistically to draw the reader's attention to and, at the same time, to distract her eyes from this homology of structure. In this instance, the reader is co-present to the text currently being read, *Les Eaux troubles de Javel*, and its predecessor, *Nestor Burma contre C.Q.F.D.*, whose events unfurl in the same Parisian locale. Here, the text, like Barbara Creed's description of an uncanny house, is "haunted by the ghost or trace of a memory which takes the individual back to the early, perhaps foetal, relation with the mother" (cited in Mulvey 1996, 14). In this case, however, Nestor Burma and his steps in this particular *arrondissement* are haunted not by memories of the mother; and "the exterior carapace of feminine beauty" does not collapse "to reveal the uncanny, abject, maternal body" (Mulvey 1996, 15). Indeed, the fetish here does not fail. Instead, what is revealed, and remembered, as abject is Burma's resolution of the case in *Nestor Burma contre C.Q.F.D.*, in which the woman passing by, Lydia Verbois, was correctly labelled as guilty and subsequently freed by the enamoured Burma, only for her to die in a train derailment. By passing by, Jeanne maps Lydia's steps and offers a chance for Burma to negotiate his trauma, in the present, by re-solving this past case. The novel that follows is therefore entirely predicated on this rewriting of a wrong in the double space of the *XVe arrondissement*.

Immediately following his encounter with Jeanne, Burma begins the investigation proper, or perhaps the overt detection-text. During his meeting with Hortense, who has hired him to trace her missing husband, Paul Demessy, Burma twice refers to the latter's elevation out of the gutter as "de l'histoire ancienne", and this, we are told, "sans mentir entièrement" (2006 [1957], 14). To lie partially is, of course, one way of describing a fetishistic negotiation of a traumatic truth: the actions that will guide Burma through this new case will hinge on a desire not only to protect Hortense and others in the *XVe* from the truth but also to redeem the actions of Burma's own past and another story. For, a story about stories is precisely what we are presented with in *Les Eaux troubles*. Both the ancient past—Burma's role in marrying the tramp Demessy to an exotic foreign beauty—and the future denouement of the investigation are equally subjective; both are reconfigurations of that other ancient past. As such, this will be a case of double fetishism, not only a retelling of the past in order to come to terms with the present, but also a manipulation of the present in order to salvage the past.

This storytelling aspect of Burma's detection comes to the fore in *Les Eaux troubles*. Amongst Demessy's things are a number of books. By providing a record of Demessy's reading habits, Burma is, of course, letting us in on the whodunit aspect of his modus operandi: he will bring about his re(-)solution not only by acting on the ground, becoming one with the *XVe arrondissement*, but also by taking a step back from the action and engaging with the clues objectively. In this way, his retracing of his steps in these Parisian streets reflexively mimics the critical stance— simultaneously subjective and objective—of Baudelaire's *flâneur*.[14] This will obviously involve a process of analytic reading; it will also lead the detective to write the story of the crime as the investigation proceeds. This act, which appears supremely objective, is in fact equally an insight into the subjective practice of writerly reading, which allows the detective of modernity to engage with the crime text as a piece of modernism, that is to say a text that simultaneously pulls the reader in and pushes her away. The following perusal of Demessy's books, therefore, is a particularly neat *mise en abyme*; its reflexivity checks Malet's reader and forces her to engage more actively, but it also reminds her that the detective is performing the same critical reading. The list of books is as follows:

> [D]eux bouquins défraîchis et un cahier d'écolier. Les deux bouquins traitaient de mécanique et le cahier était couvert de notes et de dessins s'y rapportant. [...] C'était aussi des bouquins d'étude, voisinant avec un roman d'amour, deux ou trois policiers et quelques autres d'espionnage. (2006 [1957], 16)

Any list of books would have sufficed to create a reflexive, modernist moment. The particularity of this list is to offer a commentary on how the thriller in which it appears is going to be written. The list includes a theoretical component ("des bouquins d'étude"), in this case the theory of car mechanics, some exercise books, a romantic novel, a few crime thrillers and some spy novels. Burma's search discloses the recipe for a formulaic detective novel (which might include notes on how to dissimulate truths and the distribution of red herrings—a study of how to "lie partially"), which *Les Eaux troubles* will most certainly be. More interestingly, however, it also gives specific details of the "mechanics" of the specific novel (*Les Eaux troubles*) that is both already begun and ongoing: this will be a novel set in one of the principal hubs of the French automotive industry (the Citroën plant will play a major role in the decor and plot, and Renault's famous site at Boulogne-Billancourt is just across the river). Demessy's books provide detailed information on how to write *this* book, then. There will, of course, be a love interest (indeed, the "mechanics" of this one will prove reasonably complicated); and, as we have seen, the denouement will include a somewhat fantastical espionage angle.[15]

And yet, this is no simple *mise en abyme*; this is a full list of ingredients intended both to help and hinder the reader. We should remember that the key message is that Demessy's role here is "to be a story". Burma is giving us this information, not Léo Malet himself; the information relates to a story that Burma has not as yet finished. The only way he can know (and disclose) information about the spy element is if it forms part of the story that he intends to write. The list is, thus, a red herring despite itself, and Burma is offering us a lesson in how to lie partially. This is a story about pulling the wool over the reader's eyes, and it is up to us to see which character operates in this way vis-à-vis the reader-in-the-text, played, of course, by our fetishist-detective.

Given the intertextuality created between *Les Eaux troubles* and *Nestor Burma contre C.Q.F.D.* by the common incident of the woman passing by, it would be counter-intuitive not to seek to trace the object or person onto whom the truth of the foundational, if not phallic or even necessarily *fatale*, woman has been displaced.[16] The obvious first choice is the *passante* herself. Jeanne Marigny is never under serious suspicion in the novel, however; instead, she assists Burma with the investigation, during which they develop a romantic connection (as prescribed by Demessy's books). The perfume that she wears (and which reminds Burma of his secretary, Hélène) puts him onto the scent, quite literally, of the "other woman". For, it soon becomes clear that this other woman is the prime suspect:

> Il existait peut-être un moyen—une bien faible chance—de parvenir jusqu'à la femme si délicieusement parfumée. Et ensuite, tout le monde pourrait aller se coucher. (2006 [1957], 78)

And when Burma at last finds her, her physical resemblance to Jeanne, as well as to Lydia Verbois, the woman passing by in *Nestor Burma contre C.Q.F.D.*, is as striking as the perfume that they also share: "Lorsqu'elle se glissa sous le volant, un éclair de chair jaillit d'une mousse de nylon" (2006 [1957], 85). The traditional fetish accoutrements of noir indicate, as Steve Smith has demonstrated (2000), a displacement of desire. In this case, I should argue, Baudelaire's celebrated lifting and swinging of "le feston et l'ourlet" in "À une passante" (1861) has been translated from Lydia Verbois, via the partial lying of the metonymic "culotte de nylon bleu", into the stockings of three women: Jeanne, Hélène, Burma's secretary, and this other woman, who turns out to be none other than Paul Demessy's *other* wife. For, but for the fact that he is not technically married to Hortense, Demessy is a bigamist. This is the information that Burma has been withholding since the opening pages of the novel (one of his partial lies): his ascent from the gutter was arranged by Burma as part of a green-card-style arrangement, which sees a young Scandinavian woman, Wanda, able to attain French citizenship by entering into a sham marriage with a man desperate for money to improve his position in life.

I would argue that this marriage is calqued on Baudelaire's prose poem "Le Fou et la Vénus", with its impossible synthesis of the abstract Beauty of the poetic and the vulgar reality of the prosaic, which functions as the guiding principle of the plot (and the subplots, McGuffins and red

herrings) of *Nestor Burma contre C.Q.F.D*. Indeed, the whole story of
Wanda's guilt and Burma's motives for devising the elaborate counter-
explanation that allows it to go unsaid are both pre-established in
C.Q.F.D.: if Burma has already considered Lydia's guilt, his resistance to
it has taken root at the same time, and it is fuelled by Hélène's reasoning
(which thus becomes the counterpoint to his own gut reaction): "Elle […]
s'acharna sur la jeune fille avec une insistance qui me déplut" (1985
[1945], 172). By way of a punishment, Burma sends Hélène off to visit
fashion houses all over Paris to find where Lydia works, just as he will
again in *Les Eaux troubles* when she goes around jewellers' shops to find
out the provenance of Jeanne's perfume. While Burma's desire for the
guilty party to be innocent is clearly translated from *C.Q.F.D.* onto *Les
Eaux troubles*, I would argue that the desire itself is *not* displaced. In fact,
Hélène's following comments perfectly resume Burma's (partially)
unconscious desire to believe in Wanda's freedom and, thus, to lie
(partially) both to himself and the reader:

> Ouais, siffla-t-elle, goguenarde. *L'autre chose*, c'est Lydia Verbois. Elle
> semble vous avoir fait impression. […] Et c'est pour cette raison que vous
> ne voulez pas envisager sa culpabilité. (1985 [1945], 172)

Lydia's innocent persona is the logical and ever present alter ego of her
guilty one; and it is by choosing (and performing the writerly reading of)
Wanda's innocence that Burma redeems the failed synthesis of his
communion with his own beloved woman passing by.

Wanda's motives for killing Demessy parallel Lydia's murder of
Barton in *C.Q.F.D.*: like Wanda, Lydia wants no further contact with her
estranged husband; like Wanda, too, she fires in the end because her
blackmailing husband wants to have sex with her in a sordid little room in
the XVe *arrondissement*. The displacement of other plot elements speaks of
a rewrite of the novel rather than a simple transfer of the female suspect: it
is Lydia's invented alter ego, also called Jeanne, who is said to be
remarried, living with her child in the country; in *Les Eaux troubles*, this
domestic side of Lydia/Jeanne's persona is taken up by Hortense,
Demessy's impoverished, countrified and pregnant current partner.
Wanda's feelings for her own current partner, on the other hand, come
from *C.Q.F.D.*'s other "other woman": Mme Julien Bourguet, who, it
transpires, was Thévenon's mistress and the mysterious woman seen with
him in a taxi in Paris, also wants her past liaison kept secret from her
present husband. The tragic figure of Mme Bourguet, who takes her own
life, is sacrificed to Burma's investigation and arguably inoculates him in

his 1957 reprise, in which her innocence is juxtaposed with Lydia's guilt in the composite figure of Wanda.[17]

Finally, the alternative denouement of *Les Eaux troubles* is also foreshadowed in *C.Q.F.D.*: Burma feels almost from the start that the police are wrong to ignore the famous advice of Dumas père ("cherchez la femme..."); instead, "[l]e siège de la police était fait. Il s'agissait d'un drame du milieu" (1985 [1945], 157). And yet, as Burma's gut feelings are superseded by his desire, he too considers gangsters to be likely culprits: "Il faut tout de même bien leur trouver une place dans ce scénario" (1985 [1945], 197). This line is important not only because it proleptically signals the pride of place to be given to gangsters at the end of *Les Eaux troubles* but also, and especially, because of the indication that their part in the plot is precisely to be "found", to be written in. For, clearly, theirs is a fanciful role, which we should be as naïve to consider in *Les Eaux troubles* as the police are in *C.Q.F.D.*

The most obviously oneiric part of the conclusion of *Les Eaux troubles* comes just before Burma falls unconscious in the cellar of the Arab gang's hideout. It appears that the gang's leader has himself entirely fabricated his account of Demessy's spying (in order to cover up his own part in a bank heist, the motives of which were purely financial), with the result that the spy story remains just that—a story—until the end. And as the curtain falls on Burma's alternative solution, the wall in the cellar collapses in an explosion, and out come tumbling Demessy's corpse, banknotes and all.[18] Intertextually, this element of the alternative narrative is inspired directly by Burma's mistaken assumption in *C.Q.F.D.* that Thévenon's missing gold is cemented into a wall in the cellar of a house in the Parisian suburbs, where he had temporarily stayed, where Lydia had coincidentally come to live and where Burma himself had previously stumbled thanks to a moment of objective chance. This proves not to be the case, however; instead, the cement used rather roughly to cover a cavity in which Thévenon had hidden his revolver proves a distraction from a more subtle use elsewhere in the cellar. The wall thus lies partially; it gives an alibi to the cement and steers the gaze of potential onlookers away from the bars of the cellar window, which are none other than the missing "lingots" (1985 [1945], 217). This earlier use of cellar space allows the reader of *Les Eaux troubles* to reconfigure the banknotes that rain around Burma as a (disingenuously factitious) celebration of the porous borders of open-closed space. The credibility of otherwise imaginary Arab villains with imaginary motives in an imaginary cellar full of imaginary money is, via this proleptic use of cellar space, always already grounded in Burma's case history.[19]

When Wanda and Lydia embark on their final attempt to lie partially to Burma, that is to tell him a truth made palatable to his gaze, they have both already established their fetishistic pedigree. In Wanda's case, as has already been noted, her entry into the text, as she climbs behind the wheel of her car, reveals if not her most flattering then at least her most fetishistically suggestive angle. Lydia, too, after her experience at the hands of the two thugs in the house in the suburbs, makes sure that Burma's understanding of events is passed through the filter of his desire:

> Elle s'arrêta. Sa main se crispa sur son genou, relevant un peu la jupe. Sous la fine soie des bas était visible la trace bleue d'un coup en voie de guérison. (1985 [1945], 143)

Thus, when Wanda gives her account of her presence at the scene of Demessy's murder, she begins in that fetishistic zone where polar opposites merge and run parallel:

> [E]lle ramena sa robe sur ses belles jambes, découvertes presque jusqu'à la lisière du bas depuis qu'elle s'était effondrée dans le fauteuil. Marrant ! Elle qui n'hésitait pas à montrer ses fesses, lorsqu'elle montait ou sortait de voiture. (2006 [1957], 88)

Here Burma is picking up on Wanda's apparently duplicitous sense of shame. One might argue that she is damned either way—whether she pulls her dress up or down, this will be interpreted as drawing the male gaze—but the important aspect of this scene is that we see it through Burma's eyes; and this gesture, which is diametrically opposed to what one might expect, is itself reversed as her need emerges for him to read her otherwise.

She admits to having been present at the scene and to striking Burma as he entered the room; she even admits to having gone there to kill Demessy in his sordid would-be love nest; she stops short only of having pulled the trigger, alleging instead that he was already dead. There can be no mistaking this crime, for it is a precise replica of Lydia's shooting of Barton. Her whole defence will rely on whether Burma is prepared to erect the necessary screen memory in place of the obvious truth of what has occurred. She exposes her leg in order to elicit a fetishistic response. Her gestured invitation to him to "get a good look" is therefore a call for him to believe in the myth of the innocent woman: "[S]a robe lui remonta au-dessus du genou, et elle la laissa là, pour que je me rince l'œil" (2006 [1957], 94). Like Lydia before her, Wanda asks whether Burma believes her. This time, however, Burma decides to see what will happen if he allows the myth to mask the truth: "Je vais faire comme si. Je verrai ce que ça donnera" (94).[20]

And what it gives, of course, is the gangster solution, one that resolves the traumatic truth of the present (Hortense's need for money to bring up her baby; Wanda's need to live her new life with the husband of her choice) by an exploration of the past (the story that we learn of Demessy's marriage to Wanda and Burma's part in it). Burma's rewriting of the immediate past (the truth of Demessy's murder), on the other hand, rights a wrong that is arguably simultaneously past and present (the death of Lydia Verbois). Burma thereby turns the XVe arrondissement into a double murder space that opposes and conjoins *Les Eaux troubles de Javel* and *Nestor Burma contre C.Q.F.D.* Perversely, it is Malet's fetishism that, displacement and overvaluation of female body parts notwithstanding, remakes the whole by rewriting the wrong of Lydia's death. Her guilt is now balanced out, via Wanda's liberation, with her innocence. And with this reinvention of the XVe arrondissement another aspect of Malet's *Nouveaux mystères* comes to light: the fragmentation of the city only highlights the metonymic value of such areas as Reader's Bastille, whose diversity ultimately reflects the palimpsestuous quality, and broader metropolitan self-alterity, of all Paris. For, while Paris is always itself, it is always already also its Other.

Notes

[1] See Reader 2010; see also Harvey 2003 and Higonnet 2006.

[2] This famous description of the little prose poems is taken from Baudelaire's letter to Arsène Houssaye, which acts as a preface to the collection. See Baudelaire 1973, 21.

[3] Michel Covin offers a particularly insightful chiastic analysis of the full title of Baudelaire's *Petits Poèmes en prose : Le Spleen Parisien*, according to which Paris is both opposed to Spleen, as an abstract noun, but also the locus of the abstract's encounter with the city streets, and thus the embodiment of prose poetics. See Covin 2000, 51–52.

[4] Ellen Lee McCallum refers to fetishism as the "unique intersection of desire and knowledge" (1999, xii).

[5] For a detailed analysis of Freud's theory of *le refoulement partiel*, see Rey-Flaud 1994, 27–43.

[6] Certainly, the fetishist's method of negotiating the world is deemed effective by Freud, so much so that he saw no need to treat it. In her work on the visual image in the work of the surrealists, Johanna Malt describes this phenomenon in terms of a "paradox of presence and absence" (2004, 136).

[7] The reference here is to "Le Fou et la Vénus" (Baudelaire 1973, 33–34).

[8] This expression is borrowed from Mulvey's comparison of Marxist and Freudian fetishisms (1996, 5); to this end, she is citing Thomas Richards's description of Victorian England's Great Exhibition.

[9] The reference here is to an interview given by Malet to Noël Simsolo, published in 1985.

[10] In this way, the "true"—nihilistic or other—murderer of *Les Eaux troubles de Javel* partially fulfils the *cahier des charges* of the perfect best-seller according to the bookstore owner in Vernon Sullivan's classic post-war *roman noir*, *J'irai cracher sur vos tombes*, in which "des jeunes filles pures [...] réussiront à grandir intactes au milieu de la pègre sordide des faubourgs" (Vian 2010, 245).

[11] By dismissing Malet's ending of *Les Eaux troubles de Javel*, which Emanuel herself (2006, 92) seems to find vaguely troubling in its incoherent outpouring of racist stereotypes, I shall aim to follow in the path of Pierre Bayard who offers up new murderers for *The Murder of Roger Ackroyd* and *The Hound of the Baskervilles*, in *Qui a tué Roger Ackroyd ?* (1998) and *L'Affaire du Chien des Baskerville* (2008), respectively.

[12] *Les Eaux troubles de Javel* was first published in 1957, *Brouillard au pont de Tolbiac* in 1956.

[13] For a more detailed reading of the ubiquitous woman passing by in the Parisian literature of the years immediately following the Second World War, the debt to Baudelaire's "À une passante", inter alia, and the reciprocal reflection of and impact on the historical moment, see Rolls 2010.

[14] This stepping back from the action falls under the practices that Ross Chambers (1999, *passim*) includes under his critical notion of "belatedness". As I have noted here and elsewhere, the *flâneur* is always already both inside and outside the action. He is, therefore, belated in respect of events at the very moment that he allows himself to be swept up by and to take action in them.

[15] Clearly, this is also an amusing *mise en abyme* when considered, more simply, as an author's note, in which case it suggests that writing *Les Nouveaux mystères de Paris* is as formulaic a project as writing any other *polar*: you still need the same basic elements, but the local colour is provided, perhaps more extensively than is usually the case, by a particular Parisian *arrondissement*. It is important to reiterate, however, that to treat the choice of locales as mere palettes of local colour is to do a disservice to this project, in which Paris also plays the critical, prose-poetic role that I have outlined above.

[16] The *femme fatale* in this novel, as in *Nestor Burma contre C.Q.F.D.*, is very much of the French screen variety as described by Deborah Walker, for whom the spider woman of American film noir never really survives the journey across the Atlantic. For Walker, the *femme* of French noir is more an accidental killer; she is, in other words, more *fatalitaire* than *fatale* (Rolls and Walker 2009, 132–48).

[17] Wanda and Jeanne both wear a perfume that Burma has smelt on Hélène. In *C.Q.F.D.* Mme Bourguet wears a perfume that Hélène used to wear before the war; Lydia also used to wear it before the war, and it is because she took an old handbag, still containing a bottle of this perfume, to her fatal rendezvous with Barton that the two suspects become confused. Both novels carry double (pre-war

and post-war) fragrances, and it is by this common, disjointed trace that they are conjoined.

[18] On one level, this is a convulsive, surrealistic moment: the explosion mimics the shock that occurs when two parallel worlds collide, and while not fatal—it usually ends in death in films like Luis Buñuel's *Un chien andalou*—it does cause Burma to faint.

[19] The illusory role of gold in *Les Eaux troubles*, where it is important only in the alternative, dream-denouement, also emerges in *C.Q.F.D.* When Lydia tells Burma that she fired on Barton while he was trying to force her to sleep with him in his room off the boulevard Victor, he cries out "non" (230). He forces her, perhaps out of pure jealousy, to believe that Barton was motivated by gold rather than sex. Gold, then, is used in both novels to silence the guilt of the *femme fatale* in a *crime passionnel*.

[20] A comparison of page 195 of *C.Q.F.D.* reveals that Wanda's technique is almost a word-for-word reconstruction of Lydia's veiled truth: "Ses yeux un peu humides cherchèrent mon regard. [...] Vous me croyez, dites ? implora-t-elle. [...] Elle se tassa dans le fauteuil, accablée. Elle glissa un peu sur le coussin, et dans ce mouvement sa jupe découvrit ses jambes très haut."

Works cited

Baudelaire, Charles. 1998 [first published in 1861 in the second edition of *Les Fleurs du mal*]. "À une passante." In *The Flowers of Evil*. Translated by James McGowan with parallel French text. Oxford: Oxford University Press, 188.

—. 1973. *Petits Poëmes en prose (Le Spleen de Paris)*. Paris: Gallimard [Poésie].

Bayard, Pierre. 1998. *Qui a tué Roger Ackroyd ?* Paris: Minuit.

—. 2008. *L'Affaire du Chien des Baskerville*. Paris: Minuit.

Chambers, Ross. 1999. *Loiterature*. Lincoln; London: University of Nebraska Press.

Covin, Michel. 2000. *L'Homme de la rue: Essai sur la poétique baudelairienne*. Paris: L'Harmattan.

Emanuel, Michelle. 2006. *From Surrealism to Less-Exquisite Cadavers: Léo Malet and the Evolution of the French 'Roman Noir'*. Amsterdam; New York: Rodopi.

Harvey, David. 2003. *Paris, Capital of Modernity*. New York; London: Routledge.

Higonnet , Patrice. 2006. *Paris, capitale du monde : Des Lumières au surrealism*. Paris: Tallandier.

McCallum, Ellen Lee. 1999. *Object Lessons: How to do Things with Fetishism*. New York: SUNY Press.

Malet, Léo. 1985 [1945]. *Nestor Burma contre C.Q.F.D.* In *Les Enquêtes de Nestor Burma et Les Nouveaux mystères de Paris. Œuvres completes,* vol. I, 123–236. Paris: Robert Laffont.

—. 2006 [1957]. *Les Eaux troubles de Javel.* In *Nestor Burma : Les Nouveaux mystères de Paris,* vol. II, 1–112. Paris: Robert Laffont.

Malt, Johanna. 2004. *Obscure Objects of Desire: Surrealism, Fetishism, and Politics.* Oxford: Oxford University Press.

Mulvey, Laura. 1996. *Fetishism and Curiosity.* Bloomington; Indianapolis: Indiana University Press.

Reader, Keith. 2010. "Writing the City, Writing the *Quartier*: Work-in-Progress on the Bastille Area of Paris." *Contemporary French Civilization* 34.2: 49–65.

Rey-Flaud, Henri. 1994. *Comment Freud inventa le fétichisme... et réinventa la psychanalyse.* Paris: Payot & Rivages.

Rolls, Alistair. 2010. "L'Élégante de la rue Lepic: A New Look for *une passante.*" *Contemporary French Civilization* 34.2: 91–107.

Rolls, Alistair, and Deborah Walker. 2009. *French and American Noir: Dark Crossings.* Houndmills: Palgrave Macmillan.

Smith, Steve. 2000. "Between Detachment and Desire: Léo Malet's French *roman noir.*" In *Crime Scenes: Detective Narratives in European Culture since 1945,* edited by Anne Mullen and Emer O'Beirne, 125–36. Amsterdam; Atlanta: Rodopi.

Vian, Boris. 2010. *Œuvres romanesques complètes,* vol. I. Paris: Gallimard, Bibliothèque de la Pléiade.

CHAPTER SIX

AN OVERWRITTEN MYSTERY: BALZAC, TELEVISION AND *UNE TÉNÉBREUSE AFFAIRE*

ANDREW WATTS

The indifference of scholars to television adaptations of Balzac's work is mystifying. While critics have often derided adaptation as an "unimaginative act of imitation" (Sanders 2006, 24), television provides compelling evidence of the many innovative ways in which popular culture has engaged with *La Comédie humaine*. To date, at least sixty recreations of Balzac texts have been produced for the small screen, including, most recently, Alain Berliner's 2010 adaptation of *La Peau de chagrin* for French and Belgian television. In France, films and mini-series based on *Le Colonel Chabert*, *Eugénie Grandet*, *La Duchesse de Langeais*, *Le Père Goriot*, and *La Cousine Bette* have long been staples of television drama, as have versions of numerous other works from *La Comédie humaine* (Doumens 2008). For some television directors, most notably Jean-Daniel Verhaeghe, adapting Balzac has become one of the recurring challenges of their careers. Between 1993 and 2009, Verhaeghe ensured that Balzac remained firmly in the consciousness of French viewers, directing no fewer than five adaptations inspired by the novelist's own prolific output.[1] Beyond Europe and the United States, broadcasters have continued to reinterpret Balzac's work for other national audiences. In 1956, Román Chalbaud directed *La Piel de zapa*, a serial based on *La Peau de chagrin*, for Venezuelan television, while the same novel was later recast as a mini-series in both Colombia and Mexico. Despite the frequency with which television has exploited Balzac's fiction, researchers nevertheless remain sceptical as to the value of the adaptations that this medium has spawned. According to Anne-Marie Baron, part of the role of television is to make celebrated works of literature accessible to a wider public, a process, she argues, that can dilute the complexity of the

Balzacian narrative. Of Verhaeghe's 2009 adaptation of *La Maison du chat-qui-pelote*, Baron claims that the director finds himself restricted "[à] l'illustration et à l'affadissement pour plaire au plus grand nombre", and that the end result succeeds in giving only "une petite idée de l'intrigue de cette œuvre" (2009, 355). An even greater number of scholars have simply greeted television adaptations of Balzac with silence, as if to dismiss this rich body of material as unworthy even of critical commentary.

Focusing on Alain Boudet's 1975 version of *Une ténébreuse affaire*, this chapter seeks to engage with this neglected corpus. It presents television adaptations of Balzac as artistic products that can help to deepen our understanding of the novelist's creative praxis and the ways in which it foreshadows subsequent techniques of televisual narration. Boudet's film offers an intriguing case study through which to explore the relationship between television and Balzac. Moreover, it lends itself readily to analysis in this volume given that the theme of detection plays a key role in both the adaptation and its source text. As a starting point for my discussion, I want to begin by explaining the artistic and commercial imperatives behind Boudet's re-imagining of *Une ténébreuse affaire*, and why this novel so often described as the first *roman policier* proved highly, if problematically, suited to adaptation for French television in the 1970s. In the second part of this chapter, I consider how Boudet rearticulated the mystery at the heart of *Une ténébreuse affaire* in a manner befitting both the source text and television as a medium. In particular, I wish to focus on the director's use of close-ups and fragmented camera shots, and the ways in which these techniques echo the forensic quality of Balzac's realism. Finally, my chapter probes the relationship between the concept of detection and the palimpsestic nature of the adaptive process. More specifically, I argue that, like a detective retracing past events and imposing his or her own interpretation on them, the adapter returns to earlier texts and grafts new meanings onto them. In his version of *Une ténébreuse affaire*, Boudet adds his own resonances to Balzac's story, not least by engaging with other televisual sources such as the historical drama series *Thierry la Fronde* (1963–66). In so doing, the director reveals his artistic affinity with Balzac, whose novel can be seen to "overwrite" a host of earlier texts—foremost among them Walter Scott's *Rob Roy*—while at the same time emphasizing its own status as a new work of art.

Boudet's adaptation of *Une ténébreuse affaire* first aired on TF1 on 9 July 1975, and attracted positive reviews from the press. Writing in *Le Figaro*, Jean Belot praised the director's ability to exploit the artistic possibilities of television, and identified this film as one of the few highlights of an otherwise drab summer schedule. "*Une ténébreuse affaire* séduira sans nul doute," claimed Belot, "un public déshabitué à voir des dramatiques bien construites, s'appuyant sur un scénario solide et bénéficiant d'une interprétation bien sérieuse" (1975, 19). Boudet's achievement in garnering such favourable reviews appears all the more impressive given the complexity of his source material. *Une ténébreuse affaire* is one of Balzac's most intricately woven tales of political life under the Consulate and Napoleonic Empire, and, in the words of Alain, "un des plus difficiles à lire" (Balzac 1973, 7). The first part of the novel sees the fictional policemen, Corentin and Peyrade, despatched to Aube to investigate a plot against Napoleon. Acting on the orders of the Minister of Police, Fouché, the two officers quickly turn their attention to four noblemen, the twins Marie-Paul and Paul-Marie de Simeuse and brothers Adrien and Robert d'Hauteserre, who are suspected of having returned from exile to join the royalist conspiracy. However, the police investigation is thwarted by the actions of the twins' female cousin, Laurence de Cinq-Cygne, who together with Michu, the former bailiff of the Marquis de Simeuse, intercepts the four aristocrats and hides them in the forest. Unable to flush out the conspirators, Corentin is forced to retreat to Paris, the bitterness of his defeat compounded by Laurence, who strikes the policeman across the hand with her riding crop as he rifles through her personal possessions. In the second part of the story, the young nobles are granted an amnesty and return to live at the Château de Cinq-Cygne. Their happiness is soon interrupted, however, when they are implicated, together with Michu, in the kidnapping of a government official, Malin de Gondreville. Following a trial, the Simeuses are sentenced to death and the d'Hauteserres to penal servitude. Laurence eventually succeeds in having the judgement against her cousins commuted to military service by making a personal plea to Napoleon, but she is unable to save Michu from the guillotine. The conclusion to the novel brings together the two key strands of the plot—the royalist conspiracy and Malin's abduction—as Balzac reveals that Corentin framed the men in an act of revenge for the humiliation that Laurence had inflicted on him years before with a single swipe of her riding crop.

With its emphasis on plotting and conspiracies, *Une ténébreuse affaire* proves a fascinating subject for a study of the relationship between detective fiction and the adaptive process. As René Guise points out, Balzac's novel is not a "whodunit" in which the reader must attempt to solve the crime before the fictional detectives unmask the perpetrator (Balzac 1973, 9–10). Despite the abundance of clues, false alibis, and sudden plot twists in this text—all of which are familiar features of the *roman policier* as Todorov, Narcejac, and others would come to define it in the twentieth century—Balzac always provides the reader with sufficient information to keep him or her one step ahead of the investigation. The suspense in this novel comes not from a race for the reader to solve the mystery. It results instead from waiting to discover how Corentin and Peyrade will react when they expose the truth, and what the consequences for the conspirators will be. For this reason alone, writes Guise, bluntly, "*Une ténébreuse affaire* n'est pas un roman policier" (Balzac 1973, 10).[2] If this work is not, in its formal characteristics, a detective novel, the process of detection does underpin its composition. By the time *Une ténébreuse affaire* was serialized in *Le Commerce* in 1841, Balzac was well known as a novelist who delighted in sniffing out hidden truths and tales of private distress. In his introduction to the *Études de mœurs au dix-neuvième siècle* in 1835, the novelist's secretary, Félix Davin, lauded Balzac's ability to penetrate behind the closed doors of French society. "Ce drame avec ses passions et ses types," wrote Davin, "il [M. de Balzac] est allé le chercher dans la famille, autour du foyer; [...] fouillant sous [des] enveloppes en apparence si uniformes et si calmes" (Balzac 1976–81 v.1, 1153–54). In *Une ténébreuse affaire*, Balzac took his investigative instincts a stage further by claiming to resolve one of the great mysteries of the Napoleonic period, namely the kidnapping of Senator Clément de Ris from his home near Tours in 1800. In his 1843 preface to the novel, Balzac explained that Fouché had ordered the abduction of Clément de Ris in order to recover documents implicating the Minister of Police in his own plot to overthrow Napoleon in the wake of the Battle of Marengo. Having uncovered these supposed facts—and as Armine Kotin Mortimer reminds us, Balzac's is but one of several different accounts of the kidnapping (1997, 244)—the novelist adapted them, giving Clément de Ris, in the guise of the fictional Malin, the much broader resonance of a social type.[3] "[L'auteur] a changé les lieux, changé les intérêts tout en conservant le point de départ politique," Balzac continued in his long preface to the novel, "il a enfin rendu, littérairement parlant, l'impossible, vrai" (1976–81 v.8, 493). Though not a *roman policier*, *Une ténébreuse affaire* presents itself as both a work of detection, and an adaptation whose key sources, in palimpsestic fashion, form layers of barely visible traces that Balzac boldly reinscribes into a new narrative.

    That the mystery behind *Une ténébreuse affaire* would have resonated strongly with Alain Boudet comes as little surprise. He, like Balzac, revelled in uncovering historical material and using it as a springboard for his own creativity. A graduate of the Institut des Hautes Études cinématographiques (IDHEC), Boudet directed more than eighty television films between 1960 and his retirement in 1987. Capable of completing as many as six films per year, he specialized in dramatizing ostensibly minor historical events that he saw as encapsulating the wider characteristics of the period in which they occurred. "Au sein de plusieurs de ses réalisations," explains Madeleine Ambrière, "il [Boudet] s'appuie sur un fait historique d'apparence anodine, tout comme Balzac, pour en faire un symbole historique." Boudet's 1963 film, *Un Bourgeois de Calais*, for example, took its inspiration from the figure of Eustache de Saint-Pierre, one of six men who offered themselves up for execution in order to bring an end to the English siege of Calais in 1347. More unusually, *L'Orange et le musicien*, in 1967, explored the circumstances surrounding Mozart's theft of a piece of fruit during the composer's journey to Prague in 1787. Coupled with his enthusiasm for revisiting these lesser known episodes in history, Boudet showed a predilection for adapting works of nineteenth-century French literature. Between 1961 and 1963, he oversaw a three-part recreation of *Les Misérables*, alongside which he adapted another Hugo novel, *Quatrevingt-treize*, in 1962. The director would also become well versed in the challenges of bringing Balzac's work to the small screen. In 1967, he reworked *Béatrix* for the French national broadcasting agency ORTF, before establishing a creative partnership with screenwriter Jean-Louis Roncoroni, with whom he collaborated on *Eugénie Grandet* in 1968, and *Une ténébreuse affaire* seven years later. It is perhaps unsurprising that *Une ténébreuse affaire* would prove to be the last time Boudet adapted a Balzac text, not least because this film draws together the director's interest in neglected historical events and the passion for nineteenth-century fiction that had shaped much of his career.

While the artistic motives behind Boudet's adaptation of *Une ténébreuse affaire* seem clear, the reasons for which TF1 commissioned this film nevertheless warrant further consideration. As French cinema had done during the silent era, television readily identified Balzac as a name capable of attracting audience and bolstering the medium's claims to cultural legitimacy.[4] Throughout the 1960s, adaptations of Balzac texts featured prominently in French television schedules, when the key objective of the country's broadcasting authorities, claims François Jost, was "la valorisation intemporelle du patrimoine" (2005, 10). However, the interest that television producers showed in *La Comédie humaine* took on a new dimension in France in 1974, following the break-up of ORTF. The split resulted in the creation of three separate channels, TF1, Antenne 2, and FR3, and heralded the start of a new competitive era in the French television industry. Against this backdrop—and with four out of five French homes owning a television set by 1974 (Crivello 2007, 187)—the battle for audience share became increasingly fierce. TF1 responded to these changed circumstances by striving to balance its output of "serious" drama with light entertainment. "Les programmes doivent intéresser," declared the channel's incoming president, Jean Cazeneuve, "c'est-à-dire non pas reproduire ce qui dans l'existence est banal ou vulgaire, mais ce qui est significatif. TF1 devra témoigner d'un effort de rajeunissement, de la recherche d'un style attrayant à la fois sérieux et gai" (Mousseau and Brochand 1982, 151). Alongside historical serials such as Guy Lefranc's *Marie-Antoinette* (1975–76), TF1 rebranded popular programmes from the ORTF catalogue such as the music show *Top à...* and *La Une est à vous*, an interactive series that allowed viewers to vote for the programme they most wanted to be shown on a Saturday afternoon from a selection that included American Westerns and martial arts series. Among this varied output, adaptations of Balzac, of which *Une ténébreuse affaire* was one of the first to appear under the new broadcasting regime, represented the kind of quality drama that TF1 was determined to show it could produce.[5]

The popularity of television crime dramas in the 1970s also ensured that the time was ripe to bring *Une ténébreuse affaire* to the small screen. By 1975, French viewers were well familiar with the portrayal of police investigations on television, a fact that owed much to Claude Loursais's pioneering series *Les Cinq dernières minutes* (1958–96). Originally conceived as a gameshow, *Les Cinq dernières minutes* revolved around fictional cases investigated by Commissioner Inspector Bourrel and his assistant Dupuy, and was the first detective series to be aired on French television. The programme consistently topped the country's television ratings, surviving even the death of its lead actor, Raymond Souplex, in 1972. It also marked the beginning of a golden age in French crime drama, as television producers attempted to cater to the growing appetite of viewers for programmes in this genre.[6] Between 1964 and 1965, *Rocambole*, based on the adventures of the gentleman criminal created by the nineteenth-century serial novelist Ponson du Terrail, ran for two series and a total of seventy-eight episodes. As well as captivating viewers, *Rocambole* was one of a number of drama series and serials that also illustrated the strong connection between television and nineteenth-century literature during this period. In 1967, Marcel Bluwal and Claude Loursais adapted the memoirs of the former criminal-turned-chief of police Vidocq, who had famously served as the inspiration for Balzac's own master-criminal, Vautrin. Following its initial run of thirteen episodes, the programme returned for a second series, *Les Nouvelles Aventures de Vidocq*, in 1973. A 1961 episode of *Les Cinq dernières minutes*, focusing on a plot against Louis-Philippe during the July Monarchy, also reflected television's more practical debt to nineteenth-century literature by reusing a lavish set that had previously been constructed for an adaptation of Eugène Sue's *Les Mystères de Paris* (Baudou and Schleret 1990, 29). With its depiction of a mysterious kidnapping, and based on a celebrated nineteenth-century text, Boudet's version of *Une ténébreuse affaire* thus brought together two of the key elements that were likely to appeal to 1970s viewers, and that made this project an attractive proposition for TF1.

If *Une ténébreuse affaire* was clearly well matched to the context of 1970s television, Boudet, in turn, proved that his medium could recreate the novel and its central theme of mystery in a uniquely televisual way. The opening sequence of the film calls attention to the enigmatic quality of the story from the outset. The action begins with a close-up shot of a hand pouring gunpowder into the barrel of a rifle.[7] The camera then cuts to a dog being startled from its sleep, before Michu, played by Robert Bazil, strains to see who is approaching through the forest. Boudet continues to build the sense of mystery in this sequence by delaying the moment at which the viewer sees Corentin and Peyrade. Instead, our first glimpse of the detectives is through fragmented shots that deny us a complete picture of the two men: first, a close-up of Peyrade's boots as he strides across the countryside, and then a shot of the policemen engaged in conversation, their bodies partially hidden behind an embankment as Boudet places the viewer in the position of a clandestine observer to the initial phase of the investigation. As Michu catches sight of the detectives in the distance and scrambles to hide his rifle, Corentin emphasizes the unusual nature of the events he has come to investigate. In response to Peyrade's gleeful observation that Michu has removed his coat and must already be feeling the heat of their inquiry, the more cautious Corentin replies simply: "Il cache quelque chose." The camera techniques that Boudet deploys in this sequence prove highly consonant with television as a medium. The director's use of close-up, in particular, reflects television's emphasis—at least before the advent of wide-screen technology—on tight, detailed shots that were well suited to presentation on a small screen. Moreover, his combination of close-ups and "voyeuristic" camera perspectives echoes the opening of the source text. In his description of Michu, Balzac invites the reader to imagine the mixture of fear and bewilderment he or she might experience if faced with the sight of the bailiff loading his gun:

> Quiconque eût pu contempler cette scène, caché dans un buisson, aurait sans doute frémi comme frémissaient la vieille belle-mère et la femme de cet homme. (502)

Having underlined the strangeness of this episode, the novelist then encourages us to consider why Michu has not prepared any of his other hunting equipment.

> Évidemment un chasseur ne prend pas de si minutieuses précautions pour tuer le gibier, et n'emploie pas, dans le département de l'Aube, une lourde carabine rayée. (502)

In a manner reminiscent of a forensic detective, Balzac homes in on an apparently trivial detail and, as D. A. Miller explains, invests it with much broader significance (1988, 27–28). As this first passage in the text shows, the novelist delights in generating and deciphering mystery, creating an enigmatic sequence of events that Boudet readily adapts in his own medium.

Alongside his reconstruction of the mystery that underpins *Une ténébreuse affaire*, Boudet's juxtaposition of the themes of detection and hunting further illustrates his ability to refit the source text for television. As Max Andréoli has shown in his own analysis of Balzac's novel, *Une ténébreuse affaire* contains numerous references to hunting (1975, 107–09). In his opening portrait of Michu, Balzac describes the character as wearing "une veste de chasse en coutil vert" (501). Concerned as to why her husband is loading a rifle, Marthe asks nervously whether he is intending to kill hares, prompting the bailiff to state, with sinister conviction, that he is targeting "un monstre que je ne veux pas manquer, un loup-cervier" (502). Laurence de Cinq-Cygne also exhibits a passion for hunting, while her cousins later propose this traditional aristocratic pastime as an alibi that would explain their presence in the forest at the time of Malin's abduction. However, the characters in *Une ténébreuse affaire* do not limit themselves to pursuing animals. "La chasse," writes Andréoli, "est assimilée par Balzac à la chasse à l'homme" (1975, 108). Corentin takes particular pleasure in stalking the conspirators and attempting to gather evidence of their involvement in the royalist plot. "L'homme de police a toutes les émotions du chasseur," declares the narrator, in terms which underscore the link between detection and hunting in this novel, "mais [...] là où l'un cherche à tuer un lièvre, une perdrix ou un chevreuil, il s'agit pour l'autre de sauver l'État ou le prince, de gagner une large gratification" (578). Boudet's film places special emphasis on the theme of hunting, and on the way in which the police can themselves become the hunted. As Corentin and Peyrade make their way to the Château de Gondreville following their initial encounter with Michu, they are tracked by the bailiff, who has set out on his own mission to kill Malin. Boudet again places the viewer in a clandestine position, as we watch the two detectives from Michu's vantage point in the bushes. Once Corentin and Peyrade have entered the chateau, the director evokes the enjoyment they derive from their pursuit of Malin by connecting the police investigation to images of games and strategic manoeuvring. As the policemen arrive to carry out their search, Corentin deposits his hat on a chessboard, casually moving one of the knights across the board before toppling several of the other pieces with his hand.[8] Boudet's subsequent choice of camera shots playfully dramatizes the different hunts in progress at this stage of the plot, as Michu is shown creeping around the corner of one of the chateau towers in search of Malin, before the director cuts back to the interior of the building, where Corentin and Peyrade are themselves watching Malin from a window. In this short sequence, Boudet rearticulates the theme of hunting that plays a key role in Balzac's plot, and does so in a way that exploits television's capacity to render complex narrative situations in visual shorthand.

In addition to exploiting Balzac's representation of the detective as a hunter, Boudet takes full advantage of the novelist's engagement with the theme of fragmentation and his harnessing of its symbolic potential within the context of the fictional investigation.[9] Indeed, the director pushes the notion further, highlighting the ways in which fragmentation represents both a creative and a destructive act. At the level of the film's plot, Corentin and Peyrade display particular enthusiasm for breaking into locked drawers and cabinets as they race to find the clues needed to arrest the conspirators. As the detectives search the Château de Gondreville, Boudet emphasizes the wilful destruction in which they are prepared to engage, with Corentin shown sitting on the floor attempting to lever open the drawer of an ornate writing desk. The scene anticipates the policeman's subsequent actions at the Château de Cinq-Cygne, where he tries literally to crack the case by prying open a small wooden box belonging to Laurence. As Corentin takes a knife to the lid, Boudet's soundtrack registers the loud snap of a riding crop, before Laurence throws the precious object, containing the locks of hair of her dead parents, onto the fire. These references to fragmentation prove entirely consistent with the source text and Balzac's vision of a society in decline. In his description of the lodge inhabited by Michu and his family on the edge of the Gondreville estate, the novelist underscores the dilapidated state of the building, which is gradually crumbling away. "Depuis la mort du Grand Marquis," observes the narrator, "ce pavillon avait été tout à fait négligé" (505). Fragmentation also characterizes the structure of the novel. As Gwen Thomas has argued in her earlier study of the police in *Une ténébreuse affaire*, Balzac's plot is riddled with gaps, holes, and the unexplained absences of its characters.[10] While Laurence spends days out riding, Corentin, observes Thomas, goes missing in the middle of the story to return to Paris (1994, 292). At the level of plot, and in its structural features, *Une ténébreuse affaire* proves as fragmented as the television film it inspired.

In Boudet's version of the novel, fragmentation also appears as an integral element of the director's camera technique. During Corentin's search of the Château de Cinq-Cygne, the camera closes in on actor Stéphane Bouy's face, eventually focusing on one of his eyes in extreme close-up as he promises Laurence "nous nous reverrons, Mademoiselle". The fractured portrayal of Corentin in this scene functions as a playful reference, perhaps, to nineteenth-century representations of the Napoleonic police as a single "eye" watching over society, and a metaphor for Corentin's vow to keep the royalists under surveillance. More importantly, however, fragmentation is key to the way in which Boudet organizes his material on screen. Adaptations are often faced with having to fracture their source texts in order to accommodate them within the confines of a different medium. In the case of *Une ténébreuse affaire*, Boudet excludes, most notably, the memorable episode in which Laurence pleads with Napoleon on the battlefield at Jena, an omission due most likely to the cost and technical difficulty of recreating Balzac's panoramic vision of the battle on screen. However, while sacrificing parts of the original plot, the director embraces the fragmented nature of television as a medium, using it to generate his own artistic effects. As John Fiske has argued, "television's continuous flow is actually fragmented into an often jarring experience of segments" (1989, 63). Television dramas are made up of multiple scenes, with often rapid transitions between them. Such transitions are key to the sequence depicting the abduction of Malin, in which Boudet juxtaposes shots of the Simeuses and d'Hauteserres recovering their fortune, which Michu had previously buried in the forest, with shots of the masked bandits riding towards the Château de Gondreville. The intercutting of the two events underlines their simultaneity. However, in contrast to Balzac's text, the film does not confirm explicitly the innocence of the royalists, who are shown leaving the forest after the kidnap has taken place. Instead, a shot of one of the d'Hauteserre brothers casting a nervous glance over his shoulder suggests that their day's work may, after all, have included the kidnapping. By exploiting the fragmentation inherent to his own medium, Boudet thus replicates the mystery at the heart of *Une ténébreuse affaire*, and adds another possible interpretation to the riddle of Malin's disappearance.

If Boudet's camera technique reflects his ability to articulate new meanings around Balzac's novel, so, too, do his borrowings from other televisual sources. *Une ténébreuse affaire* is an inherently palimpsestuous film that grafts itself not only onto Balzac's text, but onto earlier television programmes. The casting of Robert Bazil as Michu provides a striking example of the way in which Boudet overwrites the material provided by his own medium. A seasoned character actor, Bazil had spent much of his television career prior to 1975 playing supporting roles, and during the 1960s had appeared in episodes of *Les Cinq dernières minutes* and another detective series, *L'Inspecteur Leclerc enquête* (1962–63). However, it was his performance as Boucicault, in the historical drama series *Thierry la Fronde*, that established Bazil as one of the most recognizable faces on French television during this period. *Thierry la Fronde* ran for fifty-two episodes between 1963 and 1966, and achieved enormous popularity with viewers both in France and countries as far afield as Australia (Utz 2012, 146). Loosely inspired by the legend of Robin Hood, the series revolved around the adventures of a fourteenth-century nobleman and his fight to regain his rightful property from the King of Navarre. Bazil first appeared in episode two of the series, in which Thierry recruits Boucicault for his band of outlaws after providing him with a hot meal and a new pair of shoes. *Une ténébreuse affaire* recalls the actor's performance in *Thierry la Fronde* by exploiting the connotations of loyalty and comradeship that had come to define Bazil's screen persona. In the film, as in the novel, Michu places his personal affection for the Simeuses above his Revolutionary principles. "Avant sa mort, Mademoiselle," he tells Laurence, as he shows her where he intends to hide her cousins, "le Marquis de Simeuse, qui savait mon attachement pour lui et les siens, m'a fait le gardien de ses enfants et de leur fortune." Michu's devotion to the Simeuses, and his willingness to stand with them against Napoleon, surprises even Marthe, who learns of her husband's involvement in the conspiracy only as the plot is about to be discovered. Our ability to understand Boudet's film certainly does not depend on a prior knowledge of *Thierry la Fronde*. Nevertheless, the director clearly delights in evoking the traces of this televisual source, traces that he encourages the viewer to detect in his film, and that add further layers of resonance to his interpretation of the source text.

Boudet's enthusiasm for sifting through the resources of his own medium is a key feature of his artistic affinity with Balzac. Like the film version, *Une ténébreuse affaire* is marked by the palimpsestuous traces of earlier works of art, most notably Walter Scott's 1817 novel *Rob Roy*. The influence of Walter Scott on Balzac is well attested. As Geneviève Delattre explains:

Walter Scott est incontestablement son grand maître ès-art du roman, c'est à lui qu'il [Balzac] revient infailliblement chaque fois que sa réflexion se porte sur l'art ou la technique du roman. (1961, 309)

In *Une ténébreuse affaire*, Balzac compares Laurence de Cinq-Cygne to Scott's own heroine, Diana Vernon. "Quiconque a lu le beau roman de *Rob-Roy*," he writes, "doit se souvenir d'un des rares caractères de femme pour la conception duquel Walter Scott soit sorti de ses habitudes de froideur, de Diana Vernon" (536). The two characters are both experienced horsewomen. Diana can clear a gate with her mount "at a flying leap" (104), while her fiery temperament marks her out as an obvious precursor of Laurence. Of his first meeting with Diana in *Rob Roy*, the fictional Frank Osbaldistone remembers being "astonished with the overfrankness of her manners" (106), but is captivated by her beauty nonetheless. Balzac revels in these intertextual parallels, so much so that he denies the reader the pleasure of identifying the source being overwritten by naming Scott's novel explicitly. However, Balzac does not simply retrace or imitate *Rob Roy*. As Boudet imposes his own artistic vision on *Une ténébreuse affaire*, so Balzac tailors Scott's work to suit his own ideological concerns. The novelist's willingness to adapt his source material is evidenced, in particular, by the ending of the narrative. In contrast to the loving marriage enjoyed by her fictional counterpart Diana, Laurence agrees to marry Adrien d'Hauteserre out of sympathy and a desire to salvage something worthwhile from the wreckage of the failed conspiracy.[11] "Elle lui offrit un cœur flétri," writes Balzac, solemnly, "qu'il accepta" (684). Rejecting Scott's preference for the trite facility of a happy ending, *Une ténébreuse affaire* condemns the corrupt practices of the Napoleonic police, and the profound impact these had exerted on individual lives. In so doing, Balzac asserts his ability to create a new textual artefact that lays claim to the status of truth. His narrative, like a palimpsest, bears the marks of its literary antecedents while simultaneously overwriting them.

Balzac's rescripting of *Rob Roy* provides further clear evidence of the inherent suitability of his work for television. For more than half a century, television producers have continued to take inspiration from *La Comédie humaine*. Among the sixty films and mini-series to have appeared to date, Boudet's 1975 adaptation of *Une ténébreuse affaire* occupies a special place. Like Balzac, Boudet was drawn to stories of historical events that had been largely forgotten by posterity. With the tale of a mysterious kidnapping at its core, *Une ténébreuse affaire* appeared as a natural fit for the director's own adaptive interests. The popularity of television detective series during the 1960s and 70s, coupled with the break-up of ORTF, also served as key drivers in bringing this novel to the small screen. Boudet's film is notable for the ways in which it uses established techniques of televisual narration to reinterpret the mystery formulated by the source text. The director's use of close-up, in particular, reflects the detective instinct that underlies Balzac's own aesthetic and the novelist's ability to attribute much wider significance to the apparently inconsequential details of everyday life. As well as engaging with the fundamental tenets of Balzacian realism, Boudet contemplates the fragmented structure of his own medium, and uses this to infuse his adaptation with meanings that are not always present in the source narrative. Most importantly, Boudet's version of *Une ténébreuse affaire* exposes the link between the concept of detection and the palimpsestic nature of the adaptive process. In a manner befitting their fictional detectives, Balzac and Boudet pore over the work of their predecessors searching for material that can be used to fashion a new artistic product. Whether borrowing from earlier television series such as *Thierry la Fronde*, or from Scott's *Rob Roy*, both novelist and filmmaker illustrate the potential for redeploying the works of the past. Moreover, they demonstrate that "overwriting" these sources is not a passive act of imitation, but a dynamic part of artistic creativity. As Genette argues:

l'humanité, qui découvre sans cesse du sens, ne peut toujours inventer de nouvelles formes, et il lui faut bien parfois investir de sens nouveaux des formes anciennes. (1982, 558)

In the final analysis, Boudet's version of *Une ténébreuse affaire* proves that television, as much as Balzac himself, was equal to this task.

Notes

[1] The five Balzac adaptations directed by Verhaeghe are *L'Interdiction* (1993), *Eugénie Grandet* (1994), *La Duchesse de Langeais* (1995), *Le Père Goriot* (2004), and *La Maison du chat-qui-pelote* (2009).

[2] For further discussion of the differences between *Une ténébreuse affaire* and the *roman policier*, see Massol (2006, 70–71).

[3] For alternative accounts of the Clément de Ris affair, see Carré de Busserolle 1899 and Rinn 1910.

[4] On the relationship between early cinema and *La Comédie humaine*, see my chapter "Diamond Thieves and Gold Diggers: Balzac, Silent Cinema, and the Spoils of Adaptation", in Griffiths and Watts (2013, 47–79).

[5] On TF1 and its place in contemporary French society, see Péan and Nick 1997.

[6] For a discussion of *Les Cinq dernières minutes* and its contribution to the development of television crime drama in France, see for example Baudou and Schleret (1990, 24–60).

[7] Such images also echo the violence of Balzac's text. On representations of violence in *Une ténébreuse affaire*, see Heathcote (2007, 101–24)

[8] Boudet's film echoes the importance of games in the source text. For a discussion of games and gaming in Balzac's novel, see Schuerewegen (1990, 375–88).

[9] I am particularly indebted to Kate Griffiths for drawing my attention to the theme of fragmentation and its possible applications to nineteenth-century French literature. Within the context of television, Griffiths explores this theme in her chapter "*Chez Maupassant*: The (In)Visible Space of Television Adaptation", in Griffiths and Watts, 2013, 143–71 (146–48), while I take up my own discussion of fracturing and fragmentation in "Balzac on the BBC: Serial Breaks and Adaptive Returns in *Père Goriot* (1968)" (forthcoming in *Dix-Neuf*, 2014).

[10] In addition to the studies by Miller and Thomas, Gérard Gengembre explores Balzac's representation of the police in "La Police dans *La Comédie humaine* ou l'envers du politique contemporain", in Lyon-Caen and Thérenty (2007, 123–31).

[11] For an alternative reading of Laurence de Cinq-Cygne, see Michel (1977, 51–70).

Works cited

Ambrière, Madeleine. "*Une ténébreuse affaire* d'après Honoré de Balzac." <http://www2.cndp.fr/archivage/valid/37021/37021-4739-4547.   pdf> [accessed 1 October 2013].

Andréoli, Max. 1975. "Sur le début d'un roman de Balzac, *Une ténébreuse affaire*." *L'Année balzacienne*, 89 123.

Balzac, Honoré de. 1973. *Une ténébreuse affaire*. Edited by René Guise. Paris: Gallimard.

—. 1976–81. *La Comédie humaine*. Edited by Pierre-Georges Castex.12 vols. Paris: Gallimard, Bibliothèque de la Pléiade.

Baudou, Jacques and Jean-Jacques Schleret. 1990. *Meurtres en séries: les séries policières de la télévision française*. Paris: Huitième Art.

Belot, Jean. 1975. "*Une ténébreuse affaire*." *Le Figaro*. 9 July, 19.

Carré de Busserolle, J. X.. 1899. *La Vérité et curieuses révélations sur l'enlèvement du sénateur Clément de Ris et sur les procès des accusés à Tours et à Angers*. Paris: Mercure Poitevin.

Crivello, Maryline. 2007. "Des *Croquis* aux *Conteurs* une sensibilité au passé. 1957–1974." In *La Télévision des Trente glorieuses: culture et politique*, edited by Évelyne Cohen and Marie-Françoise Lévy. Paris: CNRS, 185–96.

Delattre, Geneviève. 1961. *Les Opinions littéraires de Balzac*. Paris: Presses Universitaires de France.

Doumens, Laure. 2008. "Répertoire des adaptations cinématographiques et télévisuelles des œuvres de Balzac." Maison de Balzac. Unpublished.

Fiske, John. 1989. "Moments of television: Neither the text nor theaudience." In *Remote Control: Television, Audiences, and Cultural Power*, edited by Ellen Seiter et al., 56–78. London and New York: Routledge.

Genette, Gérard. 1982. *Palimpsestes: la littérature au second degré*. Paris: Seuil.

Griffiths, Kate and Andrew Watts. 2013. *Adapting Nineteenth-Century France: Literature in Film, Theatre, Television, Radio, and Print*. Cardiff: University of Wales Press.

Heathcote, Owen. 2007. *Balzac and Violence: Representing History, Space, Sexuality and Death in "La Comédie humaine"*. Bern: Peter Lang.

Jost, François, ed. 2005. *Années 70: la télévision en jeu*. Paris: CNRS.

Lyon-Caen, Boris and Marie-Eve Thérenty, eds. 2007. *Balzac et le politique*. Saint-Cyr-sur-Loire: Christian Pirot.

Massol, Chantal. 2006. *Une poétique de l'énigme: le récit herméneutique balzacien*. Geneva: Droz.

Michel, Arlette. 1977. "Une femme devant l'histoire: Laurence de Cinq-Cygne ou la fidelité." *L'Année balzacienne*, 51–70.

Miller, D. A. 1988. *The Novel and the Police*. Berkeley and Los Angeles: University of California Press.

Mortimer, Armine Kotin. 1997. "Balzac: Tenebrous Affairs and Necessary Explications." In *The Play of Terror in Nineteenth-Century France*, edited by John T. Booker and Allan H. Pasco, 242–55. Newark: University of Delaware Press; London: Associated University Presses.

Mousseau, Jacques and Christian Brochand. 1982. *Histoire de la Télévision française*. Paris: Nathan.

Péan, Pierre and Christophe Nick. 1997. *TF1, un pouvoir*. Paris: Fayard,

Rinn, Charles. 1910. *Un mystérieux enlèvement: l'affaire Clément de Ris (1800–1801) d'après des documents inédits*. Paris: Lefrançois.

Sanders, Julie. 2006. *Adaptation and Appropriation*. London and New York: Routledge.

Schuerewegen, Franc, 1990. "Une ténébreuse affaire ou l'histoire du jeu." *L'Année balzacienne*, 375–88.

Scott, Walter. 1998. *Rob Roy*. Edited by Ian Duncan. Oxford: Oxford University Press.

Thomas, Gwen. 1994. "The Case of the Missing Detective: Balzac's *Une ténébreuse affaire*." *French Studies*, 285–98.

Utz, Richard. 2012. "Robin Hood, Frenched." In *Medieval Afterlives in Popular Culture*, edited by Gail Ashton and Daniel T. Kline, 145–58. New York: Palgrave Macmillan.

CHAPTER SEVEN

ENIGMAS, ERASURES AND *ENQUÊTES*:
CAMILLE LAURENS AND THE PALIMPSEST

ADRIENNE ANGELO

> Sentiments et événements vont s'inscrire sur cette étendue vide–espace et
> temps solidaires–, mais en palimpseste: tout est dit, il n'y a qu'à le redire,
> tout est vécu, il n'y a qu'à le revivre. (Laurens 1998, 43)

In 2010, following a three-year hiatus from writing, Camille Laurens published *Romance nerveuse*. It is a novel that revisits, in part, the events that transpired during the *rentrée littéraire* of 2007—namely, Laurens's accusations of *plagiat psychique* levied against Marie Darrieussecq upon the publication of Darrieussecq's novel *Tom est mort* and Laurens's subsequent abandonment by her long-time editor Paul Otchakovsky-Laurens after he publicly sided with Darrieussecq in the ensuing debacle and terminated Laurens's contract with Éditions P.O.L. While the title of this work clearly evokes the surplus of anxiety that resulted in Laurens's writing caesura, the type of plagiarism alleged by Laurens is of a very specific ilk: it is both literary (the theft or unacknowledged borrowing of another's written work) and psychological (that which concerns one's suffering, one's emotions, one's thoughts or one's imagination). We might say, in fact, that Laurens needed to articulate a new definition of literary pilfering that would best encapsulate her psychological anguish and the extent to which she was, in her words, "menacée" by Darrieussecq's fictional account of a mother coping with the death of her child, an experience that Laurens had actually lived and recounted in *Philippe*, published in 1998 (2005). It was the autonomous space of the fictional text which allowed Laurens to rearticulate her sense of being wronged while also creating a distance between the author (Camille Laurens) and the first-person narrator (Camille Laurens). In so doing, she included passages from her article "Marie Darrieussecq, ou le syndrome du coucou", first published in *La Revue littéraire* in 2007 and retitled in the novel as

"Dolorosa: Un roman stabilo". In 2003, Laurens found herself on the receiving end of her then-husband's (Yves Mézières's) charges of *atteinte à la vie privée* following the publication of *L'Amour, roman*, the rewriting of Laurens's 1992 novel *Romance*. Mézières reproached Laurens for having included his name and that of their daughter in this second and more autobiographical version of the family memoir. Although Mézières conceded the veracity of the events Laurens recounts, he has also called Laurens's depiction of his character skewed and devoid of context (Peras 2011). While Mézières's legal action was ultimately dismissed, and while a second printing of *L'Amour, roman* changed his name to Julien, the first-edition copies of the text in which he was "unmasked" remain in circulation.

By way of introduction, these two examples illustrate the extent to which literary texts have very real consequences when they encroach on the division between tragic and intimate lived experiences and the public disclosure of such events. As Laurens has both initiated and been subjected to charges of wrongdoing, the implications that lie behind such accusations also suggest that the author is vulnerable in laying bare her feelings of betrayal behind the mask of fiction. Further, as Laurens has always woven others' textual citations into the very fabric of her (auto)fictional narratives and, moreover, very often recycles various narrative scenes from her other works, it would seem that intertextuality is a vital centrepiece in her literary labyrinth. These various scenes of writing, rewriting and recitation—made all the more complex given the diverse strata of inter-fictional texts that are often echoed from novel to novel—merit further consideration of the form and function of the palimpsest in her works. The two aforementioned examples of Laurens's rewritings could be seen as the author's response to these highly mediatized feuds: self-justification in the case of *Romance nerveuse* and exculpation in the case of the second printing of *L'Amour, roman*. However, for the purposes of this chapter, I shall reconsider Laurens's earliest writings, her four-part, crime-centred novels, which are especially ripe with scenes and scenarios of palimpsestic scripting. These works include *Index* (1991), *Romance* (1992), *Les Travaux d'Hercule* (1994) and *L'Avenir* (1998).

Given that the palimpsest in its most literal definition refers to a type of literary artefact, specifically a reused manuscript over which one or more layers of text has been written but which may still allow for the original script to be read in part, it seems appropriate to examine the metaphor of the palimpsest in these earlier works. The reappearance of characters and the rewritings of certain scenes that are repeatedly staged in Laurens's earliest writings suggest a degree of porosity that would allow the author to evoke earlier episodes and alter them according to narrative perspective and strategies. The metaphor of the palimpsest accounts for a number of important gestures that figure in Laurens's writings, notably rewritings, overwritings, erasures and gaps. However, my interest in reading the palimpsest in these four novels is also connected to the genre invoked in all four: crime fiction. Sarah Dillon explains the appeal of the palimpsest in terms that reflect the pleasure one takes in reading crime fiction: "[Palimpsests embody] the mystery of the secret, the miracle of resurrection and the thrill of detective discovery" (2007, 12–13). Camille Laurens is not a name that one would readily associate with this genre; however, there does appear to be a very clear interest in crimes of passion that are re-enacted and rewritten in all four novels.[1] Insofar as the crime genre is invested with questions of wrongdoings, discovery, guilt, motives, vengeance and justice, Laurens's engagement with this genre can be said to demonstrate the ways in which reading and writing implicate the (female) author in both committing certain transgressions and in usurping authority via the act of writing with the aim of seeking vengeance.

As we shall see, an additional layer that makes her novels particularly vertiginous is one related to the fragmentation of narrative voice and the multiplicity of characters' names used in the service of self-narration. Although it could be argued that such precarious notions of self in relation to the writing subject are in fact common to any autofictional project, the specificity of self-fragmentation in Laurens's writings is one that suggests in its very gesture the need to mask one's identity in the light of revelations or accusations regarding emotional wounds. Does such a carefully crafted labyrinth of identity actually serve as a type of scriptural haven for the author in the light of more personal crises and vulnerability? Does the evocation of different forms of representation in her writings (notably cinema, theatre and the visual) also attest to an acute desire to rewrite or perhaps restage a sense of being wronged? Does the rewriting of certain narrative episodes in other works function to alleviate a sense of guilt or responsibility? Or do other examples of rewritings (sometimes contained within a single novel) belie a reassertion of authorial identity? In what ways might these crafty palimpsestic interplays allow for a reconsideration of female criminality and detection in the service of literary creation?

As mentioned above, Laurens's entire corpus is one founded on intertextuality both in terms of form—the actual citing of others' works—and theme. Yet while this intertextuality foregrounds not only a textual doubling of excerpts or rewritings of pre-existing literary works written by Laurens herself or other canonical figures in French literature, it also demands an acute engagement on the part of the reader to make connections between these texts. Thus, Laurens's highly literary texts create a space in which reading and writing represent significant and highly symbolic actions. In fact, it could be said that the emphasis placed on the exchange between reading and writing, and between (fictional) reader and (fictional) writer parallels the supposed reciprocity in amorous relationships. However, as we shall see, it is the impossibility of lasting love and the inescapable failure of the couple in these accounts that serve as catalysts for these earlier examples inspired by *faits divers*. The author's scenarios of fated and sometimes fatal love affairs reflect not only the female protagonists' complete isolation from the object of their desire but also negate the idealized happy ending of the romantic fantasy. Yet, the cat-and-mouse game of seduction played out in her works is one founded on the imagined ideal of a reading and writing exchange. In other words, although the author may reveal herself as "Camille Laurens" or "Laurence Ruel" (her birth name), or although the first-person or even third-person narrators (sometimes named Camille, Laurens, Laurence or Ruel) are themselves characters who are authors, their scripts are addressed to the men in their lives, men whose complete, and desired, difference and distance from these women leads to a number of misunderstandings, misreadings and ultimate breakdowns of communication. The male lover, as absolute Other, remains a mystery for the female author (and protagonist), a problematic that Laurens articulates as follows:

> [On] ne connaît jamais l'autre; l'autre est un secret. Il est toujours voilé, masqué, volontairement ou non. Il n'y a que des 'effets' de vérité, mais c'est encore une fois lié à la question du leurre, du désir et de l'absence. Derrière un visage, il y a toujours un autre visage. Mon obsession en fait— et c'est sans doute pour cette raison qu'il y a des figures de détective partout dans mes livres—est de voir ce que ça cache.
> (Georgesco 2011, 83–84)

These comments clearly attest to the challenge that the Other represents: he is an unknown secret or a masked mystery; moreover, the phrasing of these comments reveals the multiple levels of identity that call to the author in ways akin to the palimpsest and Dillon's aforementioned parallel between the palimpsest and crime fiction.

Bearing in mind the multi-layered nature of these narratives, it is also important to consider the link between intertextuality and palimpsestic writing as articulated by a number of scholars in the 1970s, at a time when literary criticism became especially keen on analysing the forging of multiple meanings developed principally through a crossover between reader and writer. Julia Kristeva, most often credited with the coining of intertextuality as a critical term, describes its innate interconnectedness by evoking the mosaic: "Tout texte se construit comme une mosaïque de citations, tout texte est absorption et transformation d'un autre texte" (1978, 15). Philippe Sollers writes that "Tout texte se situe à la jonction de plusieurs textes dont il est à la fois la relecture, l'accentuation, la condensation, le déplacement et la profondeur" (1971, 75). A third notable definition of this textual phenomenon comes from Roland Barthes:

> Le texte redistribue la langue (il est le champ de cette redistribution). L'une des voies de cette déconstruction-reconstruction est de permuter des textes, des lambeaux de textes qui ont existé ou existent autour du texte considéré, et finalement en lui: tout texte est un intertexte; d'autres textes sont présents en lui à des niveaux variables, sous des formes plus ou moins reconnaissables: les textes de la culture antérieure et ceux de la culture environnante; tout texte est un tissu nouveau de citations révolues.
> (1973, 1015)

However it was Gérard Genette, in *Palimpsestes: la littérature au second degré,* who proposed the term "transtextuality" to encompass five specific elements of textual relations: intertextuality, paratextuality, metatextuality, hypertextuality and architextuality. Genette defines the hypertext as: "tout texte dérivé d'un texte antérieur par transformation simple … ou par transformation indirect" (1982, 14). It is in this definition that we find the explicit evocation of the palimpsest: the hypertext functions on a par with the palimpsest in that it derives from, imitates or refers to the earlier hypotext.

While each of her four novels in this tetralogy could certainly be read independently of each other, Laurens did conceive of this project as a four-part series, with chapter headings divided according to the letters of the alphabet so as to reflect the project of telling a story from beginning to end, from "A to Z". While the alphabetical ordering of these works strives to create a sort of coherence in structuring the key themes that will be treated in each section, it also, as Florent Georgesco notes, has the effect of creating "une sorte de double invisible du récit, la trace d'un sens caché, d'une incertitude plus grande encore que celle qui marque le récit" (2011, 14). The metaphorical evocation of the palimpsest is readily apparent in Georgesco's observation, and it is one that can be extended to a number of palimpsestuous objects found or buried in each of the works and also finds a place in thinking through the female protagonist's need to discover and uncover certain truths related to herself and to her male lovers.

In the opening scene of Laurens's first novel, *Index*, Claire Desprez, an architect currently working on plans for the renovations to Guy de Maupassant's childhood home prior to its opening as a museum, stops at a news-stand on her way to the train station. As chance would have it, the store has not received newspaper deliveries for two days, and instead she purchases a detective novel to pass her two-hour journey. But she is less interested in actually reading than in appearing to read; in fact, she finds the crime genre rather tiresome. Once into her journey, she studies the book in her lap; its title, *Index*, mirrors its fragmented and alphabetized form, an obvious *mise en abyme* for the reader who notes clear similarities between the author of the work (Camille Laurens), its structure and the genre to which the work "promises" to adhere: crime fiction. Although the novel does have a plot—an unnamed individual has recruited a private detective to track down a certain Blanche—it does not seem to have any chronology. Claire continues to skim the novel, flipping through chapters at random. After a moment, however, she stops mid-page: the story she is reading reveals intimate details of her own life.

> Claire était à bout de nerfs; depuis quinze jours tout son esprit était tendu vers le seul dessein d'élucider le mystère d'*Index* : qui avait écrit ce livre, comment, pourquoi? (1991, 130)

Convinced that "Camille Laurens" must be the pseudonym of her former lover, Jacques Millière, her initial quest to locate her former lover is subsumed by another, founded on the desire to rewrite her history:

> Elle voulait compléter sa table des matières à l'aide de ses souvenirs personnels, qui contredisaient ici et là le texte imprimé; elle imaginait d'imposer à l'éditeur sa correction du récit sous forme de petits feuillets glissés entre les pages, erratum […] addendum… (154)

Upon learning from Jacques's mother that he died three years ago, thus before the publication of *Index*, Claire's own investigation begins anew and she seeks out a "real" Camille Laurens who lives in Paris on the rue Saint-Jacques. He, however, turns out to be a dance instructor, not a writer. Coincidentally, another minor character in *Index*, Constance Fabre de Cazeau, an editor of the literary review *Boustrophédon*, opens a submission that is sitting atop a pile on her desk.[2] It is titled *Enquête* and recounts a very familiar story: the first-person (male) narrator, a private detective, shares details of his latest job. He is paid by an unknown individual to ensure that a certain young woman read a particular novel. The man follows her for a time so as to learn her routine. As chance would have it, her regular news-stand near the train station has not received newspaper deliveries for two days, and he takes this opportunity to place a few copies of the novel on top of some stock in the hope that she will purchase a copy. The detective closes his story with an admission that his investigation is ongoing and that he does not quite know what to make of the purpose of his search. The submission is signed "Camille Laurens".

From the very first pages of this work, there is an aura of suspicion surrounding the female protagonist. Not only does she seem to partake in the compulsive theft of trivial objects—for example a pen, and, later, a book left on the train—but Claire is also implicated in having abandoned Jacques and her child years earlier. The suspicion levied against Claire is even evident in the title of the work (*Index*) and its numerous references to the index finger, "un doigt accusateur" which points at Claire, at certain objects (which may or may not have an importance in solving the initial mystery at stake in this work), a finger that is raised to the lips in a gesture meant to silence, and thus keep secret, certain mysteries of Claire's past (1991, 17). Yet, the gesture of indexing, beyond the apparent formal organization of this work, also suggests the act of revisiting and unearthing the past. While Claire assumes the role of detective on the hunt for a man who might have betrayed her past secrets in the publication of this novel, she nonetheless feels vulnerable and violated by revelations in the work, a vulnerability that is activated by her reading. In fact, she refers to the charge of "atteinte à sa vie privée", the same charge that would be levied against the author Camille Laurens herself over a decade later by her husband, thus eerily foreshadowing the over-revelatory powers of even the most fictional of texts (1991, 16):

> Le livre s'est simplement ouvert à une page où dort un signet d'herbe sèche—notre passé—et nous lisons noir sur blanc le texte impossible et clair du secret que nous croyions gardé, telle Claire redécouvrant dans son livre, une main devant la bouche, tant d'années après, comme sur l'ardoise magique où ne s'effacent pas les choses qu'on efface, cette chose abominable qu'elle a faite, un jour. (1991, 114–15)

While Laurens's evocation of the "ardoise magique" in the above passage is cited in relation to the book Claire (and we) read, this highly charged object imbued with palimpsestuous qualities also evokes Freud's metaphor for describing the indelible, porous nature of memory. In her article "Temps, mémoire, transmission", Anne Muxel, describing Freud's specific comparison of memory-work to this object, writes:

[Le] fonctionnement de la mémoire [que Freud] compare à un 'bloc-notes magique' (l'ardoise magique) sur lequel l'empreinte de l'écriture, bien qu'effacée dans sa couche la plus superficielle, peut toujours se lire dans une zone profonde. Le jeu de la mémoire et de l'oubli serait comme ce va-et-vient auquel il est si tentant de jouer lorsque l'on a entre ses mains cet objet magique, écrire, effacer, écrire, effacer à nouveau…. (2002, 22–23)

The link between writing and memory and, especially for Claire, between reading and the triggering of memory, suggests a careful interplay between past scenes that are never wholly effaced just as the written word is never wholly erased.

Beyond the dictionary-like structural division that continues in the next work, *Romance*, there would not appear to be a direct link between this second work and *Index*. None of the previous characters resurfaces, and the only event that would tie the works together is the suggested car accident at the end of *Index*, the scene which opens *Romance*. Nonetheless, the themes of ill-fated love, betrayal and the revelation of secrets remain a centrepiece of this second work. *Romance*, the title of which evokes love songs and, for anglophone readers, would also conjure up the notion of a more traditional love story, centres on Lise Imbert, a young woman who is in love with Yves Morand, a psychoanalyst. Lise suspects Yves's infidelity, and her worries are confirmed by her friend, Max Grangier, a filmmaker who also happens to be in love with Lise. Although the bulk of this narrative (also rewritten in *L'Amour, roman*) focuses on Lise's family history, there is a very real crime scene at the conclusion of this work: Lise's vengeful murder of Yves.

Initially at least, it would seem that Max, as a filmmaker, is granted authorial power as he describes his forthcoming cinematic project to Lise; however, Max's work is an adaptation of a novel by an unnamed woman who, we learn in the very final pages of the text, is currently serving time in prison for the murder of her lover, "un crime qu'elle nie depuis toujours d'avoir commis" (1992, 283). The title of this novel-within-the-novel— *GK1991*—shares an obvious reference, in terms of its structure, to the actual novel that the real Camille Laurens writes, and again, the very novel that we read. *Romance* is itself organized between the letters G and K, and while the year 1992 marks the date of its publication, it is more than likely that Laurens was writing the text in 1991. Thus it is tempting to read female authorship here as a means of connecting the anonymous, fictional criminal and the real author, Camille Laurens, herself. Max's mastery over the narrative is therefore actually undermined for two reasons. First, the idea for the story originated from an incomplete manuscript that Max discovered by chance:

> C'était un livre qui l'avait aussitôt inspiré, enfin, ce qu'il en restait. Il l'avait trouvé sous le pied d'un vieux bahut qu'on déplaçait, dans une maison de plage louée quelques jours pour un tournage. (1992, 22)

The discovery of this buried text, one which serves as the narrative catalyst, could be seen as another example of the palimpsest as it comes to bear on the rewriting of a number of ensuing scenes. Second, the real author of Max's fragmentary text is a woman who is serving a prison term for a crime she denies having committed:

> C'est incroyable, non: je veux faire un film d'amour, et je me retrouve malgré moi dans une nouvelle intrigue policière. Mais vécue, cette fois! Réelle. Cette femme a été jugée pour le meurtre de son amant, un homme qu'elle connaissait à peine. (283)

Thus, Max's initial filmmaking project, one based on the titular "romance", is negated by the real events that inspired the writing of the discovered artefact—the incomplete manuscript by an accused murderess—which, in turn, is unknowingly realized by Lise who similarly murders her lover. Of course, the female author writing from prison is a figure that will be taken up in the next work, but in this second work, it would seem that the act of detection is most necessary to Lise who soon learns the truth of Yves's infidelities.

Upon returning to her family's home in Viorne following an extended absence, the only trace of Yves that remains is a postcard he leaves her informing her that he has decided to return to Paris, a postcard which he initially bought during his visit to a museum/chateau, once inhabited by Honoré d'Urfé, as a sort of alibi or proof of his faithfulness.

> Yves Morand a payé sa carte comme on monnaye un alibi; il a acheté la preuve de son passage en ces lieux, le témoignage de sa fidélité envers Lise qui, sinon, le soupçonnerait peut-être de mentir. Il ne la connaissait pas encore très bien. (169)

Both this citation and the one above, in which the murdered lover is a man whom she "hardly knew", recall Laurens's comments cited at the beginning of this chapter about the ultimate lack of recognition that exists between men and women, and the way in which that lack of recognition sets into motion the desire to investigate. Lise reads Yves's farewell message and mirrors Claire's reaction to reading that we have seen in *Index*: "Lise a mis la main devant sa bouche en écarquillant les yeux, comme si elle se souvenait d'avoir oublié quelque chose d'important" (254). Examining the postcard more closely, she notes the image on the

front of "le lac d'indifférence", a clear sign that her suspicions about Yves
are confirmed (254). Consumed with rage, Lise confronts and kills Yves in
Chartres, an act that restages the events described in the anonymous text
found by Max at the beginning of the novel:

> Elle lui demande s'il y a une autre femme. Il fait non de la tête. Il ment. …
> Alors elle saisit quelque chose sur la table, un coupe-papier, un serre-
> livres, un tisonnier, un outil de jardinage, et elle le frappe violemment à la
> tête. … Elle frappe de plus en plus fort, offensive, agressive. … Elle
> s'enfuit sans hâte, avec le calme de quelqu'un qui vient d'exposer
> simplement sa version des faits. (278–79)

This citation is recounted from the viewpoint of an omniscient
narrator; however, the narrator's vagueness in describing the murder
weapon—"quelque chose"—is tempered with the certainty of Lise's
murderous impulse and inner rage. Lise does not seem to feel remorse for
her actions; in fact, her killing of Yves is likened to another mode of
rewriting a story—it is that of a woman who simply offers her version of
the facts.

The third text, *Les Travaux d'Hercule*, very clearly deconstructs the
highly codified genre of crime fiction by establishing the entire quest as a
ruse created by the unnamed first-person female narrator. She tracks down
a detective in Paris named Jacques André and chooses him not for his
successful reputation but because of his name: "Il ne sait évidemment pas
que je l'ai pris parce que son nom commence par A et qu'il s'appelle
Jacques" (1994, 16). Jacques's assignment is to track down someone in
Zigliara who has sent her a postcard on March 21 every year for the past
six or seven years but who, this year, has stopped writing to her. The
messages on these cards are insignificant for the narrator, and she has not
saved any of them. They are all signed "Jacques", but the narrator is
convinced that this is a pseudonym. What is more, the date is insignificant
to her. Jacques has very little to go on, but he accepts this "entreprise
absurde" because he enjoys challenges and his trip is already financed. His
investigation, funded by this mysterious woman, leads him to the unsolved
disappearance of the Chambon family: Simon, his wife Laure Nemours
and their son Tristan. Jacques dutifully sends his progress reports to "la
cliente", while she, growing frustrated with his lack of progress, pushes
him to delve further into the mystery.

> Au bas de la page, sous sa signature, la Voilette avait griffonné quelques
> lignes–c'était ce qui s'appelait répondre par retour du courrier! Elle le
> sommait de ne pas enterrer l'affaire, elle voulait qu'il creuse encore; une

espèce de paragraphe illisible fermait le message, un C peut-être, un L aux contours embrouillés... (148–49)

The revelation of what we, as readers, know to be the initials of the "real" Camille Laurens—CL—remain hidden from Jacques, the man employed by her. Later in his investigation, Simon Chambon, who becomes a likely target of Jacques's inquiry, has no link to the anonymous client who, we learn, is herself serving a six-year prison term for having murdered her lover, "un certain Jacques quelque chose" (64). The crime committed in this novel is revealed to be akin to the myth of Hercules who, killing his wife Megara, then exiled himself with the help of Theseus. Simon, in a fit of jealous rage about Laure's infidelities, kills her and their son and flees with the help of his friend Robert. But Jacques is the one duped by his client, whom he names "La Voilette". Ultimately, she uses an investigation as the pretext for setting him up in the service of her writings:

La Voilette l'avait manipulé. Emprisonnée, elle l'avait envoyé au hasard dans le monde, outre-mer, à seule fin de rechercher pour elle non des personnes mais des idées, des images, ou même seulement des mots peut-être, des mots dont le halo aboutisse à un livre. (244)

Like the anonymous author of the incomplete work found by Max in *Romance*, this woman writer is, too, in prison and is preparing a manuscript for publication; however, in this work, the woman employs Jacques as a surrogate investigator for a crime that is itself a red herring for the true goal of this exercise in authority.

En ce qui concerne Jacques, tu savais bien qu'il faudrait le sacrifier, tu savais depuis le début qu'écrire serait un jeu de massacre. Il te manquait seulement le dénouement de l'histoire et d'une certaine manière, il te l'a fourni. (230)

L'Avenir was written as a means of completing the A to Z project that Laurens began with *Index* and it evinces a clear split in narrative voice: between "je" (Laurence Ruel) and "elle" (Camille). Laurence, an author of an unnamed autobiographical novel that shares a number of similarities to stories from Claire's past recounted in *Index*, has recently signed a contract for its adaptation to cinema. Laurence's autobiography traces her failed love story with Jacques. In fact, towards the end of this work, we learn that the narrator, who is pregnant, turned back to writing during her time in prison. This is information that would seem to link the narrator's identity both to the unnamed author mentioned in *Romance* and also the unnamed client, and later narrator of *Les Travaux d'Hercule*. However, although Laurence is our narrator, her authority over her story is undermined by the director of the film, Francesco Fellini, who refuses to collaborate with her on the script. Laurence travels to the movie set in North Africa, disguised as a journalist for the newspaper *L'Avenir*. Once there, she spies a certain Camille and Jacques who will both play a role in the film. Camille, although married, falls for Jacques, the actor who also plays Jacques in the film, and sets out to seduce him. What follows during the filming (which is also the fiction we are reading) are a number of repetitions and substitutions already demanded by the very medium staged in this work. In this regard, *L'Avenir* is especially revelatory from an intermedial perspective which creates multiple doubles (and triples) for the three protagonists who make up this quasi-love-triangle. But what seems to be most important is Laurence and Camille's respective views on reading and writing. For Laurence in particular writing affords her a certain power in the domain of seduction. In a moment of first-person narration, she likens the written word to "une arme offensive", thus attesting to the power of words to provide her greater self-assurance and, ultimately, to assist in her seduction of Jacques.

> On peut séduire n'importe qui avec des mots tracés pour lui sur une feuille de papier. ... [Les] mots touchent. Pourquoi? Je ne sais pas au juste. Peut-être sont-ils pleins non seulement du temps passé à les former sur la page, mais aussi du temps traversé depuis des siècles pour arriver jusque-là, entre les mains de celui qui maintenant les lit. Les mots écrits ont une mémoire, ils sont chargés d'histoires, comme s'ils commençaient tous par 'Il était une fois...' (1998, 69)

Laurence wants to relive and rewrite her relationship with Jacques, but in order to do so must find a way to "double" herself:

> C'est alors que j'ai eu cette idée d'apparaître dans le film de ma propre vie, tout en jouant non moins anonymement une partie beaucoup plus importante, être l'ombre de moi-même, la doublure de mon double, voilà qui devrait pimenter ce tournage lamentable. (76)

Although these comments do suggest a certain self-effacement, we should not lose sight of the fact that the novel we are reading—organized between the letters O and Z—does seem to usurp the film from which she is banished. (The film is also entitled *Oz*.) Just as Laurence seeks a way to regain control over her life, Camille, too, expresses a need to master her life, and she will do this through writing:

Elle n'a qu'à sublimer cet amour impossible envers Jacques et en faire un livre… elle va renoncer à Jacques pour le récit de Jacques, elle va l'oublier dans les mots. (102)

In this example, then, both Camille and Laurence, despite playing roles in the film within the novel, the primary plot of which could be said to revolve around Jacques, ultimately do find a space in which to reassert their voices.

All of these references to Laurens's pleasurable, maddening or frustratingly slippery texts affirm a self-aware playfulness that will be most appreciated by the reader alert to intertextual citations and multiple rewritings of scenes that overlap from novel to novel. If the examples in this four-part series include elements of what one would expect to find in crime fiction—a victim, a suspect, a motive, some type of crime, a detective, an investigation—these criminal narratives nonetheless challenge our narrative expectations of the genre. Elements which would normally occupy a privileged place within the crime fiction narrative, the crime and the investigation, are in fact secondary to identificatory ruses related to the act of writing and the important and symbolic roles bestowed on the acts of reading and writing in Laurens's works. With such a focus on literacy, it is unsurprising that tangible written objects, be they manuscripts, books or postcards, serve as indelible remnants of the past linking time and text to women's memory. In her literary crime narratives, Laurens engages with the *roman policier* as a means of exploring memory and crimes of passion, and in order to articulate woman's desire to have the last word while at the same time rewriting the sense of being wronged. Laurens's novels stage the struggle for control and mutual understanding in any collaboration between the sexes via the act of reading and rewriting. Self-fragmentation plays a key role in creating an often necessary distance between the narrator and her protagonist in recalling particularly painful events and, in other cases, creating a transparent sense of privacy to ward off others' accusations. In both cases, however, we are reminded of the traces of her other works whose echoes demonstrate the palimpsestic role that intertextuality and intermediality play in Laurens's crafting of her autofictional project.

Notes

[1] Both Sarah Capitanio (2002) and Jutta Fortin (2011) have also considered Camille Laurens's engagement with and evocation of the genre of crime fiction. Although I am treating the first four texts of Laurens's *œuvre* as the urtext of her project, readers will also note the detective figure that reappears in *Ni toi ni moi*, as

Fortin mentions: "*Ni toi ni moi* utilise le canevas du roman policier: il s'agit d'enquêter sur la disparition mystérieuse de l'amour, de trouver le coupable du 'crime'" (2011, 262).

[2] Interestingly, even the title of this fictional review, *Boustrophédon*, takes on great importance in the revelation of the palimpsest. Boustrophedon refers to a type of writing, commonly found in ancient scripts, that runs left to right and then alternates on the next line from right to left. Such multidirectional writing also ties in to Dillon's analysis of other examples of palimpsestic writing in which "[the new writing] runs in the same direction as the original script, either written directly over the top of the old one, or between its lines; in others, the overlying script is at right angles to the original script, the scribe having turned the pages on their side" (2007, 14).

Works cited

Barthes, Roland. 1973. "Texte (Théorie du)." *Encyclopédie Universalis* 15. Paris: Encyclopédie Universalis: 1013–17.

Capitanio, Sarah. 2002. "Authorial Inscription and its Subversion in the Novels of Camille Laurens." *Romance Studies* 20.1: 5–16.

Dillon, Sarah. 2007. *The Palimpsest: Literature, Criticism, Theory*. London: Continuum.

Fortin, Jutta. 2011. " 'Au bal masqué de l'amour, cavalier, cavalière, on danse toujours avec sa mère': *Ni toi ni moi* de Camille Laurens, *Adolphe* de Benjamin Constant." *Modern and Contemporary France* 19.3: 253–64.

Genette, Gérard. 1982. *Palimpsestes: la littérature au second degré*. Paris: Éditions du Seuil.

—. 1997. *Paratexts: Thresholds of Interpretation*. Translated by Jane E. Lewin. Cambridge: Cambridge University Press.

Georgesco, Florent. 2011. "Camille Laurens: Entretien avec Florent Georgesco." *Écrivains d'aujourd'hui: Camille Laurens*. Paris: Éditions Léo Scheer.

Kristeva, Julia. 1978. *Sémiotikè, recherches pour une sémanalyse*. Paris: Éditions du Seuil.

Laurens, Camille. 1991. *Index*. Paris: Éditions Gallimard. Collection Folio.

—. 1992. *Romance*. Paris: Éditions Gallimard. Collection Folio.

—. 1994. *Les Travaux d'Hercule*. Paris: Éditions Gallimard. Collection Folio.

—. 1998. *L'Avenir.* Paris: Éditions Gallimard. Collection Folio.

—. 2007. "Marie Darrieussecq ou le syndrome du coucou." *La Revue littéraire* 32 <http://www.leoscheer.com/la-revue-litteraire/2009/12/15/

22-camille-laurens-marie-darrieussecq-ou-le-syndrome-du-coucou>
[accessed 21 April 2014].

Maniquis, Robert. 2011. "De Quincey, Varieties of the Palimpsest, and the
Unconscious." *Romanticism* 17.3: 309–18.

Muxel, Anne. 2002. "Temps, mémoire, transmission." *Histoire et
anthropologie* 24:13–28.

Peras, Delphine. 2011. "Ils se sont reconnus dans un roman." *L'Express*,
June 2. <http://www.lexpress.fr/culture/livre/ils-se-sont-reconnus-dans-
un-roman_998186.html> [accessed 21 April 2014].

Sollers, Philippe. 1971. *Théorie d'ensemble*. Paris: Éditions du Seuil.

PART III:

IMITATION, PARODY, METAFICTION

CHAPTER EIGHT

TAKING BACKGROUND RESEARCH TOO FAR? CARYL FÉREY'S CROSS-CULTURAL BORROWINGS

ELLEN CARTER

Bestselling crime writer Caryl Férey, born in 1967, has been hailed as the future of French crime writing (Busnel 2012a). His first two major novels—*Haka* (1998) and *Utu* (2008 [2004]; English translation 2011)— use contemporary Maori and New Zealand society as a backdrop and together have sold over 140,000 French-language copies (Daniell 2012, 24). In *Haka*, Jack Fitzgerald, a half-Maori policeman, investigates the sexual mutilation and murder of a young Polynesian woman on an Auckland beach. His investigation reveals incest, a transgender Samoan serial killer and a cannibalistic Maori separatist sect, and ends in Fitzgerald's suicide. In *Utu*, Pakeha (a New Zealander of European origin) policeman Paul Osborne, the friend of *Haka*'s hero Fitzgerald, is asked to tie up the loose ends after Fitzgerald's suicide. Osborne has to deal not only with members of *Haka*'s cannibal sect—including his childhood sweetheart, Hana Witkaire—but also a cabal of corrupt Pakeha politicians and businessmen who are dynamiting an ancient Maori village site to make way for a golf course. Having chosen to narrate both novels from the perspective of New Zealanders, Férey, who had visited New Zealand on three occasions for a total of seven months, had to find a way to bolster the ethnographic authenticity and credibility of his representations in order to write himself inside these cultures (Carter and Walker-Morrison 2012, 9). One technique he employed was an unacknowledged importing and rewriting of portions of two other texts: Booker Prize-winning *the bone people* by New Zealander Keri Hulme (1985), and *Les Immémoriaux*, an ethnographic novel set in Tahiti, by early twentieth-century French writer, Victor Segalen (first published in 1907). In this chapter, I identify how

Férey uses these borrowed texts, then explore how his cross-cultural bootlegging might be described from a literary critical perspective.

Case one: borrowing from Keri Hulme for *Utu*

Throughout *Utu*, Férey includes text in Maori either as single words, usually glossed in French within the main text, or as conversations between characters, usually with the French translation footnoted. This is not surprising given Férey's interest in how Maori:

> have reclaimed their language because there are many words that only exist in Māori – that only have meaning in Māori – and that have no meaning for us. If they lose their language, they'll lose their sense of their culture and of what they're doing on the Earth.
> (Férey, cited in Piquet 2011)

I was intrigued by how Férey had mastered this language, until I traced the vast majority of the Maori words and phrases he uses to the French translation of New Zealand author Keri Hulme's Booker Prize-winning novel *the bone people* (1985; French translation 1996), which Férey cites in *Utu*'s bibliography (2008, 469).[1] While Hulme, born in 1947, wrote *the bone people* mostly in English, she includes Maori words and phrases, which are neither translated nor explained in the English text, though she provides a glossary for some of them at the end of the novel (1985, 446–50). When the French translation by Françoise Robert appeared in 1996, these endnote glosses had moved to footnotes, augmented by linguistic and cultural explanations added by the translator.

I identified thirty-two direct "borrowings" in *Utu* from the French translation of *the bone people*, and another twelve more tangential borrowings. Some of these are single words or short phrases incorporated into the text with glosses or footnotes. However, the more striking examples of Férey's borrowings occur in conversations involving three pairs of characters each of which has a different purpose. The first pairing is Paul Osborne and Hana Witkaire, Osborne's half-Maori first love who becomes a separatist fighter. They speak to each other in Maori on two occasions (see Table 1): once when they are children when Paul reveals to Hana that he has been secretly studying Maori to impress her (Férey 2008, 73–76), then again as young adults when Hana has sex with Paul before telling him that she was raped by a gang of schoolboys in the neighbourhood where they grew up (169–70). Férey's intent is to bolster both Osborne's character development as a Maori expert and his lifelong yearning for Hana.

	Utu (Férey 2008)		*the bone people ou les hommes du long nuage blanc* (Hulme 1996)		
page	**Maori**	**French (footnote)**	**page**	**Maori**	**French (footnote)**
73	Tena koe	Bonjour	25	Tena koe	Bonjour (lorsqu'on s'adresse à une seule personne)
74	E korero maori ana koe ?	Tu parles maori ?	83	E korero Maori ana koe ?	Vous parlez maori?
74	He iti iti noa iho taku mohio	Oh! Je le parle un peu	83	He iti iti noa iho taku mohio	Oh! je le comprends un peu
74	Ka pai... E noho ki raro	C'est bien. Assieds-toi	84 / 82	ka pai / E noho ki raro	C'est bien / Assieds-toi
74	Tena koe, kei te pehea koe?	Comment ça va?	155	Tena koe, kei te pehea koe?	Comment allez-vous ?
74	E ke pai [*sic*]	Très bien	179	E ka pai	Très bien
74	He puku mate, nei ?	L'estomac qui se retourne comme une chaussette, hein ?	155	He puku mate, nei ?	L'estomac qui se retourne comme une chaussette, hein ?
76	Aue	Exclamation exprimant la consternation ou le désespoir	24	Aue	Exclamation qui exprime la consternation ou le désespoir
169	Haere : mou tai ata, moku tai ahiahi	Nous partirons : toi par la marée du matin, moi par celle du soir	467	Haere. Mou tai ata, moku tai ahiahi	Nous partirons. Toi par la marée du matin, moi par celle du soir
169	Ka tata te po : haere	La nuit va bientôt tomber : viens	317 / 245	Ka tata te po / Haere mai	La nuit va bientôt tomber / Viens ici
170	Taipa	Tais-toi	407	Taipa	Tais-toi, tiens-toi tranquille
170	Ki a koe	Prends-moi	463	Ki a koe	Prends-moi

Table 1: Similarities between extracts from *the bone people* and Maori spoken during conversations between Paul Osborne and Hana Witkaire in *Utu*.

Férey's second character pairing occurs when Osborne tracks down Pita Witkaire, Hana's grandfather and a tribal elder (2008, 383–89). The fact that Osborne opens in Maori (see Table 2) has a dual purpose: to show respect, but also to signal that Osborne is not an uncouth Pakeha whom Witkaire can ignore. Witkaire responds in "English"—showing that this conversation belongs to the white world—and they continue in that language until Witkaire refuses to tell Osborne what Hana is doing. Osborne tries to provoke an answer by speaking Maori but Witkaire dismisses him by calling him "tama" (son), indicating both Osborne's non-elder status and that Witkaire knows of Osborne's history with Hana.

Utu (Férey 2008)			*the bone people* ou *les hommes du long nuage blanc* (Hulme 1996)		
page	**Maori**	**French (footnote)**	**page**	**Maori**	**French (footnote)**
383	Tena koe	Bonjour	25	Tena koe	Bonjour (lorsqu'on s'adresse à une seule personne)
389	Whakautua mai tenei patai aku	Répondez à ma question	560	Whakautua mai tenei patai aku	Répondez à ma question
389	E noho ra, tama	Adieu, fils	168	E noho ra	Au revoir (dit par celui qui s'en va aux personnes qui restent)
			58	Tama	Fils

Table 2: Similarities between extracts from *the bone people* and Maori spoken during conversations between Paul Osborne and Pita Witkaire in *Utu*.

Férey shows Pita Witkaire speaking Maori to his granddaughter, Hana, only when she rushes back from Europe to attend her grandmother's funeral (see Table 3). Férey shows Pita trying to reconnect Hana to her land and family through language. It does not work as her grandfather hoped; Hana reconnects with a more militant version of her Maori roots and joins the separatists.

Utu (Férey 2008)			the bone people ou les hommes du long nuage blanc (Hulme 1996)		
page	Maori	French (footnote)	page	Maori	French (footnote)
283	Tihe mauriora	Je salue le souffle de la vie qui est en toi	218	Tihe mauriora	Signifie littéralement éternuement de vie et veut dire: « Je salue le souffle de la vie qui est en toi »
284	Kia koa koe	Je te souhaite toute la joie possible	501	Kia koa koe	Je vous souhaite toute la joie possible
284	E taku hine, e taku hine	Ô ma femme, ô ma femme	459	E taku hine	Ô ma femme

Table 3: Similarities between extracts from *the bone people* and Maori spoken by Pita Witkaire to Hana Witkaire in *Utu*.

In borrowing from Hulme, Férey chose a writer with a complicated position in the New Zealand and Maori literary landscape. While Hulme defends her cultural affiliation—"I think of myself as a Maori writer rather than Pakeha" (Hulme, cited in Worthington 1998)—, Pakeha writer and academic C.K. Stead (1985) attacked her right to win the 1984 Pegasus Award for Maori literature on the grounds that:

> as Hulme is only one-eighth Maori, her upbringing was substantially European and she was raised speaking English, she has no right to write as and for Maori. (Worthington 1998, 248)[2]

Despite this, *the bone people ou les hommes du long nuage blanc* was the only French/Maori resource then available to Férey. Even using Hulme's novel did not leave Férey's text fault-free: Hulme's French translator made two errors that Férey perpetuates in *Utu* (see Table 4).

Given that the original and translated versions of *the bone people* constitute a rare (and mostly accurate) trilingual Maori/English/French resource, Férey could have helped his English-language translator, Howard Curtis, complete the same triumvirate for *Utu*. However, it seems as if Férey did not pass on this resource: Table 5 gives five examples of footnotes in *Utu*'s English translation that would have benefited from more linguistic and cultural knowledge on the part of the translator.

the bone people (Hulme 1985)			the bone people (Hulme 1996)		Utu (Férey 2008)	
page	Maori	English (glossary)	page	French (footnote)	page	French (footnote)
113	He puku mate, nei?	Crook stomach, eh?	155	L'estomac qui se retourne comme une chaussette, hein ? [overtranslation]	74	L'estomac qui se retourne comme une chaussette, hein ?
354	Ki a koe	To you	463	Prends-moi [mistranslation]	170	Prends-moi

Table 4: Translation errors between English and French editions of *the bone people* perpetuated by Férey in *Utu*.

Utu (Férey 2011)			the bone people (Hulme 1985)		
page	Maori	English (footnote)	page	Maori	English (glossary)
64	He puku mate, nei?	Stomach turning like a sock, eh?	113	He puku mate, nei?	Crook stomach, eh?
81	rangitira [sic][3]	Aristocrat	99	Rangatira	Chiefly, or noble person / people
124	Hapu	Subtribe	253	Hapu	Next tribal division down from 'iwi'
141	Haere: mou tai ata, moku tai ahiahi	We shall leave: you on the morning tide, I on the evening	357	Haere, mou tai ata, moku tai ahiahi	Go, the morning tide for you, the evening tide for me
142	Ki a koe	Take me[4]	354	Ki a koe	To you

Table 5: Problems in *Utu*'s English-language translation stemming from Férey's use of phrases from *the bone people*.

When I interviewed him on 8 November 2011, Férey volunteered that he had used this rare French/Maori resource, adding: "I don't know if it's reasonable; maybe I was wrong." He went on to explain the parallel between his borrowing from Hulme, and Osborne's trying to impress Hana:

It's almost funny because it's as if I could speak Maori, which isn't at all true, and I just inserted... in fact, like Paul Osborne who tries to learn Maori and says something and when Hana says to him 'ah, your stomach is churning', he doesn't understand anything. But I pretend to understand. So it's a little game... (personal communication)

Whatever his excuse, it is worth making two final observations about these numerous borrowings. First, the phrases themselves are everyday utterances reminiscent of a tourist's phrasebook. Second, Férey uses them in a relatively anodyne manner; they serve to bolster his characters' Maori credentials rather than contribute to *Utu*'s plot or style. Such mitigating factors are not true of my next case.

Case two: borrowing from Victor Segalen for *Haka*

Three-quarters of the way through *Haka* we find a ritual sacrifice scene in a forest where a character called Térii—draped in priestly robes, daubed with saffron, bare-chested and tattooed—invokes his gods. Table 6 shows the resemblance between eight passages from Férey's description and extracts from *Les Immémoriaux* by Victor Segalen, first published in 1907. Born in 1878 in Brest, Victor Segalen was sent to French Polynesia in 1903 as a Navy doctor (Nicole 2001). He returned to France in 1905 then, in 1907, self-published under the pseudonym "Max-Anély" *Les Immémoriaux*, a novel written from a Tahitian perspective depicting the Tahitians' first contact with Europeans—particularly missionaries—and its impact on Tahitian culture, religion and identity. As well as reading European accounts of Tahiti—reports of voyages by Cook, Bougainville, Wilson and Radiguet; the missionary memoirs of William Ellis; anthropological accounts by Moerenhout, Huguenin and de Bovis; and books and dictionaries on Tahitian culture, religion and language (Nicole 2001, 132)—, Segalen's two years of direct contact with islanders through his medical practice gave him first-hand access to their culture, stories and religion (133). Segalen died in 1919, so his works are out of copyright under France's seventy-year system and have entered the public domain. Thus they can be used without charge so long as Segalen's moral rights— enforced in perpetuity—are respected, including the right of attribution, which holds that his name and the work's original title must be given, something that Férey did not do.

Leaving aside Férey's implicit belief that early twentieth-century Tahitian exoticism seen through French eyes parallels contemporary New Zealand Maori cultural practices, the wisdom of his choice of source is debatable, since recent critical reception of *Les Immémoriaux* is mixed.

Les Immémoriaux (Segalen 2009)		Haka (Férey 2003)	
page	**text**	**page**	**text**
23	guerrier furieux qui marche dans l'ombre	324	guerrier furieux qui marche dans l'ombre
22	Le maro blanc, insigne du premier savoir	329–30	le maro blanc, signe du premier savoir
21	ses chairs, encerclées de bandelettes, fussent macérées d'huiles odoriférantes	330	Térii recouvrit les corps des prisonniers de bandelettes macérées d'huiles odorantes
14	comme un cochon sacré renifle, avant l'égorgement, la fadeur du charnier	330	Avant l'égorgement, la bête [un cochon sacré] renifla le charnier
22	les offrandes : les cochons égorgés en présages ; les hommes abattus suivant les rites ; les chiens expiatoires, éventrés. De ces bas-fonds — où rôde et règne Tané le mangeur de chairs mortes – levaient d'immondes exhalaisons	330	un charnier où exhalaient toutes sortes d'immondices. Les offrandes : cochons égorgés en présage, chiens expiatoires éventrés. De ces bas-fonds régnait Tané, le mangeur de chairs mortes.
22	des têtes aux orbites vides	330	des têtes aux orbites vides
18	Vêtu du maro sacerdotal, peint de jaune et poudré de safran, le torse nu pour découvrir le tatu des maîtres-initiés, Paofaï marchait à la manière des incantateurs.	331	vêtu du maro sacerdotal, peint de jaune et poudré de safran, marchait à la manière des incantateurs, le torse nu pour découvrir le tatu des maîtres-initiés
19	— Que les dieux qui se troublent et s'agitent dans les neuf espaces du ciel de Tané m'entendent, et qu'ils s'apaisent.	331	— Que les dieux qui se troublent et s'agitent dans les neuf espaces du ciel de Tané m'entendent, et qu'ils s'apaisent!

Table 6: Textual similarities between Segalen's *Les Immémoriaux* and Férey's *Haka*.

On the one hand, the novel is regarded as "the only French literary work about Tahiti that has been taken seriously and accepted by Maohi [indigenous people of Tahiti]" (Nicole 2001, 139), while Ollier (1997, 294) notes that the Académie Tahitienne, charged with conserving and promoting the Tahitian language, considered translating the novel into Tahitian in the 1970s. Others are less complimentary, notably Chantal

Spitz, author of *L'Île des rêves écrasés* (1991), Tahiti's first indigenous novel (Nicole, 2001, 193). Spitz feels that Europeans such as Gauguin and Segalen robbed Tahitians of their expression (Staszak 2004, 360).

It also seems as if Férey did not get past the first dozen or so pages of Segalen's novel from which all eight of Férey's borrowings are taken. Férey even named his cannibalistic master of ceremonies "Térii", after the main character of *Les Immémoriaux*, an unlikely name for a New Zealand Maori. Two publishers have further complicated the issue by their choices of cover art: Folio policier's edition of *Haka* (2003) uses an image of Tahitian tattooing, while Pocket's edition of *Les Immémoriaux* (2009) uses an image of New Zealand Maori tattooing.

When I asked Férey about this resemblance between *Haka* and *Les Immémoriaux*, he emailed: "Segalen inspired me for *Haka*'s forest scene with Tane prowling around. The reason was that at the time there was no internet and what little info I had came from books, often accounts of travel" (personal communication, 29 May 2012). Unlike Férey's unacknowledged borrowing of what are essentially phrasebook entries from Hulme for *Utu*, his speaking in Segalen's voice is more egregious because these borrowings contribute to *Haka*'s style and tone. This forest sacrifice scene resolves one of the novel's two investigations and does so in a manner that French readers are likely to find memorable because it uses images of non-noble Pacific savages that have haunted accounts of French explorers since d'Entrecasteaux (Ledru 2007, 489; Douglas 2009, 177; Smith 1985, 141). As a result, Férey's cross-cultural and cross-temporal entanglement of textual and stylistic layers leads to an interconnectedness between his source and final texts and creates analytical problems for a (cultural-insider) reader.

Férey's borrowings viewed through literary theory

To try to understand why Férey borrowed from Hulme and Segalen, as well as the effect his borrowings have on his texts and his readers, I now read his actions through five literary theoretical lenses, proposed by Julia Kristeva, Gérard Genette, Marie Darrieussecq, Roger Little, and Pierre Bayard. Given Férey's borrowing from textual sources, I start with Julia Kristeva's concept of intertextuality, which posits the existence of "several texts within a text" (Kristeva 2002, 8).[5] It supposes a reader might recognize the underlying source texts, engendering literary pleasure and dialogue. As a concept, intertextuality has not remained static:

Since Kristeva proposed the concept of intertextuality, this has been developed and refined, effectively ousting the unidirectional notion of influence. The notion of tribute remains present, but the later author is recognized as participating actively in a relationship of his or her creation. (Little 2006, 20)

So can I use intertextuality to understand Férey's borrowings?[6] In *Haka* and *Utu*, is Férey participating in a relationship he created with Hulme's and Segalen's novels? Do his readers link his texts back to the west coast of New Zealand's South Island in the 1980s? To early nineteenth-century Tahiti? Do Férey's texts aid the comprehension of Hulme's and Segalen's works? To make such claims would constitute a perilous interpretative strategy or, in Sarah Dillon's words, a "risky reading" (2007, 63–84): connecting elements that are not supposed to be linked or seeing resonances where none are present in order to develop a convenient model to support a spurious claim.

My second theoretical lens attends to textual transcendence or transtextuality: "everything that brings [a text] into relation (manifest or hidden) with other texts" (Genette 1992, 81). Gérard Genette identifies five types of transtextual relationship (1997, 1–5), of which two— intertextuality and hypertextuality—are relevant to Férey's borrowings. Since Genette (1979, 87) references Kristeva in matters intertextual, here I concentrate on hypertextuality, which Genette defines as:

any relationship uniting a text B (which I shall call the *hypertext*) to an earlier text A (I shall, of course, call it the *hypotext*), upon which it is grafted in a manner that is not that of commentary. (1997, 5)

Adopting this definition, we could say that Férey borrowed hypertextually by grafting *Haka* and *Utu* (his hypertexts) onto Segalen's and Hulme's novels (the hypotexts), thus creating the possibility for the reader to "engage in a relational reading, the flavour of which, however perverse, may well be condensed in an adjective coined by Philippe Lejeune:[7] a *palimpsestuous* reading" (Genette 1997, 399). As Dillon notes, this

'[p]alimpsestuousness' – a simultaneous relation of intimacy and separation – provides a model for this form, preserving as it does the distinctness of its texts, while at the same time allowing for their essential contamination and interdependence. (2007, 3)

But was Férey seeking this dialogue between his novels and their hypotexts? I think not because, although it is faintly feasible that he felt his

French readers might scent Segalen in *Haka*, it is highly unlikely he believed them familiar with Hulme.

For my third theoretical lens, I turn to a French author to examine whether Férey deliberately plagiarized in order to make a literary or political point. Novelist Marie Darrieussecq published an essay (2010) in response to accusations of plagiarism levelled against her by two other novelists: Marie NDiaye and Camille Laurens (Cottille-Foley 2010). In her essay, Darrieussecq went beyond commenting on how these accusations had affected her, to read leading thinkers in the field in an attempt to understand the occurrence of, and attitudes to, plagiarism in its various guises, claiming that:

> [p]lagiarism is a journalistic term. Counterfeit a legal term. Intertextuality an academic term, hypertextuality a term for comparative literature specialists. (2010, 128, my translation)

While she contends that all writers of fiction—and of autobiography—imagine the world they describe to a greater or lesser degree (17), and she argues that fictional borrowing could be understood—even condoned—under certain circumstances, the situations she identifies do not apply to Férey: he is not (in literary critical terms) a modernist (143), not a post-colonial author reappropriating colonial pillage (138), not exploring a literary topos (157), not a "great" writer (133), not seeking an authentic voice (17), and not seeking to express the inexpressible (172). So, if I were to apply the plagiarism label to Férey's novels, he would not find an apologist in Darrieussecq.

My fourth theoretical lens follows from Darrieussecq's suggestion of the reappropriation of colonial pillage as a justification for fictional borrowing: "intertextual rewriting is a way to reclaim stolen History and refuse 'literary slavery'" (2010, 138, my translation). Férey is not alone as a French metropolitan author borrowing from post-colonial writers. Little (1999a) denounced as "intellectual neo-colonialism" the plagiarizing of poet Léopold Sédar Senghor—the first president of the Republic of Senegal and the first African elected to the Académie Française—by a French popular novelist, Guy des Cars, arguing that des Cars perhaps "holds black writers in such neocolonialist contempt that the standard rules of intellectual property were felt not to apply" (11) and noting that des Cars "cannot claim to be writing against the background of an oral tradition where the reworking of others' material is a necessary and integral part of the art" (11–12). Little continued this theme in a later article:

For those interested in stereotypical colonialist attitudes persisting beyond colonialism, whether towards Blanche/Noir relations, towards *métissage*, towards French colonial policy and practice in Africa, or more generally towards the depiction of racism, *Sang d'Afrique* provides clear, if dismal, examples compounded by the conservatism of the author. That Guy des Cars should have plagiarised Senghor so flagrantly, yet apparently with impunity, suggests that there is something rotten in the state of Parisian publishing. (1999b, 20)

However, intellectual neocolonialism is not Férey's reason for borrowing from Keri Hulme. Rather, Férey's actions can be read as signs of respect both for his reading public and, perversely, for his source author. He wanted to provide his French readers with as accurate a portrayal of New Zealand as possible despite his dual handicaps of lacking personal knowledge and experience, and having no access to today's catholic research tool: the Internet.[8]

For my final theoretical lens, I play devil's advocate and ask: what if Férey's portrayal of New Zealand is all the truer for his lack of personal experience of the country and its culture(s) and his attendant need to borrow this knowledge from others? To do so, I turn to Pierre Bayard who, in *Comment parler des lieux où l'on n'a pas été ?* (2012), suggests that:

In fact, nothing says that travelling is the best way to discover an unknown city or country. There is every reason to think the opposite—and the experience of numerous writers reinforces this feeling—that the best way to talk about a place is to stay at home. (14, my translation)

Bayard addresses the part plagiarism can play when discussing whether journalists need to visit a place in order to write about it, citing the case of Jayson Blair, sacked in 2003 from the *New York Times* for plagiarism and fabricating his stories, including one filed from West Virginia about the family of a soldier missing in Iraq (2012, 75–85). Bayard defends Blair's approach, arguing that, just as one can be physically present at, but psychically absent from, an event, so the reverse can also be true; that there are multiple ways of being "present". Blair's physical absence from, but meticulous research on, the places he wrote about might disqualify him from the ranks of journalist but, Bayard argues, earn him a place amongst fiction writers. While Blair's colleagues questioned whether or not he had visited West Virginia, Bayard believes that they should have been asking whether Blair's article helped readers understand what life is like for the families of missing American soldiers. A similar question could be asked of Férey: rather than counting the months he spent in New Zealand—or his factual errors—did his portrayal help French readers understand what life is like for contemporary Maori and New Zealanders? Férey has claimed that what interests him is the contemporary situation of indigenous peoples in formerly colonized countries (Busnel 2012b; Piquet 2011). *Utu* is broadly sympathetic to Maori, thus French readers close the novel with a new appreciation for their situation. Perhaps both Hulme, who defends her Maori affiliation, and Segalen, moved by the plight of Tahitians under missionary influence, might approve of Férey's ends, all the while questioning his means.

Conclusion

By reading Férey through the work of these five literary critics, I hoped to find explanations for his borrowings. I failed, perhaps because "the sliding scale between reminiscence, imitation, parody, pastiche, influence, intertextuality, and plagiarism is not clearly calibrated" (Little 2006, 17), just as the reasons for, and effects of, textual borrowing are also slippery. Although Férey is not an insider to the cultures he examines, and thus does not have built-in authenticity, he shores up the believability of his settings by implication, by establishing the credibility of other elements. His borrowings are a means to shortcut his acculturation. But they are only one tool among many (Carter and Walker-Morrison 2012), including his credentials as a traveller; his lengthy passages of narratorial diegesis detailing the country's political, economic, social and historical background; his resort to the crime genre, where readers expect to suspend disbelief; and credibility bleed, a phenomenon known from travel writing whereby the reader must believe the author undertook the voyage described (Bassnett 2004, 68). The danger lies in Férey's methods drawing a veil of authenticity over his novels in their entirety, leaving outsider readers with no way of telling either true from false or first- from second-hand knowledge. Férey's conflation of Tahitian with New Zealand culture in *Haka* is an obvious example, but even in the more carefully researched *Utu* we find problems (Carter and Walker-Morrison 2012, 15–16). Alongside Férey's largely accurate description of the dire socio-economic situation of Maori compared to Pakeha New Zealanders (2008, 54), we find inaccuracies such as his claim that each gang has its own distinctive facial tattoo design (360), or that there are Maori-language secondary schools (49). Readers have no markers within the text to help them decide how much of the background to believe. Férey tries to make up for his lack of personal knowledge by using secondary sources, but why single Férey out for this analysis when the meticulous preparatory research of Gustave Flaubert for *Madame Bovary* (Culler 2007, 684) or Émile Zola for

Germinal (Zakarian 1972) is celebrated? Despite his failure to cite his sources, we should perhaps applaud Férey for offering to French readers a perspective on New Zealand and Maori culture that extends beyond rugby.

And one final thought. Férey emphasizes that the main difference between indigenous peoples and their colonizers lies in their respective attitudes to private property (cited in Busnel 2012a). While one of the first acts of colonizers was to seek title to land and other resources, indigenous peoples regard themselves as custodians rather than owners. Perhaps Férey's lax attitude to Hulme's copyright and Segalen's right of attribution is his way of honouring the indigenous beliefs of these Pacific peoples for whom "the very notion of authorial copyright [is] utterly alien to oral tradition" (Little 2006, 16).

Notes

[1] Europa Editions chose not to reproduce the bibliography in its English-language translation of *Utu* (2011).

[2] This debate extended beyond New Zealand's shores when a Canadian academic, Margery Fee, supported Stead's stance, claiming that "a White writer should not write as Other: the risks are too great that privilege has obliterated that writer's awareness of difference" (1989, 27).

[3] Error introduced by translator; correctly spelt "rangatira" in original French editions of *Utu*.

[4] The error stems from a literal translation into English of the French phrase Férey took from the French translation of *the bone people*, which itself was incorrect.

[5] Kristeva was interested in detective fiction, publishing three detective novels— *The Old Man and the Wolves* (1991), *Possessions* (1996), *Murder in Byzantium* (2006)—and using the genre to explore her interest in the "society of the spectacle" (Keltner 2011, 131). Reading detective fiction requires engagement in two concomitant stories—that of the crime and that of the detection—with intratextual resonances that engage the reader's imagination and desire to create meanings (138–39).

[6] Here I use a Kristevan intertextuality that allows for authorial intent, rather than a Barthesian "Death of the Author" variety whereby an "intertextual reader/interpreter then is free and unfettered in tracing the relations between texts; there is no authorial intention to defer to, since the will of the author is not capable of fixing meaning" (Irwin 2004, 230).

[7] Although Genette cites Lejeune as the coiner of this term, Dillon (2007, 4) explains that Genette was the first to introduce it into print, having read it in a manuscript version of Lejeune's article.

[8] The Internet, of course, makes knowledge available to outsiders while also facilitating both the act, and the detection, of plagiarism.

Works cited

Bassnett, Susan. 2004. "Travelling and translating." *Journal of Postcolonial Writing* 40.2: 66–76.

Bayard, Pierre. 2012. *Comment parler des lieux où l'on n'a pas été?* Paris: Éditions de Minuit.

Busnel, François. 2012a. "Caryl Férey." In *Le Grand entretien*, edited by A. Kobylak. Paris: France Inter.

—. 2012b. "Caryl Férey." In *La Grande librairie*, edited by A. Soland. Paris: France 5.

Carter, Ellen, and Deborah Walker-Morrison. 2012. "Cannibalistic Māori behead Rupert Murdoch: (mis)representations of antipodean otherness in Caryl Férey's 'Māori thrillers'." In *The Foreign in International Crime Writing: Transcultural Representations*, edited by J. Anderson, C. Miranda and B. Pezzotti, 9–21. London: Continuum.

Cottille-Foley, Nora. 2010. "Un texte en cache-t-il un autre ? Le palimpseste chez Marie Darrieussecq." In *Stealing the Fire: Adaptation, Appropriation, Plagiarism, Hoax in French and Francophone Literature and Film*, edited by J. Day, 129–40. Amsterdam: Rodopi.

Culler, Jonathan. 2007. "The Realism of *Madame Bovary*." *MLN* 122.4: 683–96.

Daniell, John. 2012. "Culture vulture." *The Listener*, 25 August, 24–26.

Darrieussecq, Marie. 2010. *Rapport de police: accusations de plagiat et autres modes de surveillance de la fiction*. Paris: P.O.L.

Dillon, Sarah. 2007. *The Palimpsest: Literature, Criticism, Theory*. London: Continuum.

Douglas, Bronwen. 2009. "In the event: indigenous countersigns and the ethnohistory of voyaging." In *Oceanic Encounters: Exchange, Desire, Violence*, edited by M. Jolly, S. Tcherkézoff and D. Tryon, 175–98. Canberra: ANU E Press.

Fee, Margery. 1989. "Why C.K. Stead didn't like Keri Hulme's *the bone people*: who can write as other?" *Australian and New Zealand Studies in Canada* 1: 11–32.

Férey, Caryl. 1998. *Haka*. Paris: Baleine.

—. 2003. *Haka*. Paris: Gallimard.

—. 2008 [2004]. *Utu*. Paris: Gallimard.

—. 2011. *Utu*. Translated by Howard Curtis. New York, NY: Europa.

Genette, Gérard. 1979. *Introduction à l'architexte*. Paris: Éditions du Seuil.

—. 1992. *The Architext: An Introduction*. Translated by Jane E. Lewin. Berkeley, CA: University of California Press.

—. 1997. *Palimpsests: Literature in the Second Degree*. Translated by
Channa Newman and Claude Doubinsky. Lincoln, NE: University of
Nebraska Press.

Hulme, Keri. 1985. *the bone people*. Baton Rouge, LA: Louisiana State
University Press.

—. 1996. *the bone people ou les hommes du long nuage blanc*. Translated
by Françoise Robert. Paris: Flammarion.

Irwin, William. 2004. "Against intertextuality." *Philosophy and Literature*
28.2: 227–42.

Keltner, Stacey K. 2011. *Kristeva*. Cambridge: Polity Press.

Kristeva, Julia. 2002. "'Nous deux' or a (hi)story of intertextuality."
Romanic Review 93.1–2: 7–13.

Ledru, Jean-Pierre. 2007. *D'Entrecasteaux à la recherche de la Pérouse:
deux sabots sur la mer*. La Rochelle: La Découvrance.

Little, Roger. 1999a. "Plagiarism as neocolonialism." *French Studies
Bulletin* 20.70: 10–12.

—. 1999b. "More on plagiarism as neocolonialism." *French Studies
Bulletin* 20.73: 19–20.

—. 2006. "Reflections on a triangular trade in borrowing and stealing:
textual exploitation in a selection of African, Caribbean and European
writers in French." *Research in African Literatures* 37.1: 16–27.

Nicole, Robert. 2001. *The Word, the Pen, and the Pistol: Literature and
Power in Tahiti*. Albany, NY: State University of New York Press.

Ollier, Marie. 1997. *L'écrit des dits perdus: l'invention des origines dans
Les Immémoriaux de Victor Segalen*. Paris: L'Harmattan.

Piquet, Laurence. 2011. "Interview with Caryl Férey." In *Un soir au
musée*, edited by C. Aventurier. Paris: France 5.

Segalen, Victor. 2009 [1907]. *Les Immémoriaux*. Paris: Terre Humaine
Pocket.

Smith, Bernard. 1985. *European Vision and the South Pacific*, 2nd ed.
New Haven, CT: Yale University Press.

Spitz, Chantal. 1991. *L'Ile des rêves écrasés*. Papeete: Éditions de la Plage.

Staszak, Jean-François. 2004. "Primitivism and the other. History of art
and cultural geography." *GeoJournal* 60.4: 353–64.

Stead, C.K. 1985. "Keri Hulme's 'The Bone People' and the Pegasus
Award for Maori Literature." *Ariel* 16: 101–08.

Worthington, Kim. 1998. "Hulme, Keri." In *The Oxford Companion to
New Zealand Literature*, edited by R. Robinson and N. Wattie, 247–
49. Auckland: Oxford University Press.

Zakarian, Richard H. 1972. *Zola's 'Germinal': a Critical Study of its
Primary Sources*. Geneva: Librairie Droz.

CHAPTER NINE

FILATURES DE SOI:
DETECTIVES, DISAPPEARANCES AND DECEIT
IN THE CRIME AUTOFICTIONS
OF CALLE, LAURENS AND NOTHOMB

ELISE HUGUENY-LÉGER

Many critics and readers view autofiction as a crime against literature, perpetrated by authors who delve tirelessly into their private lives to produce works devoid of any literary value. When Philippe Vilain published *Pas son genre* in 2011, a jury member of the "Prix des lecteurs de L'Express" wrote:

> Bref, ce roman est à ajouter à la longue liste de cette production française nombriliste et sans générosité, au style vaguement prétentieux, qui n'apporte rien au plaisir de la lecture, rien à la littérature, rien au débat d'idées. (Poirson 2011)[1]

This assessment is characteristic of reviews which make autofiction the *mauvais genre* of contemporary French literature. Despite their popular success, writers such as Christine Angot, Frédéric Beigbeder, Catherine Cusset, Chloé Delaume or Camille Laurens rarely trigger consensus amongst critics and readers: if they write about everyday life in unadorned styles, they are said to lack literary flair; when they favour complex narrative threads peppered with ample metanarrative, their texts become unmistakably highbrow. Despite clear affinities with other genres on the literary spectrum, the label "autofiction" is consistently avoided by writers of other categories, even of genres also written in an autodiegetic voice, such as autobiography, memoirs, or autobiographical novels. A fiercely debated notion in literary criticism, autofiction encompasses a multitude of definitions and practices, which rapidly broadened and challenged Serge Doubrovsky's initial 1977 definition of the genre.[2] The term autofiction appeared at the end of the 1970s, at a time of transformation in autobiographical practice and criticism in France. Under the impulse of structuralist theorists (Barthes, Genette, Lejeune) and New Novelists (Duras, Robbe-Grillet, Sarraute, Simon),[3] life-writing (in particular, the writing of childhood memories) took a new turn, including fragmented narratives, visual components, and increasingly tenuous frontiers between fiction and reality,[4] and receiving major critical attention. Many "new autobiographies" and autofictions were to follow in the experimental footsteps of the *nouveaux romanciers*, with autobiographical texts experimenting with complex narrative structures, with the idea of a recognizable and unified character and author, and with the inclusion of photographic and cinematic devices.

A recurring theme to be found in many autofictions is that of the quest: narrators embark upon a journey to uncover a blurred identity (that of the author-narrator), to chase up past images of a self that may not exist any longer, making use of clues and traces—often photographs—found along the way.[5] Such is the case in Perec's innovative *W ou le souvenir d'enfance*, in Duras's *L'Amant* or in *Le Voile noir* by Anny Duperey, in which photographs act as triggers for a literary "investigation". It is not surprising, then, that many writers of autofiction should decide to write their quest of the self as inquiries and *filatures*, using some of the components of crime fiction and *enquêtes journalistiques* to construct their searches and their narratives. Emmanuel Carrère's film *Retour à Kotelnitch* and novel *Un roman russe*, or Patrick Modiano's *Dora Bruder*, develop from *faits divers* and use the investigatory format, which eventually aims as much at finding information about the narrators' own history and History as about that of a missing person (Jewish teenager Dora Bruder in Modiano; the last prisoner of war, and the author-narrator's own grandfather in Carrère). The very nature of autofictional quests sheds light on the reasons why many works of autofiction also actually portray crimes, disappearances and investigations, often in parodic mode—a mode in itself characteristic of the crime fiction genre (Kemp 2006). This chapter will focus on the use of crime fiction elements within the framework of autofiction, but does not purport to build artificial bridges between two genres which are unquestionably distinct in terms of their use of plot and character, their narrative devices, their intentions, and their readership. Fred Vargas is amongst those who, in her *Petit traité de toutes vérités sur l'existence*, deem this genre unworthy of attention (Platten 2011), and it is easy to see what separates the *polar* from a genre devoted to exhibiting the self through fiction and imagination. But since the motifs of crime, disappearance, deceit and inquiry do feature recurrently in autofiction, it is worth exploring what the rewriting of crime fiction can contribute to the experimental genre of autofiction, and vice versa. The three authors chosen as case studies here—Sophie Calle, Camille Laurens and Amélie Nothomb—all integrate into their (auto)fictional works elements such as mysterious disappearances, investigations, crimes, processes of shadowing, and the solving (or non-solving) of enigmas, and create ludic echoes with other works, genres and expectations. This chapter will focus on features which make autofiction a mode of inquiry heavily reliant on parody, playfulness, and connivance with the reader: among these, the use of *filatures*, investigations and *mises en abyme* emerge as key tools in processes of rewriting.

Conceptual artist Sophie Calle is well known for two projects in particular: one which consisted of shadowing unknown people on the streets of the French capital (*Filatures parisiennes*, 1978–79), and a second targeting one specific man and tracking him down in Venice (*Suite vénitienne*, 1980). Calle was then tailed herself for a day, by a detective hired by her mother, at Calle's behest, and also hired a second detective to shadow the first. In this project, entitled *La Filature* (1981), the series of *mises en abyme* seems designed to blur traces and uncover multiple identities. In 1981, she returned to Venice for another project, entitled *L'Hôtel*: after being hired as a maid to clean hotel rooms, she used this disguise to search through people's belongings, take pictures which resembled police evidence, and deduce information about the guests' lives and occupations. Calle's projects, which question the nature of privacy and private identity, inevitably feature a mixture of tangible reality and fiction: whilst the content of her "experiments" involves mostly verifiable events, Calle often blurs the boundaries between reality and fiction, acknowledging that in most of her projects,

> Everything is real, everything is true…, there is just generally one lie included… So every time there is a lie, and generally there is one in each work: it is what I would have liked to find, and I didn't.
> (Curiger 2009, 55)

With Calle, the chosen form is always that of a very subtle *mise en scène*, a manifestation of freedom and risk-taking set within strict constraints and rules, in Oulipian fashion. Camille Laurens merges reality and fiction in different ways: this writer, who has become one of the key advocates of autofiction and regularly contributes to academic conferences on the topic (Laurens 2010), has always displayed an acute interest in crime fiction and has created many complex narratives which are either built around, or function as, enigmas. Her first, unpublished text was a *polar* entitled *Casablanca*, co-written with her then husband, and she has acknowledged the influence of Dashiell Hammett, author of hard-boiled detective novels, on her writing practice. But whilst her first texts leaned quite clearly towards fiction, her production shifted towards the autobiographical after the death of her newborn son and the publication of the eponymous text *Philippe* in 1995. Since then, whilst retaining its ludic qualities, her writing has become a way of reflecting on loss and absence. Therefore, whilst the content of her texts has become more explicitly intimate and autobiographical, the topos of disappearance has remained one of her preferred narrative triggers. Crime fiction elements continue to play a central part in her work, even in texts which integrate many "true" elements of her life within fictional frameworks. For instance, *Ni toi ni moi* is described in its blurb as a type of "roman policier: on enquête sur la disparition de l'amour" (Laurens 2008a). In this book, Laurens uses cinematic metaphors and film sets as framework for the "investigation" to take place—a context which aptly suits autofiction, as cinema merges mimetic possibilities of representation with the possibilities of telling a story from different angles, of making several shots of the same scene, of assembling fragments of life into one piece. Doubrovsky also used this metaphor when he wrote: "le récit de soi est toujours mise en forme, scénarisation romanesque de sa propre vie" (Doubrovsky 2010), expressing the idea that we are all actors in our own lives, subject to the various modes of projection of our dreams and desires.

Calle and Laurens therefore provide variants of Doubrovsky's original definition of autofiction: a narrative in which the content is strictly true,[6] but the form invented. The term autofiction was inaugurated in the text ambiguously entitled *Fils*, which conveys images of filiation, lineage and inheritance[7] as well as processes of spinning and weaving threads.[8] The latter reading works as an effective metaphor in what we might term "crime autofiction": authors carefully construct their works, using intricate structures which allow the scattering of clues and narrative threads, but also the weaving of voices. But autofictions borrowing from crime fiction also use the very topos of shadowing, or *filature*, a term whose polysemy lends itself well to multi-layered autofictional projects, since its various meanings are:

1. ensemble des opérations industrielles qui transforment les matières textiles en fils à tisser
2. usine où est fabriqué le fil
3. action de filer, de suivre quelqu'un pour le surveiller (prendre qqn en filature)

(*Le Petit Robert* 2000)

The metaphor of weaving, spinning and the fabric of the text is a common one, but applies particularly well to autofictions, which often include sequels, rewriting and re-creation,[9] producing works which can be described as patchworks of reality. Language plays a crucial part in creating these multiple layers, with authors often interested in the innovative possibilities found in juxtaposing sounds or in playing with the multiple meanings of words. Laurens certainly enjoys spinning the threads of language, and has pursued the metaphor herself in texts dealing exclusively with language and its creative possibilities. In *Tissé par mille*, she writes:

> On peut tout faire avec un dictionnaire, virtuellement toutes les histoires s'y trouvent—un vrai fictionnaire en puissance. C'est sans doute pourquoi l'autre nom du dictionnaire est Thesaurus, qui veut dire "trésor". Le dico, c'est de l'or, des tomes d'or, des pépites dont nous sommes les orpailleurs. Tout y est—père et mère, ciel et terre, impair et manque, toujours ouvert pour cause d'inventaire. Dictionnaire, univers. (Laurens 2008b, 46)

In crime (auto)fiction, the investigator's act of tailing someone and that of spinning threads cannot be separated. Crime fictions include at least two layers of narrative. As Sarah Dillon notes in her study of the palimpsest:

> The classical whodunit contains two texts: the story of the "true" version of events which the perpetrator has erased, or attempted to erase; and the story of the ostensible version of events superimposed upon it. (Dillon 2007, 65)

In a traditional crime fiction narrative—a format often challenged, especially in the *roman noir* (Todorov 1971)—the aim of the investigation is firstly to look at all possible threads, then to see how they join together, in order, hopefully, to weave together a reconstruction of the crime so as to make it coincide with the actual events, and eventually uncover the identity of the culprit. This scattering of clues and leads across several layers of narrative gives the reader an active role in unveiling, decoding and assembling these multiple layers, producing a pattern which will, inevitably, be both different from the original one and unique to each reading.

The palimpsestuous nature of crime fiction narratives is echoed in the process of superimposition and erasure at work in autofiction, as can be seen by looking more closely at Laurens's work. Laurens views autofictions as a quest to uncover what has been kept unsaid or secret, whilst being aware of the limitations of language in this process of unveiling and transcription:

> A mon sens, toute autofiction réussie apporte de l'inouï, littéralement. En cela il s'agit toujours d'une sorte d'investigation qui trouve, à travers les mots et donc incomplètement, sa résolution. (Laurens 2011, 106)

In a genre defined by tenuous borderlines between reality and fiction, Laurens invariably uses highly complex narrative structures which include a reflection on the role of literature in the formation of identity. Strongly influenced by *polars* and often marked by formal constraints, her texts follow in the footsteps of Oulipo writers such as Perec, who made *la disparition* one of the core themes of his works, and who always dealt with this theme in multi-layered, playful ways (Gascoigne 2006). In that respect, there is a strong filiation between Laurens and Perec, in terms of content as well as form: Laurens puts great emphasis on the assembling of her texts, and indexes are one of her favourite narrative devices. Her first books formed a tetralogy linked by the letters of the alphabet—the first chapter of *Index* starting with A, the last chapter of *L'Avenir* starting with Z.[10] Laurens's third published novel, *Les Travaux d'Hercule* (1994), bears the trace of both Perec's *La Disparition* (1969) and his unfinished novel, *"53 jours"* (1989), a series of *mises en abyme* in which each embedded story is a crime novel. In *Les Travaux d'Hercule*, the mysterious disappearance of a man is recounted and investigated in multiple layers of narrative with an intricate web of inter- (and intra-)textual references. The main narrative is framed by two short sections written by a first-person female narrator looking for a detective (for an assignment which is not really explained). She chooses one who specializes in "[f]ilatures, disparitions" (Laurens 2003, 17), mostly on the basis of his name, Jacques (the name of the male lover in many of Laurens's books). The main section of the narrative consists of a third-person account of this investigation: detective Jacques André—who pretends to work in the film industry, so as not to reveal his true identity—is sent, (we assume) by the first-person narrator of the opening section, to an exotic location with a closed French community, in order to investigate the sudden disappearance of a man and his family. The *consulat* puts him up in the abandoned family house, which is still haunted by their presence, and where he tries to conduct his investigation by talking to people who knew the family. As always in Laurens, the narrative thread of the investigation keeps meeting other lines of inquiry and metatextual references. Enigmas around the family thicken as the narrative progresses; they remain a mystery, the resolution of which lies in the hands of the writer herself. As with Perec's

"53 jours", we witness the very weaving of the fabric of the narrative: the reader is given the sense that each outcome is just a possibility which the narrator may or may not elect to pursue. As Michael Sirvent declares, in "post-*nouveaux romans*" such as those of Perec (and, we might add, those of Laurens):

> [e]ndings are always illusory, incomplete and/or virtually infinite: they seem at least to propose a rereading of endings that never stop ending. [...] After a period of deconstructing the detective genre in the *nouveau roman*, the strategy of the post-*nouveau roman* seems to be to construct the pragmatic conditions of an interactive rapport between text and reader. (Sirvent 1999, 173)

In the final pages of *Les Travaux d'Hercule*, the detective realizes that he has been manipulated all along by La Voilette, the woman who asked that the investigation be carried out in the first place, who has deliberately sent him on an impossible mission and used his investigation as material for a book that she is writing:

> La Voilette l'avait manipulé. Emprisonnée, elle l'avait envoyé au hasard dans le monde, outre-mer, à seule fin de rechercher pour elle non seulement des personnes mais des idées, des images, ou même seulement des mots peut-être, des mots dont le halo aboutisse à un livre. Il s'était démoli en quête du néant pour qu'elle remplisse des pages! il avait voyagé, s'était forgé une identité nouvelle, avait perdu tous ses repères, tous ses ancrages, tandis qu'elle inventait une histoire! (Laurens 2003, 244)

As an avatar of the author figure, la Voilette represents the deceitful and demiurgic power of the writer, which is a core, self-reflexive theme in autofiction. Laurens has acknowledged that with *Les Travaux d'Hercule*: "j'ai voulu mener une réflexion sur la littérature elle-même, sur l'écriture romanesque comme investigation du réel, autour de l'idée de leurre" (2011, 37).

Processes of *dédoublement* and deceit are central to *polars* and are also a core feature of autofictions, where the author plays repeatedly with the boundaries between reality and fiction, between author, narrator and main protagonist, and between past, present and projected images of the self. Jacques Dubois's assertion that "[l]e récit policier est, par excellence, texte du double jeu" (2006, 80) also fits perfectly the autofiction subgenre—in fact, one of Calle's collections of projects is actually entitled *Doubles-jeux*.[11] In Calle however, clues (very often photographs which are presented like pieces of evidence in a police report) have an amateur quality which denotes her parodic use of investigatory procedures. The *doubles jeux* which she plays destabilize not only the content and message of her works, but also the very foundations of narrative and, more crucially, authorial presence.[12] Her parodic use of the *policier* is also to be found in the fact that projects which involve tailing are often inconclusive, stopping when the thrill of discovery and danger has gone. This ludic, parodic dimension, coupled with an emphasis on process at the expense of outcome, also prevails in Amélie Nothomb, many of whose novels feature crimes, disappearances and imprisonments as initial springboards from which the narrative unfolds.[13] Nothomb's rich production of novels is not easily pinned down to one generic category: whilst she has published a few novels which are clearly informed by her own life and can, as such, be labelled "autofictions" (*Métaphysique des tubes* (2000) and *Stupeur et tremblements* (1999) being the best-known examples), most of her novels include playful allusions to her well-known biography and persona (the author's name, her childhood spent in Asia, her Belgian origins and her other published books) alongside the rewriting of myths, allusions to real and invented authors, reflections on beauty, violence and human nature, and a proliferation of fairy-tale characters. Several of her more clearly fictional novels are built around elements of crime fiction (especially mysterious disappearances) which allow fictional projections into enigmatic worlds. *Péplum* (1996), *Mercure* (1998), *Journal d'hirondelle* (2006), *Le Fait du prince* (2008) all blend invention, biographical allusions and features of crime fiction. In these texts, mysteries often remain unsolved, secrets are valued, enigmas are often pretexts to probe the workings of the human mind, and trivial aspects of everyday life are afforded metaphysical significance. The process of unveiling and questioning supersedes any potential outcome, and in many of her texts which resemble investigations, this process is very often conveyed by long dialogues which help to create suspense and unravel clues before our eyes.[14] *Mercure* is a modern rewriting of a fairy tale, in which an old sailor, Omer Loncours, holds Hazel, a beautiful young woman, captive on an island, convincing her that she has been disfigured. To prevent her from discovering the truth, Loncours must ensure that she has no access to any mirrors or reflections. The first ending is akin to the positive outcome of most fairy tales: a nurse who befriends Hazel reveals the secret, the old man lets them leave the island; he then commits suicide, and the two women live happily ever after. However, this is followed by another, more disturbing epilogue, in which the nurse causes the death of Loncours. The second denouement is presented as an "impérieuse nécessité" by the narrator (Nothomb 1998, 205), and this inconclusive twist acts as a reminder that only the narrator holds the power to change the outcome of the story.[15]

Le Fait du prince highlights Nothomb's parodic use of crime fiction and her capacity for rewriting and echoing other contemporary types of text. It begins with these lines:

> Si un invité meurt inopinément chez vous, ne prévenez surtout pas la police. Appelez un taxi et dites-lui de vous conduire à l'hôpital avec cet ami qui a un malaise. Le décès sera constaté en arrivant aux urgences et vous pourrez assurer, témoin à l'appui, que l'individu a trépassé en chemin. (Nothomb 2008, 7)

The day after hearing this advice at a dinner party, the main character, Baptiste Bordave, is witness to the mysterious death of a man who collapses in front of him after asking for permission to use his telephone, as his car has broken down. Bordave, remembering the discussion of the night before, starts panicking that he may fall under suspicion if he calls the police. Thus, "comme dans les romans policiers, se posait la question capitale: que faire du corps?" (Nothomb 2008, 20). After searching the belongings of the dead man, whose passport reveals that he is Swedish, named Olaf Sildur and lives in Versailles, Bordave decides to swap his monotonous life with that of the dead man, who conveniently happens to be of the same age[16] and physical appearance as him. He takes his sports car (which is in perfect working order), retraces Sildur's steps to his house and settles into his life, which looks indeed far more *romanesque* than his own: there awaits Sildur's beautiful, mysterious wife who drinks champagne all day long, and does not seem at all surprised at the intrusion of this stranger into her life. Bordave's main activity will be to investigate (mostly through conversations with the woman, whom he calls Sigrid) the identity and occupation of the man whose identity he has adopted, and whom he believes to be a spy or a drug dealer. His "investigation" is based on very little concrete evidence and is mostly the product of his effervescent imagination: "Et si j'étais le chef d'un important réseau de contre-espionnage ? J'aimais cette idée" (Nothomb 2008, 86). As such, the entire text is full of *invraisemblances,* unverified leads—"Mon cerveau se mit à sécréter hypothèse sur hypothèse" (Nothomb 2008, 115)—, and mysteries which remain unsolved: can Bordave really leave his job and life overnight without anyone noticing? Will anyone actually realize that the dead body is not his? Why did Sildur pretend that his car had broken down? Who is the mysterious wife? Whom did Sildur try to ring before he died? Was his death part of a wider plot? None of the questions which would be central to an investigation are answered, but another one emerges: how far can one go in taking someone's identity, in intruding in their lives, in tailing them, and in mixing fiction with truth? In *Le Fait du prince*, the arguably weak and far-fetched "plot" of the novel serves to articulate wider, more serious questions about identity, surveillance, and the role of art and the media in contemporary society.

Although Nothomb often creates stories which seem out of (their) time, her novels also display an interest in modern modes of communication and the impact of the media on cultural production, the most notable example being *Acide sulfurique* (2005) which reflected on reality television, a few years after the first programme of the kind, "Loft Story", aired in France. In *Le Fait du Prince*, Sigrid eventually discovers that her husband is dead, and that she and Bordave are being spied on. They decide to escape through a fortuitous "galerie qui va de la cave à la banque" (Nothomb 2008, 154); they leave France and end up in Sweden, where they settle in a "gigantesque espace qui exprimait fabuleusement la notion de vide. Comme il était d'un seul tenant, d'aucuns l'auraient qualifié de loft" (Nothomb 2008, 167–68). Not only does this description bear an uncanny resemblance to the setting of a reality TV show, but Bordave and Sigrid's new occupation also raises questions of intrusion and privacy. Bordave, who has always been suspicious about modern art, undergoes a conversion:

> Le déclic fut une exposition de Patrick Guns intitulé *My Last Meals*. Au premier regard, cela correspondait à l'idée que je me faisais de l'art contemporain: des photos un peu moches avec des commentaires sans intérêt. (Nothomb 2008, 163)

Bordave drops his stereotyped misconceptions about conceptual art and, with Sigrid, they become avid collectors. Nothomb uses both invented and real references to art and to literature in her work, but in this case this is a genuine reference to the works of a fellow Belgian artist, whose exhibits in "My Last Meals" contrast the final fare ordered by prisoners on death row in Texas with pictures of the renowned chefs enlisted by Guns to prepare the dishes. This controversial exhibition reflects on intrusion into the intimacy of final moments. Just like Calle in her own daring projects, Nothomb in *Le Fait du prince* raises the question of boundaries between reality and fiction: Bordave's impersonation is seen as a game, and he tells Sigrid "Il faut glisser des fictions dans la vie. Cela donne des conséquences intéressantes" (Nothomb 2008, 141). Alongside its parodic and subtle use of crime fiction elements, this book also offers interesting reflections on the demiurgic power of the author and artist, asking how far people are entitled to go for the sake of art, a question which is central to many autofictional projects and has led to some contentious cases. In *Le Fait du prince*, in order to find out more about Olaf Sildur's identity, Bordave goes through his address book and rings every contact, hoping to talk to the person whom Sildur was trying to reach the day he collapsed and died. This investigatory method is reminiscent of one of Calle's most controversial projects entitled *Le Carnet d'adresse* (1983),[17] a notebook which Calle supposedly "found" on the street, then perused and photocopied before returning it to its rightful owner, having rung all of the contacts, inferred information about the owner, published the results of her so-called investigation in the daily newspaper *Libération*, and provoked the anger of the notebook's owner when he found out about it. This never led to a public "work of art", other than the articles published in *Libération*, as the owner never gave his authorization for it to be published.

Although one might argue that *Le Fait du prince* is not *stricto sensu* an autofiction (in that it does not encourage us to question the identity of the author-narrator as most autofictions do), it contains playful allusions to Nothomb's life and to contemporary culture,[18] and raises the same questions as those central to autofictional controversies, in particular, that of the boundaries between the public and the private sphere, the invasion of privacy, and the disclosure of details. Privacy and secrets are highly valued in Nothomb's books and in her personal life. In *Journal d'hirondelle* (2006), as Damlé (2009) remarks, the violation of privacy— in this case, a father reads the diary of his daughter—is viewed as a crime which deserves the highest form of punishment: death. Many of Nothomb's novels bring to light complex interplays between love, crime and creation,[19] and play out the demiurgic power of the author—literally demiurgic in the autofictional *Métaphysique des tubes*, in which the writer-to-be is presented as a demigod. This is also true of Calle: the multiple and sometimes contradictory facets of the author-artist do not suggest a "dissolution de l'identité" (Sauvageot 2007, 195) which may question or annihilate the authorial presence. Rather, they create a strong authorial voice which is never completely absent and controls the narrative and the reader's reactions. Marcel confirms this observation when she notes that for Calle, "the only effacement has to do with the erasure of traces and memories" (2003, 20).[20] *Suite vénitienne* offers us only a fragmented picture of the couple followed by Calle: the photographs show poor-quality representations of parts of their bodies; in the report, "their legs" is used as synecdoche for "they", which contributes to reinforcing the presence of the authorial figure. In contrast, in *La Filature*, the report from the real detective about Calle's wanderings ends with "the subject returns home. The surveillance ends" (Calle 1981b, 108): the representation of Calle the author as whole subject thus affirms her subjectivity as an artist.

Autofiction is normally defined in relation to the tradition of autobiographical writing and to the identity between author, narrator and character, partly because the genre seems to have emerged from a playful attempt by Serge Doubrovsky to fill a gap left by Philippe Lejeune in his *Pacte autobiographique* (1975). However, autofiction and its metanarrative share many formal features with the *nouveau roman* and the Oulipo, as the genre playfully questions the solidity of conventional narrative strategies (unity of plot and character) and the reliability of authorial presence. As we have seen, Calle's *filatures* dating from the end of the 1970s are ludic ways of dealing with the serious question of traces of authorship and narrative control in art. More recent autofictional works have also presented readers with a new age of suspicion, where author, narrator and character are not necessarily who we believe them to be. Motifs such as crimes, disappearances, investigations and shadowing are both fruitful narrative triggers and useful tools to renew the perennial question of the uncovering and exhibition of the self in autobiographical writing, and it seems quite appropriate that the traditional features of crime fiction and their parodies should be used widely in texts aimed at reflecting on the possibilities of language and the uncovering of identity. Through the use of stereotyped crime fiction topoi, writers such as Laurens and Nothomb also contribute to the ludic facet of autofiction, and to the extensive possibilities of rewriting and reinvention inherent to the crime fiction genre.

The parodic rewriting of crime fiction in contemporary autofiction is aptly represented by the metaphor of the *filature*, as this term evokes both the process of tailing someone (usually, a suspect), and the action of spinning threads. Robbe-Grillet's *Les Gommes* (1953), one of the founding texts of the *nouveau roman*, experiments with the structure and convention of the *roman policier*, and is described by Robbe-Grillet himself as a rewriting of previous texts and myths, expressed via the metaphor of the *filature*: "L'idée de remettre mes pas sur une trace ancienne était pour moi plutôt exaltante" (Robbe-Grillet 1997, 266). The "new" autobiographies identified by Robbe-Grillet in his essay "Du nouveau roman à la nouvelle autobiographie" (such as *Le Miroir qui revient* or *L'Amant*) are now widely studied as autofictions, and the genre lends itself well to this metaphor: by following in someone's (very often one's own) footsteps, by weaving and unravelling the voices of characters (be they accomplices, culprits or victims) with those of the narrator, Sophie Calle, Camille Laurens and Amélie Nothomb all create multi-layered narratives in which the self is never unveiled in a straightforward manner. Like all writers and artists experimenting with representations of their own existence, they have to retrace their own personal and artistic steps to include this "narrative" (that of the portrait of the writer as an artist) in their fictions. The texts and projects analysed in this chapter echo Dillon's definition of the palimpsest, that of "an involuted phenomenon where otherwise unrelated texts are involved and entangled, intricately interwoven, interrupting and inhabiting each other" (2007, 5), as they generate intricate referential webs in which the authorial figure evolves and takes many (dis)guises. Ghosts, puzzles and traces of absence inhabit these works, and the parodic use of elements of crime fiction helps to question traditional modes of self-discovery, and to invent novel ways of unveiling and creating narrative identities. By using different narrative techniques, such as dialogues in Nothomb, sequels in Calle, and formal constraints in Laurens, these writers all emphasize the ways in which their quests unfold. Their works require the active participation of the reader, whose role it is to weave together various layers of narrative, to decipher multiple levels of references, and to decide eventually: where does the truth lie?

Notes

[1] For more scathing attacks (on Angot, Beigbeder, and Laurens, among others), see Jourde 2003.

[2] See Jones 2010 for an overview.

[3] Respective authors of *L'Amant*, *Le Miroir qui revient*, *Enfance*, and *Les Géorgiques*, all published between 1981 and 1985.

[4] There is no doubt that all of these components can be found in earlier practices. But the 1970s and 80s marked the start of a visible shift in autobiographical writing, influenced in particular by new media.

[5] Photographs have played an increasingly significant part in recent autobiographical and autofictional enterprises and criticism, as a growing body of critical material demonstrates. But one of the first uses of photography following its invention in the nineteenth century was that of retaining evidence in police investigations.

[6] But the content may include dreams, aspirations, and obsessions. The definition given on the back cover of *Fils* is "Autobiographie? Non. Fiction, d'événements et de faits strictement réels. Si l'on veut, *autofiction*, d'avoir confié le langage d'une aventure à l'aventure d'un langage en liberté" (Doubrovsky 2001).

[7] If read as [fis], the term translates as "son".

[8] If read as [fil], the translation is "threads".

[9] In her latest publication to date, *Encore et jamais: variations* (2013), Laurens focuses on the process of repetition and variation.

[10] The tetralogy comprises *Index* (1991), *Romance* (1992), *Les Travaux d'Hercule* (1994), and *L'Avenir* (1998).

[11] The pattern of *filature* which she has used extensively in her work is also a good metaphor for her *œuvre* itself, where one piece leads to another, where author and reader are led to retrace her artistic footsteps, with a scattering of clues in space and in time. In 2001, twenty years after her original *filature* project, Calle asked a friend to hire a detective to follow her. The art installation juxtaposes her own report on the day (which combines factual information on the day's events, anecdotes about acquaintances, and notes on the continuous presence of the detective), with the *privé*'s own report. The detective loses sight of Calle for two and a half hours, during which she meets the mother of a young woman who has disappeared, embedding even more deeply the motif of disappearance in her reflection on art and reality.

[12] As Gratton (2009) suggests, Calle plays with the cliché of the photographer as predator, as well as the idea of photographer as, variously, journalist, paparazzo, detective, *flâneur*, voyeur, and amateur.

[13] To name but a few, *Les Catilinaires* (1995), *Péplum* (1996), and *Attentat* (1997).

[14] One of the best examples of the role of language in the investigation is Nothomb's first published novel, *Hygiène de l'assassin* (1992). For a study of dialogue in Nothomb, see Jordan 2003.

[15] For an analysis of Nothomb's use of rewritings, in particular in *Mercure*, see Oberhuber 2004.

[16] Both characters, like Nothomb herself, were born in 1966.

[17] Also entitled "L'homme au carnet", this was presented in *Libération* as a project designed to "dresser le portrait d'un inconnu" (Calle 1983, 98–99).

[18] Sildur and Bordave are *clins d'oeil* to another popular Belgian author: *Syldave* and *Bordure* are the nationalities of the fictional countries created by Hergé in *Tintin et le sceptre d'Ottokar*.

[19] The link between the three is explored in Amanieux 2005.

[20] In this essay, Marcel also comments on the generic classification of Calle's works and on the original hypertextual links between Calle and Paul Auster.

Works cited

Amanieux, Laureline. 2005. "Amour, meurtre, et langage, dans l'œuvre d'Amélie Nothomb." *L'Esprit créateur* 45.1: 79–86.

Calle, Sophie. 1978–79. *Filatures parisiennes*. Excerpts reproduced in *Sophie Calle, m'as-tu vue*, catalogue of the exhibition presented at the Centre Pompidou, 61–72. Munich: Prestel, 2003.

—. 1980. *Suite vénitienne*. Excerpts reproduced in *Sophie Calle, m'as-tu vue*, 85–94.

—. 1981a. *L'Hôtel*. Excerpts reproduced in *Sophie Calle, m'as-tu vue*, 157–68.

—. 1981b. *La Filature*. Excerpts reproduced in *Sophie Calle, m'as-tu vue*, 101–10.

—. 1983. *Le Carnet d'adresse*. Excerpts reproduced in *Sophie Calle, m'as-tu vue*, 97–100.

—. 2001. *Twenty years later*. Excerpts reproduced in *Sophie Calle, m'as-tu vue*, 113–24.

—. 2002. *Doubles-jeux*. Paris: Actes Sud.

Carrère, Emmanuel. 2005. *Retour à Kotelnitch*. TF1 Vidéo [on DVD].

—. 2007. *Un roman russe*. Paris: P.O.L.

Collectif. 2011. *Camille Laurens*. Paris: Léo Scheer.

Curiger, Bice. 2009. "Sophie Calle in conversation." In Collectif, *Sophie Calle: The Reader*, 49–58. London: Whitechapel Gallery.

Damlé, Amaleena. 2009. "'Death and the Maiden': Murder and Eroticism in the Work of Amélie Nothomb." In *Aimer et Mourir: Love, Death, and Women's Lives in Texts of French Expression*, edited by Eilene Hoft-March and Judith Holland Sarnecki, 98–126. Newcastle-upon-Tyne: Cambridge Scholars Publishing.

Dillon, Sarah. 2007. *The Palimpsest: Literature, Criticism, Theory*. London: Continuum.

Doubrovsky, Serge. 2001 [Galilée, 1977]. *Fils*. Paris: Gallimard.

—. 2010. "Le Dernier moi." In *Autofiction(s), colloque de Cerisy*, edited by Claude Burgelin, Isabelle Grell and Roger-Yves Roche, 383–93. Lyon: Presses Universitaires de Lyon.

Dubois, Jacques. 2006. *Le Roman policier ou la modernité*. Paris: Colin.

Duperey, Anny. 1992. *Le Voile noir*. Paris: Seuil.

Duras, Marguerite. 1984. *L'Amant*. Paris: Minuit.

Gascoigne, David. 2006. *The Games of Fiction: Georges Perec and Modern French Ludic Narrative*. Oxford: Peter Lang.

Gratton, Johnnie. 2009. "Sophie Calle: écriture blanche, photographie, photo-textualité." In *Ecritures blanches*, edited by Dominique Rabaté and Dominique Viart, 155–67. St Etienne: Publications de l'Université de St Etienne.

Jones, Elizabeth. 2010. "Autofiction: a Brief History of a Neologism." In *Life Writing: Essays on Autobiography, Biography and Literature*, edited by R. Bradford, 174–84. Basingstoke: Palgrave Macmillan.

Jordan, Shirley Ann. 2003. "Amélie Nothomb's Combative Dialogues: Erudition, Wit and Weaponry." In *Amélie Nothomb: Authorship, Identity and Narrative Practices*, edited by Susan Bainbrigge and Jeanette den Tooden, 93–104. New York: Peter Lang.

Jourde, Pierre. 2003. *La littérature sans estomac*. Paris: Pocket.

Kemp, Simon. 2006. *Defective Inspectors: Crime Fiction in Late-Twentieth-Century France*. London: Legenda.

Laurens, Camille. 1991. *Index*. Paris: P.O.L.

—. 1992. *Romance*. Paris: P.O.L.

—. 1995. *Philippe*. Paris: P.O.L.

—. 1998. *L'Avenir*. Paris: P.O.L.

—. 2003 [P.O.L., 1994]. *Les Travaux d'Hercule*. Paris: Gallimard.

—. 2008a [P.O.L., 2006]. *Ni toi ni moi*. Paris: Gallimard.

—. 2008b. *Tissé par mille*. Paris: Gallimard.

—. 2010. "Qui dit ça?" In *Autofictions, colloque de Cerisy*, edited by Claude Burgelin, Isabelle Grell and Roger-Yves Roche, 25–34. Lyon: Presses Universitaires de Lyon.

—. 2011. "Entretien avec Florent Georgesco, avec la participation d'Angie David." In Collectif, *Camille Laurens*, 5–109. Paris: Léo Scheer.

—. 2013. *Encore et jamais: variations*. Paris: Gallimard.

Lejeune, Philippe. 1975. *Le Pacte autobiographique*. Paris: Seuil.

Marcel, Christine. 2003. "The Author Issue in the Work of Sophie Calle." In *Sophie Calle, m'as-tu vue*, catalogue of the exhibition presented at the Centre Pompidou, 17–28. Munich: Prestel.

Modiano, Patrick. 1997. *Dora Bruder*. Paris: Gallimard.

Nothomb, Amélie. 1992. *Hygiène de l'assassin*. Paris: Albin Michel.

—. 1995. *Les Catilinaires*. Paris: Albin Michel.

—. 1996. *Péplum*. Paris: Albin Michel.

—. 1997. *Attentat*. Paris: Albin Michel.

—. 1998. *Mercure*. Paris: Albin Michel.

—. 1999. *Stupeur et tremblements*. Paris: Albin Michel.

—. 2000. *Métaphysique des tubes*. Paris: Albin Michel.

—. 2005. *Acide sulfurique*. Paris: Albin Michel.

—. 2006. *Journal d'hirondelle*. Paris: Albin Michel.

—. 2008. *Le Fait du prince*. Paris: Albin Michel.

Oberhuber, Andrea. 2004. "Réécrire à l'ère du soupçon insidieux: Amélie Nothomb et le récit postmoderne." *Etudes Françaises* 40 (1): 111–28.

Perec, Georges. 1969. *La Disparition*. Paris: Denoël.

—. 1975. *W ou le souvenir d'enfance*. Paris: Denoël.

—. 1989. *"53 jours"*. Paris: P.O.L.

Platten, David. 2011. *The Pleasures of Crime: Reading Modern French Crime fiction*. Amsterdam: Rodopi.

Poirson, Véronique. 2011. "Un roman qui n'apporte rien au plaisir de lecture", review of *Pas son genre*. *Lexpress.fr*, June 11. <http://www.lexpress.fr/culture/livre/un-roman-qui-n-apporte-rien-au-plaisir-de-lecture_1001523.html?xtor=x> [accessed 13 June 2013].

Robbe-Grillet, Alain. 1953. *Les Gommes*. Paris: Minuit.
—. 1985. *Le Miroir qui revient*. Paris: Minuit.
—. 1997. "Du nouveau roman à la nouvelle autobiographie." In *Texte(s) et intertexte(s)*, edited by Eric le Calvez and Marie-Claude Canova-Green, 263–73. Amsterdam: Rodopi.
Sarraute, Nathalie. 1983. *Enfance*. Paris: Gallimard.
Sauvageot, Anne. 2007. *Sophie Calle, l'art caméléon*. Paris: Presses Universitaires de France.
Simon, Claude. 1981. *Les Géorgiques*. Paris: Minuit.
Sirvent, Michel. 1999. "Reader-Investigation in the Post-*Nouveau Roman*: Lahougue, Peeters, and Perec." In *Detecting Texts: The Metaphysical Detective Story from Poe to Postmodernism*, edited by Patricia Merivale and Susan-Elizabeth Sweeney, 157–79. Philadelphia: University of Pennsylvania Press.
Todorov, Tzvetan. 1971. "Typologie du roman policier." In *Poétique de la prose*, 55–65. Paris: Seuil.
Vilain, Philippe. 2011. *Pas son genre*. Paris: Grasset.

CHAPTER TEN

THE MANY-LAYERED PALIMPSEST: METAFICTION, GENRE FICTION, AND GEORGES PEREC'S "53 JOURS"

SIMON KEMP

Detective fiction is, virtually without exception, a story about a story. As Tzvetan Todorov famously points out in his typology of detective fiction, the crime novel recounts the story of an investigation, which is itself the fragmentary reconstruction of another story, the story of the crime itself. The story of the crime will then, in traditional detective stories, reappear *en abyme* at the denouement, shorn of its ambiguities and false trails, as the detective reveals the solution. If we go back to the origins of the classic detective story, we find, in Conan Doyle, Agatha Christie and others of their eras, that the text is also writing about writing. The detective's narrator-sidekick chronicles the progress of the investigation in a written account, which affords the opportunity for the story to comment on its own construction. Sherlock Holmes offers sardonic views on Watson's previously published tales; Hercule Poirot famously solves the murder of Roger Ackroyd by reading the very text of the novel itself. In doing so, he discovers the clues the reader has missed in the account his neighbour, Dr Sheppard, has written of the investigation into the murder he, Sheppard, has himself committed.

Crime fiction itself may now largely have moved on from such implausible self-conscious play with the basic formulas, but it is these drastic inversions—the narrator as murderer, the detective as murderer, the victim as murderer—that attract the attention of literary authors for whom writing about writing, stories about stories, are a concern. So it is no surprise that postmodern, self-conscious authors in France and beyond frequently take their inspiration from the structures of the detective story, and from the classic clue-puzzle in particular, which from its earliest days would dismantle and recombine the essential elements of the crime fiction plot in ways limited only by the writer's inventiveness. We might note in American literature Paul Auster's *New York Trilogy* (1985–86), which displays its use of the bare formulas of detective fiction with a volume entitled *The Locked Room* and another in which the characters and places are denoted only by randomly assigned colours, and demonstrates its self-consciousness by presenting us with characters who are themselves writers of detective fiction, along with two characters going by the name Paul Auster. Similar elements could be noted in the German novel *Das Versprechen* (1958) by the Swiss writer Friedrich Dürrenmatt, subtitled "Requiem auf den Kriminalroman", in which a carefully plotted investigation narrative is derailed at the last moment by the accidental death of the culprit in a car accident, or in Haruki Murakami's *Hard-Boiled Wonderland and the End of the World* (1985) in Japanese, which connects a noir pastiche with a fantastical dream narrative in ways which only gradually become apparent, or, in British fiction, Kazuo Ishiguro's *When We Were Orphans* (2000), in which a surreal genre mismatch sees a Holmesian detective called upon to save war-torn China from the invading Japanese. In French literature, the combination of self-conscious writing about writing and an interest in the structural conventions of narrative are most evidently to be found in the post-war schools of literary experiment, Oulipo and the *nouveau roman*, and predictably, there are several texts drawing on crime fiction in both. Michel Butor's *L'Emploi du temps* (1956) features a detective-story writer who offers a short disquisition on the art, and a hero-turned-detective whose investigation principally involves the reading of a detective story, convinced that it holds the key to a real crime. Alain Robbe-Grillet's first published novel, *Les Gommes* (1953), wrenches a stereotypical crime novel plot into a circle as the detective ends up being the killer. The novel is sprinkled liberally with erudite allusions to *Œdipus Rex*, but not to crime novels which have employed the same device, including Sherlock Holmes's "Final Problem" and Wilkie Collins's *The Moonstone* (1868). Agatha Christie will later follow suit with *Curtain: Poirot's Last Case* (1975). Robbe-Grillet's next novel, *Le Voyeur* (1955), shadows the genre even more closely, leaving as it does an "ackroydal" gap in its narrative where the protagonist apparently commits a murder. Several of Robbe-Grillet's later novels are also parasitic on crime-fiction structures, sometimes presenting themselves explicitly as a collage of pulp-fiction stereotypes recombined in impossible variations. Among the work of the Oulipo group, Raymond Queneau's *Pierrot mon ami* (1942) laments at the end that it contained all the elements of a detective story, but failed to recount them in the right order, while Jacques Roubaud's *Hortense* trilogy (1985–90) merrily stages disputes between writer, reader and publisher as it shamelessly plagiarizes whole pages of Simenon for its parodic crime plots.

There are two notable characteristics shared by all of these crime metafictions. One is that they *differentiate* themselves clearly from the crime fiction on which they are parasitic by drawing on deliberately hackneyed, outdated forms of the genre and by refusing to offer their readers the traditional pleasures of the mystery story: their own mysteries either remain unsolved, or resolve themselves in ways too deliberately implausible to satisfy. The second is that they are palimpsests only in Gérard Genette's sense of pastiching an intertext, or an intertextual genre. They remain some distance from the literal meaning of a palimpsest, in which one text is literally written over another, which remains as a separate, self-contained piece discernible on the shared parchment. Butor's *L'Emploi du temps* and Robbe-Grillet's *Projet pour une révolution à New York* (1970) may each include a crime-novel-within-the-novel, but we learn very little of these texts, and what we do know is learned at second hand, reported to us by the reader-in-the-text. Within this field, George Perec's *"53 jours"* is both paragon of and exception to the crime metafiction subgenre, as I aim to demonstrate over the coming pages.

Perec was the brightest star of the Oulipo movement, and embodied most fully their ethos of combining literary creativity with generative devices from language, logic and mathematics. His most famous use of self-imposed constraint as a spur to literary invention comes in novels such as *La Disparition* (1969), written without the use of the letter "e", or *La Vie mode d'emploi* (1978), in which the succession of chapters was decided by a knight's tour of a chessboard, and the contents of the chapters partly determined by mathematical bi-squares selecting unique combinations from forty-two different lists of material, from food items to literary quotations, to be slipped into the narrative. Both these texts overtly display Perec's love of classic clue-puzzle detective fiction: *La Disparition* includes an e-free rewrite of Poe's "The Purloined Letter", and resolves its own plot in an Agatha-Christie-style country house murder mystery. *La Vie mode d'emploi* includes Agatha Christie among its generative mechanics, and incorporates several short detective stories within its ninety-nine chapters.[1]

"53 jours" was the novel Perec was working on at the time of his death from lung cancer in 1982. He had completed a full draft for just under the first half of the story, and left voluminous notes, including some fragments of the narrative, for the remainder. Jacques Roubaud recalls how he and fellow Oulipian Harry Mathews approached the task of creating a publishable version of Perec's last work:

> Devant le dossier, Harry Mathews et moi-même avons été en présence de la difficulté suivante: fallait-il essayer de saisir ce que devait être la suite de la partie déjà dactylographiée, en utilisant les fragments les plus rédigés qui se trouvaient dans les notes? ou bien fallait-il, c'était la deuxième solution extrême, donner de manière presque brute les éléments dont nous disposions, sans essayer d'interpréter. Les deux hypothèses présentaient des difficultés: la première, d'intervenir de façon grave par rapport à ce que nous avions en main; et la deuxième, de fournir le dossier brut sans faire le travail nécessaire pour la restitution de tels objets, travail pour lequel nous n'étions pas préparés. La demande nous était faite de fournir un livre lisible, c'était donc assez catastrophique. La solution que nous avons choisie est une solution intermédiaire; nous avons essayé de prélever un fil narratif dans les éléments rédigés dont nous disposions et, par ailleurs, nous avons reproduit, fidèlement j'espère, la totalité de ce qui nous a été confié. (Neefs and Roubaud 1990, 95)

The two-part structure of the novel's original plan is thus overlaid in the published edition by a tripartite division, with eleven chapters of a recognizably Perecquian, if slightly unpolished narrative, followed by thirty-three pages of narrative fragments arranged in order under the chapter headings for which they were destined, followed by 135 pages of notes relating to the novel as a whole, from which the lacunae of the second part can be to some extent reconstituted. The experience of reading the text is thus doubled: we reach the planned final lines of Perec's novel at the end of the second part, and then plunge back into the story through the notes, which help to supply some of what is absent and elucidate what is present. To long-time readers of Perec, it presents a strangely familiar experience. Doubled narratives, fragmentation and retrospective reconstitution are common features of his *œuvre*. *W ou le souvenir d'enfance* (1975) reveals only gradually the connection between its alternating chapters of childhood memoir and fantasy narrative, requiring the reader to reflect back on earlier parts of the text in order to integrate them into a coherent story. *La Vie mode d'emploi* slices up the stories of its characters' lives and distributes them at intervals through the ninety-nine chapters which correspond to the rooms of the apartment building in which they live. The vast apparatus of appendices and indexes that greets us when we reach the end of the book invites us to take up the novel again in order to unpick individual threads of story or shuffle the chapters into new combinations. Involuntarily, Perec's final work offers the possibility of an archetypally Perecqian mode of reading, a fact that was surely not lost on Mathews and Roubaud as they decided to publish in this form.

For those unfamiliar with the novel, a brief sketch of its workings is necessary before we analyse it further. Like *If on a Winter's Night a*

Traveller (1979) by his fellow Oulipian, Italo Calvino, or more recently David Mitchell's *Cloud Atlas* (2004), Perec's novel has a nested structure, setting several stories *en abyme* within one another. Unlike Mitchell's or Calvino's novels, however, all of the stories in Perec's novel are crime fictions, and all of them play a role in the plot of the stories in which they are embedded. The resulting structure is considerably more complex, and rather than being a gratuitous arrangement, is essential to the development of the story and the unravelling of its mysteries. Part One of the novel is entitled *53 jours*, a title which few readers will notice has quietly lost its quotation marks. The scene is set in Grianta, a fictional African nation and former French colony, in which the despotic President-for-life has declared a state of emergency to quell unrest. The narrator, Veyraud, is summoned to a meeting with the French consul, who informs him that the celebrated French writer, Robert Serval, who was resident in the town, has disappeared in mysterious circumstances. The only clue is an unfinished manuscript for a crime novel called *La Crypte* left behind by Serval, with the suggestion that the solution lies within, and that Veyraud, whom Serval claims was a former schoolmate, may be able to discover it. The consul hands over the manuscript with the words, "Vous saurez certainement mieux que moi le lire entre les lignes" (26). With Veyraud, the reader begins to explore *La Crypte*, the first inset novel, a Scandinavian noir in which a detective, also named Robert Serval, investigates a mysterious disappearance. We are given a detailed enough summary of the plot and portraits of the characters to form our own opinions, which we can compare with those of Veyraud, who is not reticent with his own critique. He declares at one point that "on ne peut pas dire que ça soye bien ficelé" (63), and makes specific criticisms of implausibilities in the plotting, such as when the identity of the disfigured body found in the missing man's car is belatedly questioned:

> Cette évidence, que Serval-détective énonce d'une façon si 'matter-of-fact' que l'on se dit que Serval-auteur aurait quand même bien pu, de temps en temps, la faire venir à l'esprit des autres protagonistes de son livre […]. (57)

Veyraud's commentary guides us not only in our interpretation of *La Crypte*, however. It also establishes, at least with hindsight, the *mise-en-abyme* relationship between the texts. Veyraud's summing up of *La Crypte* as "Un roman policier en deux parties dont la seconde détruit méticuleusement tout ce que la première s'est efforcée d'établir" (38) will prove to be the device of the novel as a whole. In *La Crypte* this is demonstrated by the detective's discovery of a crime novel, *Le Juge est l'assassin*, hidden in the bathroom of the missing man. We read Veyraud reading Serval reading *Le Juge est l'assassin*, in which an apparently straightforward murder is solved, only for the case to unravel as it emerges that the apparent killer has been framed by the apparent victim, who is very much alive. Detective Serval deduces that the missing person of *La Crypte* was inspired by *Le Juge est l'assassin* to fake his own death in order to frame the prime suspect, but the manuscript ends on a hesitation between two hypotheses: the missing man has organized everything to frame the prime suspect, or the prime suspect is in fact the murderer, and has organized everything to appear to have been framed. Veyraud struggles to fit the plots of both novels to his own problem of the missing Serval, and tracks down Serval's typist in search of the missing ending. Here, the novel's structure explodes into truly Perecquian complexity. We learn that *La Crypte* and Serval's other novels have been written by a method that we might call intertextual, or we might call plagiarism: "Ne croyez surtout pas, Mademoiselle, que j'invente," the author once told his typist. "Je ne fais que chiper de-ci et de-là divers détails dont je me sers pour agencer ma propre histoire" (81). Of the four models which "inspired" *La Crypte*, three are genuine crime stories by Agatha Christie, Bill Ballinger and Maurice Leblanc, and the fourth is an espionage thriller, *K comme Koala* invented by Perec, an extract from and summary of which is included in *"53 jours"*. "La vérité que je cherche n'est pas dans le livre," Veyraud realizes, "mais entre les livres" (93). This truth we then search for, using our own intertextual knowledge and research if we wish. In each case the significant resemblances are to be found in that most unliterary quality of the novel, its plotting.

This is about as far as we get in the completed part of Perec's novel. What follows is a startling pair of narrative reversals, firstly on the narrative level of Veyraud, then on an entirely new level of narrative. In the story of Veyraud, the protagonist reaches a conclusion on the basis of his reading that the author Serval has been murdered by the consul of Grianta. In fact, as he discovers too late, the opposite is true, and the whole business with the manuscript and the typist has been carefully stage-managed to frame Veyraud himself as the culprit. Part Two of the novel then opens with a masterly *coup de théâtre*, as we learn that everything we have read so far is the text of a manuscript entitled *53 jours*, which was discovered in the car of French businessman and former resistance fighter, Robert Serval, the third character of this name, who has disappeared. The novel's quotation marks now make sense: *"53 jours"* is a novel about the manuscript, *53 jours*. We then follow the investigations of detective Salini who must explore all seven of the inset stories to discover the truth about

Serval's disappearance. In a final flourish, Salini uncovers the presence of two master intertexts running through the manuscript, Balzac's *Le Colonel Chabert*, and, most particularly, Stendhal's *La Chartreuse de Parme*, famously written in fifty-three days. The word *Chartreuse* is encoded in the differences between a passage which appears in both *K comme Koala* and *La Crypte*. Names and places from Stendhal are scattered throughout all narrative levels of the first part, including Stendhal himself, anagrammatically, in a certain Professor Shetland. The first line of every chapter in the manuscript mirrors the first line of the corresponding chapter in *La Chartreuse*. What Salini cannot notice, however, is that this conceit continues through the second half of the novel, Salini's own story, which retains the intertextual link.

Unlike the other crime metafictions mentioned earlier, *"53 jours"* wraps up its mystery with a satisfying and complex solution, which Salini works out by reading intertextually between *53 jours* and *La Chartreuse de Parme*. Key to the mystery is the Stendhalian line, "Un Roman est un Miroir qui se Promène le Long de la Route",[2] which is taken very literally in the novel, as the various narrative levels offer mirror images of the same story, redistributing the roles of killer, victim, accomplice and *pigeon* across a corresponding cast of characters at each level. The outermost level flirts with reality as it presents us with a certain GP or Georges Perec (this part of the story exists in note form only) hired by the villains to write the *53 jours* manuscript. More seriously, the trail leads to what seem to be references to a real wartime massacre of resistance fighters at the Chartreuse massif, once again encoding historical trauma at the heart of the textual play as Perec did in both *La Disparition* and *W ou le souvenir d'enfance*.

"53 jours" is a paragon of crime metafiction first and foremost because it does not hold the genre at arm's length. Other literary metafictions on the crime genre often appear anxious to ensure the reader does not mistake them for crime fiction proper, employing knowing parody of genre stereotypes, as we find in Dürrenmatt, Auster, Butor, Murakami, Ishiguro and Robbe-Grillet, who advertise their ironic stance and require a reading in the second degree. In *"53 jours"* there is neither a country house nor a West-Coast gumshoe in sight: all of Perec's invented crime fictions are recognizable genre homages, but are fresh and original in their characters, settings and plots, even, with *La Crypte*, giving a remarkably prescient foretaste of Scandi-noir three decades before it became fashionable. Rather than distinguishing itself from the genre, the novel positively encourages us to read its various narrative levels as detective stories, and the textual analyses engaged in by the various

readers-in-the-text are those of typical crime-fiction aficionados, testing hypotheses, worrying at plot-holes. This is crime writing about crime writing, an exploration of the genre on its own terms, rather than a hostile deconstruction to mock its "naïve" faith in truth and reason or its "simplistic" teleology of structure, in the manner of the *nouveaux romanciers*.

Perec enjoyed crime fiction, and discussed its relationship to his own literary concerns in an interview shortly before embarking on the *"53 jours"* project:

> En tant que producteur de fiction, le roman policier continue de m'intéresser, et de me concerner, dans la mesure où il fonctionne explicitement comme un jeu entre un auteur et un lecteur, un jeu dont les intrications de l'intrigue, le mécanisme du meurtre, la victime, le coupable, le détective, le mobile, etc., sont ouvertement les pions: cette partie qui se joue entre un écrivain et son lecteur et dont les personnages, les décors, les sentiments, les péripéties ne sont que des fictions renvoyant au seul plaisir de lire (d'être intrigué, ému, séduit, etc.) est pour moi un des modèles les plus efficaces du fonctionnement romanesque.
>
> (Perec and Sidanier 1979, 10)

The comment shows the connection between the crime fiction of *"53 jours"* and the word games, jigsaws, chess problems and mathematical puzzles that inspire so much of Perec's other writing. Perec's fascination with crime fiction is not for its exploration of violence, nor for the moral questions it raises, and most definitely not for its representation of social disorder and real-world law enforcement. Crime fiction is a game and a puzzle, with the internal battle of wits between the culprit and detective mirrored extra-textually by the writer as puzzle-setter and the reader as the solver. *"53 jours"* encodes this vision of the genre into its own story at two points: most obviously, in the final-line revelation of "Georges Perec" as central to the Salini murder plot (a self-referential trick also employed in *La Disparition*), but also in one of the deepest levels of the nested narrative, where the author of *Le Juge est l'assassin*, Laurence Wargrave, is named after the culprit of Agatha Christie's *And Then There Were None* (1939).

While Perec's novel is by no means a conventional work of crime fiction, it stands apart from other literary metafictions by its retention and celebration of the genre's pleasures of game-playing and puzzle-solving. *Nouveaux romanciers* like Butor and Robbe-Grillet express a pessimistic epistemology by setting up a mystery, only to have the complexity and randomness of their worlds frustrate any "naïve" expectation on the reader's part that it might be satisfactorily resolved, and similar procedures are evident in Ishiguro, Auster and Dürrenmatt. The unravelling of an intricate and coherent plot, with unexpected twists, hidden clues and surprise revelations, is prized within the genre but undervalued among literary writers, who, since modernism, have been able to advertise their adherence to high-culture values precisely through their disdain for such matters.

Perec makes use of crime fiction's puzzle-plotting to create a rhapsody on the genre-fiction theme, in which crime-fiction intrigues lead first inwards, then outwards, through the *roman à tiroirs* itself. Sidney Lévy has suggested that the network of interrelated stories is characterized by "emergence", a concept from nineteenth-century philosophy more recently adopted by cognitive science to describe the phenomenon in which "interesting, non-centrally-controlled behaviour ensues as a result of the interaction of multiple simple components within a system" (Clark 1997, 108). Lévy suggests that "reading for Perec is a bottom-up, top-down emergent phenomenon where, from a linear succession of elements, emerges an organization, which in turn determines the elements" (Lévy 2004, 44–45), and links this to Perec's appreciation of the structures of free jazz, which, as Perec says in interview, balance internal disruption with "operators of unity" such as repetition and quotation (1993, 63). This is certainly a plausible approach to a novel in which the whole is very much more than the sum of its parts: each of the nested crime fictions may be clever and entertaining in its own right, but it is the dizzying imbrication of narratives that bewilders and delights. David Gascoigne draws attention to the "frame games" the novel plays between its various levels of fictionality. The "metalepses"—shifts between the nested stories—destabilize the reader's epistemological grounding in discerning the "truth" of a particular narrative, as an authoritative narratorial voice is retrospectively unmasked as itself a fictional creation with possibly criminal motivations to its narration. As Gascoigne puts it:

> What the "frame games" make evident is that these [conventional detective-story] distinctions between fictional "truth" and non-truth are dependent on the conventions of narrative, and in particular on the frame or context which is drawn around any particular version of events. To change the frame is also to change the rules of the truth/non-truth game, and in consequence to draw attention to the relativity and potential instability of any given narrative. (2006, 294–95)

These shifts themselves are subject to deliberate destabilization, for instance through the use of the same name for characters on three different levels of diegesis, or vagaries in tense, style and amount of detail which serve to obscure the reported or quoted status of the passage we are reading.

This blurring of levels, which confuses reality and fiction, readers and investigators, authors and criminals, finally serves to make of the novel what Bernard Magné has dubbed "une sorte de mise-en-scène de la lecture intertextuelle" (1990, 185), as the connections spread outwards beyond the nested stories into "real" detective stories by other authors and Perec's own wider *œuvre*,[3] and thence into the master-intertext of Stendhal's *Chartreuse de Parme*, and beyond that into Perec's own life and his troubled wartime childhood. The "unfathomably complex hedges of self-inscription" (Bellos 1993, 700) of the novel serve not only to bring the seriousness of personal trauma and historical atrocity into what might otherwise seem a frivolous exercise, but also to merge life and art, reality and fiction, in a way that brings our own activity to our attention, as we sit with Perec's novel in our hands. The choice of crime fiction as the medium for such a meditation as this is not an arbitrary one. Perec is interested in a very particular kind of reading associated with the genre, one which attends closely for hidden clues, dismantles structures to reassemble them in hypothetical sequences of events, and creates its own crime story from the materials available in the story of the investigation. Crime fiction is not only a story about a story, it is a story woven around an absent story, spurring the reader to fill the gaps with their own creative imagining of the solution. Perec's novel is built on this creative reading, his characters are creative readers, whose wavering hypotheses encourage the actual reader to out-think them and build their own stories from the clues in the text. It's a tragedy that Perec's untimely death left the book unfinished, but it's a smaller tragedy than most unfinished works: Perec's gaps are the reader's opportunity to follow in the footsteps of the readers-in-the-text and complete the story by themselves.

Notes

[1] I explore Perec's relationship with crime fiction in more detail in *Defective Inspectors: Crime Fiction Pastiche in Late-Twentieth-Century French Literature* (Kemp 2006).
[2] "Un R est un M qui se P le L de la R" is the title of the unfinished second half of Perec's novel, and refers to a mysterious message found on a slip of paper in the manuscript of *53 jours*. The second half of the story was to include various attempts by the detective to solve the riddle, such as "un Rhinocéros est un Monsieur qui se Prive le Luxe de la Résistance", before revealing its solution in the (mis)quotation from Stendhal.

[3] To offer just one among many possible examples of intertextuality between *"53 jours"* and Perec's other work, *Le Juge est l'assassin*, with the same author and plot, made its first appearance in *La Vie mode d'emploi* as a character's bedtime reading, where it is referred to as "un roman policier de Laurence Wargrave, *Le Juge est l'assassin*: X a tué A de telle façon que la justice, qui le sait, ne peut l'inculper. Le juge d'instruction tue B de telle façon que X est suspecté, arrêté, jugé, reconnu coupable et exécuté sans avoir jamais rien pu faire pour prouver son innocence" (Perec 1978, 334–35).

Works cited

Bellos, David. 1993. *Georges Perec: A Life in Words*. London: Harvill.

Clark, Andy. 1997. *Being There: Putting Brain, Body and World Together Again*. Cambridge, MA: MIT Press.

Dangy, Isabelle. 2006. "Du roman comme machine à égarer les soupçons: '*53 jours*' de Georges Perec." In *Les Supercheries littéraires et visuelles, la tromperie dans la culture française*, edited by Catherine Emerson and Maria Scott, 159–74. Bern: Peter Lang.

Decout, Maxime. 2012. "*« 53 jours »* de Georges Perec: la génétique, mode d'emploi." *Littérature* 168: 43–55.

Gascoigne, David. 2006. *The Games of Fiction: Georges Perec and modern French ludic narrative*. Berne: Peter Lang.

Genette, Gérard. 1982. *Palimpsestes: la littérature au second degré*. Paris: Seuil.

Kemp, Simon. 2006. *Defective Inspectors: Crime Fiction Pastiche in Late-Twentieth-Century French Literature*. Oxford: Legenda.

Lévy, Sidney. 2004. "Emergence in Georges Perec." *Yale French Studies* 105: 36–55.

Magné, Bernard. 1990. "'53 jours': pour lecteurs chevronnés ..." *Études littéraires* 23: 185-201.

Neefs, Jacques and Jacques Roubaud. 1990. "Récit et langue, à propos de *53 jours* de Georges Perec." *Littérature* 80: 95–100.

Perec, Georges. 1978. *La Vie mode d'emploi*. Paris: Hachette.

—. 1989. *"53 jours."* Edited by Harry Mathews and Jacques Roubaud. Paris: POL.

—. 1993. "La Chose." *Magazine littéraire* 316: 55–63.

Perec, Georges and Jean-Marie Le Sidanier. 1979. "Entretien avec Jean-Marie Sidanier." *L'Arc* 76: 10.

Todorov, Tzvetan. 1971. "Typologie du roman policier." In *Poétique de la prose*, 55–65. Paris: Seuil.

CHAPTER ELEVEN

FINISHINGS OFF:
MURDER À LA MALET IN SIMSOLO'S
LES DERNIERS MYSTÈRES DE PARIS

AMY WIGELSWORTH

Il faut toujours terminer ce que l'on a commencé, même si c'est un autre qui s'en charge ! (Simsolo 2002, 11)

The hypertextual category of "continuation", predicated as it is, according to Gérard Genette (1982), on the completion of an unfinished work, seems an especially apt one to form the basis of our discussion in this concluding chapter.[1] Drawing on a literary and a musical example of posthumous continuation, namely Baro's continuation of D'Urfé's *L'Astrée* and Süssmayr's continuation of Mozart's *Requiem* (1982, 223–27), Genette explains how important it is that a continuation conform to the design of the original author:

l'hypertexte doit rester constamment dans le prolongement de son hypotexte, qu'il doit seulement mener jusqu'à une conclusion prescrite ou congruente, en veillant à la continuité de certaines données comme la disposition des lieux, l'enchaînement chronologique, la cohérence des caractères, etc. Le continuateur travaille donc sous le contrôle constant d'une sorte de scripte intérieure, qui veille à l'unité de l'ensemble et à l'imperceptibilité des raccords. (1982, 224)

Genette describes continuations which do not observe the congruity and the conclusion prescribed by the hypotext as "infidèles, voire meurtrières" (1982, 271). And yet he also hints at the seemingly contradictory imperatives at play in any continuation, his reference to "ce privilège du génie qu'est une continuation *imprévisible*" (1982, 283, my emphasis) a clear acknowledgement of the value of innovative and unpredictable elements which, far from being precluded by the conservative, conformist agenda, can in fact rescue the continuation from a descent into banality. The obvious, and yet problematic, equilibrium to be struck, between conformity and closure on the one hand, and innovation and open-endedness on the other, takes on a new resonance in Noël Simsolo's *Les Derniers mystères de Paris* (2002). When an enigmatic serial killer commits murders in a series of Parisian *arrondissements*, bookseller Pierre de Gondol is enlisted to help solve the case and realizes that the crimes are based on Léo Malet's *Les Nouveaux mystères de Paris.*[2] The criminal investigation is thus transformed into a literary research project, made all the more fascinating by the fact that Malet's series of novels was left unfinished. The assumption that Malet's *œuvre* can be subjected to a palimpsestuous completion by the serial killer is an intriguing one. The idea that crime, like popular fiction, follows a pre-existing formula and, as such, can be continued and completed by the criminal, and predicted by the bookseller-cum-detective, is offset by the degree to which crimes, and crime narratives, are characterized by disorder, surprise and a pervading sense of mystery, all of which come to dominate the diegesis as the murderer's design becomes more convoluted and the links to Malet more tenuous.

In attempting to determine the significance of this novel, I will begin by exploring the Romantic analogy between art and murder and demonstrate how the affinity between serial narratives and serial murders is a particularly compelling one. I will then explore the relationship of Simsolo's novel, to conformity and closure on the one hand, and to innovation and open-endedness on the other. Umberto Eco refers to this binary in terms of "the 'modern' dialectic between order[3] and innovation" (1990, 96). Finally, I will show how these two, apparently contradictory, impulses are reconciled in this novel which, I will argue, exemplifies Eco's radical, postmodern aesthetics of the serial.

"On Murder, Considered as One of the Fine Arts"

In 1827, and in the context of a growing interest in aesthetic, as opposed to religious or moral, approaches to crime, Thomas De Quincey published a satirical essay proposing an analogy between art and murder. "On Murder, Considered as One of the Fine Arts" contended that:

> one murder is better or worse than another in point of good taste. Murders have their little differences and shades of merit as well as statues, pictures, oratorios, cameos, intaglios, or what not. (De Quincey 2004 [1827])

By positing an equivalence between the law-breaking criminal and the ground-breaking artist,[4] De Quincey crystallized the anxiety provoked by the Romantic emphasis on pioneering individuality and originality, and its concomitant rejection of classical models. The appeal of the analogy has endured, with serial murder seeming to lend itself particularly well to the comparison with art. Philip L. Simpson writes of a "near-obsessive linkage of serial murder to art" (2000, 22) and explains that:

> [the] contemporary narrative obsession with serial murder [...] substitutes repetition for creativity, pattern for design, and the spilled blood of corpses for paints. (2000, 18)

The "modernist concept of 'high art'" has co-opted De Quincey's "murder as fine art" to create what Simpson terms a "metadiscursive culture". The serial killer becomes an "artist manqué" (2000, 23), who struggles to impose a "private and romantic vision" but, blighted by isolation and lack of appreciation, fails repeatedly in his endeavour.[5] In *Les Derniers mystères*, we learn of the testicular cancer, and consequent impotence, of killer Jean Dupont, as his background is uncovered, and of his reaction to a series of crimes committed by a fellow-sufferer. On his deathbed, Aumère confesses to having murdered three translators in the first, second and third *arrondissements*, a feat which Dupont resolves to better:

> Ses crimes n'avaient rien du chef-d'œuvre et il me fallait établir un dispositif qui soit susceptible de faire œuvre d'art avec les suivants. Mais d'autres tueurs en série avaient déjà procédé de la sorte. Tableaux vivants en relation avec les sept péchés capitaux, les douze apôtres ou les 36 positions sexuelles. Je devais trouver mieux et m'inspirai alors de la série des *Nouveaux Mystères de Paris*, écrite par l'original Léo Malet.
> (Simsolo 2002, 227)

Playing on the traditional analogy between paternity and authorship, the sexual handicap of both Aumère and Dupont is an unmistakable echo of their artistic impotence.

The relationship of serial murder to serial narrative is a particularly interesting one. Simpson's failed "artist", tirelessly churning out imperfect versions of his would-be *chef-d'œuvre*, can be likened to the writer sold out to popular culture and obliged to produce a steady stream of mediocre potboilers or serials to fund his loftier literary aspirations. Serial form also provides an apposite echo of diegetic content. Simpson finds the roots of this echo in folklore, explaining that:

folklore, essentially verbal in nature, considers repetition of key images and phrases a vital structural component to begin with, and so finds a metaphoric parallel to a series of murders. W.F.H. Nicolaisen professes that counting is equivalent to narrating in the European mind-set ([1989] 77–89): an applicable concept to explain the kinship between multicide and narrative. (2000, 3)

Invoking Richard Dyer (1997), Simpson goes on to observe that "[t]he serial killer's commodification possibilities are virtually limitless" and, as such, "the serial killer is a natural character type for a modern media based on the pleasure of seriality" (2000, 22). Eliot Borenstein notes the same felicitous coincidence of form and content, observing that:

[s]erial narrative provides a comfortable home for the serial killer. What could be more dismal and horrifying then [sic] the story of a bloody, violent murder? An endless story where each gruesome killing is followed by an even more appalling atrocity. (2007, 115)

Accustomed as we are to the insistent association of serial murder and art, our reading of Simsolo's *Derniers mystères* is inevitably a cautious and self-conscious one. At times, the metadiegetic implications are subtle, to say the least, as in the following example, in which *commissaire* Yèble (the official detective to Gondol's amateur sleuth) notes an apparent change in the murders: "Avec elle, c'est une autre *série* qui commence. Nous ne savions alors pas si c'était *l'œuvre* du même type […]" (41, my emphases). The association becomes more pronounced as the novel progresses. Gondol is initially unaware of the literary *source* of the murders, mistaking it for literary *potential*:

Les propos de Yèble me revenaient à l'esprit. Un tueur s'attaquait aux putes parisiennes. « L'étrangleur des filles du minitel rose. » Un titre idéal pour un polar bien sanglant. Déjà, onze victimes. Dans onze différents arrondissements de Paris. Le sixième, le quatorzième, le dixième, le huitième, le seizième, le treizième, le quinzième, le neuvième, le douzième, le cinquième et le troisième. Un ordre qui me rappelait quelque chose. Mais quoi ? (Simsolo 2002, 49)

A series of books, cultural artefacts and other objects referring to Malet's life and work are used as accessories and clues to the murders. For example, a copy of Daphne du Maurier's *Rebecca* left at the scene of one of the murders provides a link to Malet's *Du rébecca rue des Rosiers*, while a victim poisoned with bleach is a nod to *Les Eaux troubles de Javel*. After realizing that the crimes are based on Malet's work, Gondol praises the murderer's mental aptitude, while bemoaning the fact that he has chosen to work with "still life" (the equivalent French term is, fittingly, "nature morte"), rather than settling for crime fiction as the showcase for his clever intertextual referencing:

> Je me mis à potasser *Les Nouveaux Mystères de Paris* et déduisis sans trop de peine que l'assassin de Marie Torma s'en était inspiré. Ce mec avait la fibre sacrément oulipopoupienne. Dommage pour la gent femelle qu'il soit du genre à s'adonner aux tableaux vivants avec nature morte plutôt qu'à se plaire à rédiger de simples romans policiers aux multiples références. (Simsolo 2002, 75–76)

This insistent and, increasingly, explicit linkage of serial murder to art (and to serial forms in particular) has important implications for our reading of the text. We find ourselves obliged to acknowledge that this is perhaps a novel less about serial murder per se and more about the questions raised by serial fiction itself. It is to these questions, and in particular to the dialectic between order and closure on the one hand, and disorder and open-endedness on the other, that I now turn.

The Sense of an Ending: conformity, closure and order

Etymologically, notions of success and completion are closely linked. The Oxford English Dictionary tells us that the English "achieve", for example, has its roots in the Anglo-Norman *aschever* and the Anglo-Norman, Old and Middle French *achever*, *achiever* or *achiver*, meaning to complete or accomplish (a task, etc.). Frank Kermode explored the literary implications of the human fascination with completion in *The Sense of an Ending* (1967), arguing that, since we are born and die *in media res*, we require "fictions" or "coherent patterns" to provide or imply endings. Teleology and eschatology are part of a fictive order (Kermode also refers to "form", "structure", "rationality" and, echoing the links made by Northop Frye between literature and mathematics, a "mystical geometry") which provides a comforting antidote to real chaos.[6]

The need for conclusion, even in the form of catastrophic apocalypse, is keenly felt throughout *Les Derniers mystères*. When Madame Quentin (whose murder Gondol will later discover when delivering an order to her home, drawing him further into the case), looks for a gift for her lover, her reaction to the news that Gondol doesn't have what she is looking for is somewhat exaggerated:

Son minois se chiffonnait. Des larmes perlaient de ses yeux. Sa main se
posa sur son front pour ponctuer le terrible malheur qui l'envahissait.
–Quelle catastrophe ! (Simsolo 2002, 26)

This prompts the wry narratorial observation that "Chacun voit
l'apocalypse où il peut." Later, as the novel gathers pace and Yèble and
Gondol rush through torrential rain in an effort to stop Jean Dupont
committing another murder, a gleeful tramp declares from his shelter:
"Messieurs, c'est la fin du monde !" (175). References to apocalypse are
also, almost certainly, an acknowledgement of the self-conscious
palimpsesting at work in Simsolo's text. Sarah Dillon explains that both
phenomena are characterized by a curious coexistence of destructive and
creative impulses:

> Palimpsesting and apocalypse are processes of partial destruction - the
> trace of the erased text remains in the palimpsest, certain of God's chosen
> people remain in the new age - that enable creation. (2007, 79)[7]

The emphasis on endings is just one way of demarcating, and thereby
harnessing, time. Beginnings are almost as important, most notably in the
form of regular customer Féodor Atkine's curious request to
Gondol, repeated throughout the novel, that he scour the annals of
literature in order to provide an answer to the question "Mais où sont les
neiges d'antan?", famously posed by fifteenth-century poet and criminal
François Villon:

> Le comédien m'avait demandé de lui retrouver les neiges d'antan si chères
> à François Villon. [...]
> –J'ai déjà relu *Les Neiges du Kilimandjaro* et *La Neige en deuil*, dis-je
> à l'acteur. Sans aucun succès. Pas un flocon du passé ne subsiste sur ces
> neiges éternelles. J'espère obtenir de meilleurs résultats avec *Pavillon de
> neige*, *Le Chevalier des neiges* et *La Classe de neige*. (33–34)

In fact, many of Gondol's literary "enquêtes" involve attempts to
divide narrative time into manageable portions, identifying origins,
sequences and specific periods of time within various novels, as Yèble's
teasing of him attests:

> Sur quoi tu enquêtes en ce moment ? La vie de Javert entre sa jeunesse au
> bagne et sa seconde rencontre avec Jean Valjean ? La petite enfance de
> Dorian Gray ? L'identité réelle du professeur Faustroll ? Les derniers jours
> de Des Esseintes ? Le huitième péché capital ? (45)

The preoccupation with harnessing time is linked, as in Kermode, to a more general preoccupation with order and predictability. After an argument with his actress girlfriend, Iris,[8] Gondol considers going back with champagne to apologize, and imagines the denouement his actions, coupled with her characteristic thespian posturing, would surely produce:

> il y aurait la réconciliation sur le palier, avec des regards de tragédienne classique. Une ou deux citations piquées à Marivaux ou à Bernstein. Tout un cirque avant le baiser voluptueux et le radada sur la moquette. (75)

Theatrical allusions sum up particularly well the balance between familiarity, or repetition,[9] and variation, which is at the heart of all hypertextual transformation. The relationship between a single dramatic text and the numerous possible interpretations of it is clearly analogous to the relationship between a hypotext and the hypertextual transformations it inspires.

The sense of order and predictability reflects the organization of the serial murders, modelled on "la grille Léo Malet" (83 and 125). The foregrounding of Malet's hypotext is underlined by the mischievous decision of Simsolo's publisher to wrap a misleading, bright red "bande publicitaire", announcing "LÉO MALET", around an unassuming grey and blue book cover, so that the real author's name fades into the background. Gondol realizes that the names of the victims are linked to the number of the *arrondissement* in which they have been murdered:

> j'ai remarqué la première lettre du nom ou du pseudonyme des victimes. Elle correspond chaque fois au numéro de l'alphabet en rapport à celui de chaque arrondissement. D. pour Dora dans le quatrième. E. pour Eva dans le cinquième. Etc., etc. (84–85)

The patterns are not merely precise, but self-consciously so, with the murderer deliberately leaving "une clef plus facile que les autres" in the fourth *arrondissement*: "[p]our qu'on puisse bien identifier son projet" (84). The killer's sense of design persists, somewhat incongruously, into the final four *arrondissements*, for which Malet has set no precedent. Increasingly tenuous links, to the author's lesser-known works, point to the fragility of the design:

> –Ce gus continue la série en s'appuyant toujours sur Malet. Il frappera dans les quatre derniers arrondissements.
> –En improvisant, vu que tu m'as dit que les romans n'existaient pas.
> –Ce n'est pas le genre à improviser. Bien trop maniaque pour ça. [...]
> [J]e suis certain que, pour ses prochaines exécutions, il va se baser sur des

indices qui sont éparpillés un peu partout dans les autres bouquins de Léo Malet. [...] (108)

The apparent order becomes, in itself, a source of disquiet. Gondol points out that the regularity of the attacks should allow them to plan ahead and protect potential victims, but his lack of conviction is premonitory: "–S'il suit son rythme d'un meurtre chaque mois, tu as le temps d'organiser des planques et des protections, ajoutai-je sans trop y croire" (109).

An open book: innovation, open-endedness, disorder

There is, needless to say, a school of thought diametrically opposed to that of Kermode and his fellow advocates of closure and order. Genette explains that incompleteness is sometimes a defining feature of a text, giving the example of Marivaux's *La Vie de Marianne*, in which "l'inachèvement [...] est [...] la vérité de l'œuvre" (1982, 239). He refers to "le respect, sinon le culte, voué à l'inachèvement" (235) and notes the growing respect for unfinished works since the nineteenth century (225). He points out the fundamental contradiction at the heart of all continuations: "on ne peut achever l'inachevé sans trahir, au moins, ce qui lui est parfois essentiel – l'inachèvement, bien sûr" (241–42). De Quincey makes similar remarks about the unfinished design of one of the murders he evokes:

> There was [...] an unfinished design of Thurtell's for the murder of a man with a pair of dumb-bells, which I admired greatly; it was a mere outline, that he never completed; but to my mind it seemed every way superior to his chief work. I remember that there was great regret expressed by some amateurs that this sketch should have been left in an unfinished state: but there I cannot agree with them; for the fragments and first bold outlines of original artists have often a felicity about them which is apt to vanish in the management of the details. (De Quincey 2004 [1827])

Disorder, much like incompleteness, has its advocates. Kermode is particularly critical of Morse Peckham who, in *Man's Rage for Chaos* (1965), attempts to establish an identification of art with disorder. The dialectic is echoed in Simsolo's novel where, despite the ostensibly rigorous plan of the serial killer, chaos and contingency are ever present. Note the coexistence of order and disorder in the following quotation, in which we see the full irony of the serial killer's meticulous adherence to

Malet's "plan", which in fact saw him abandon his treatment of the *arrondissements* by numerical order:

> –L'ordre dans lequel l'assassin choisit les arrondissements parisiens où il tue, c'est exactement celui de la parution des *Nouveaux Mystères de Paris* de Léo Malet, à partir du quatrième volume. [...] En 1954, il entreprend d'écrire des enquêtes de son détective de choc qui se déroulent chacune dans un arrondissement de Paris. La première est parue en décembre de cette année chez Robert Laffont : *Le Soleil naît derrière le Louvre*. Les deux mois suivants, il traite du deuxième et du troisième dans *Des kilomètres de linceuls* et puis *L'Ours et la Poupée*, un ouvrage réédité ensuite sous le titre de *Fièvre au Marais*. Deux mois passent avant que la série reprenne, mais Léo Malet abandonne alors l'ordre numérique et continue sa série dans le désordre. Les VI, XIV, X, VIII, XVI, XIII, XV, IX, XII, V, IV, XVII paraissent encore jusqu'en février 1959. Arrondissements où ton tueur a sévi dans ce même ordre.
> (Simsolo 2002, 78–79)

As Gondol explains why he thinks that Dupont's final killing will be different to the others ("La touche finale ne peut être une victime comme les autres" (219)), Yèble forces him to admit the random quality of the literary and, by extension, real-life enigmas with which they are grappling:

> –Si je te comprends bien, j'ai beaucoup plus besoin de chance que de ton art à dénicher les énigmes dans les textes littéraires ?
> –J'en ai bien peur. (219)

The pervading sense of disorder has a significant effect on temporality. In line with Gondol's fears, Dupont soon abandons his monthly schedule and the murders become more frequent. As the case takes on a new urgency, Gondol's sleep patterns are disrupted. He works through the night, fearful that the killer could strike again at any time (141), then later falls asleep surrounded by his work: "Le sommeil m'avait saisi en plein travail et je m'étais endormi sur les romans de Léo Malet" (157).

A series of odd meteorological phenomena reinforces the impression of warped temporality. First, a "canicule hivernale" (158) descends on the capital:

> Un magnifique soleil contredisait toujours la logique des saisons. Quelques femmes portaient des robes d'été avec décolletés révélateurs et jambes plutôt découvertes. Pas si désagréable en la matière, le dérèglement météorologique. Sauf pour un père Noël qui transpirait sous sa barbe de coton. (77–78)

News kiosks report the absence of snow in mountain resorts, reminding Gondol of his quest, on behalf of Atkine, for the evanescent "neiges d'antan" (Simsolo 2002, 78), and the heat continues into the new year: "Les fêtes de fin d'année se déroulèrent sous un chaud soleil tropical" (101).

The unseasonal heatwave is followed by a period of exceptionally heavy rainfall, which gives rise to an abundance of aquatic images. Gérard Louvert, a cinema enthusiast who helps Gondol with his investigations, wearing "un grand ciré de pêcheur breton et des bottes en caoutchouc" is likened to "un marin égaré" (159). Serge, one of Gondol's regular clients, enters the bookshop "laissant des mares ruisselantes sur le sol et s'ébrouant comme un phoque en pestant comme un fou", declaring :

> –Temps de merde. Les bouquinistes des quais ne vont pas ouvrir. Et si ça continue demain samedi, on fera du ski nautique sur les marchés aux puces. (160)

Flooding ensues:

> L'eau débordait du caniveau et inondait en partie les trottoirs de la ville. On entendait la sirène des voitures de pompiers. Les soldats du feu devaient s'occuper de toute la flotte répandue dans les caves. (167)

Those working on the serial killer case are dismissive of pronouncements of a watery apocalypse:

> À quelques mètres de la librairie, un clochard réfugié sous un porche nous interpella.
> –Messieurs, c'est la fin du monde !
> Yèble lui jeta une poignée de pièces de monnaie et accéléra le pas. (175)

Yèble's reaction to the tramp's warning is significant in that the threat of impending conclusion is dismissed via an offer of money, in much the same way that a successful serial can be prolonged at the behest of an editor, working on behalf of a reading public, willing to pay an author or continuator.[10]

The water imagery would also appear to be a self-conscious nod to the intertextuality at work in Simsolo's novel. As Judith Still and Michael Worton explain, with reference to Quintilian's metaphor of liquefaction, liquid imagery is a particularly apt way of evoking the conflation of reading and writing activities and the transformation of the read into the written (1990, 7 and 32) which characterize intertextuality. What we write is "a pulped version of what we have read", and reading is "a performative act of criticism and interpretation" (1990, 7),[11] rather than an independent and passive act. Gondol struggles to protect his stock of books from the rain ("La pluie s'engouffra et je me hâtai de refermer l'huis afin que les bouquins restent intacts" (Simsolo 2002, 176)), but the intertextual "pulping" implied by the image is as inexorable as the rain is unrelenting. These images are all the more significant in light of the fact that Malet's *Nouveaux Mystères* is not the only series at stake in Simsolo's novel. *Les Derniers mystères* is itself part of Baleine's "Le Poulpe" series, a collective literary project inaugurated in the 1990s and an early manifestation of "fan fiction",[12] and specifically of a sub-group of titles within the list which have Pierre de Gondol as their central character. Just as Dupont seeks, via his crimes, to prolong the series initiated by Malet, so Simsolo contributes to the ongoing, collaborative depiction of the bookseller-detective, thus reinforcing De Quincey's analogy once again.[13]

In a final meteorological twist, a sudden drop in temperature sees the winter ice-cream men unceremoniously replaced by sellers of roasted chestnuts (192) and prompts the hitherto lethargic Gondol to return to his investigations:

> un froid glacial me réveilla avant l'aube. Le gel s'était formé sur les vitres. J'allumai le chauffage et repris la lecture de l'intégrale de Malet en songeant aux messages envoyés par le tueur. (191)

The arctic temperatures are also significant in drawing Gondol's attention, along with that of the reader, to the police officer assigned to follow him, whose efforts at discretion are continually thwarted by the extreme weather. His incognito is betrayed and ridiculed as he is beset by uncontrollable shivering (191) and a conspicuous blue face (192), succumbs to a debilitating cold, and takes a spectacular fall on the ice, landing against the bookshop window:

> Un terrible bruit nous fit tourner la tête vers la vitrine du magasin. C'était le flic chargé de ma surveillance qui en était la cause. Le pauvre type avait glissé sur le verglas et s'était cogné contre la devanture de la librairie. (203)

These slapstick moments in fact serve quite a serious purpose. With the reader, along with Gondol, repeatedly reminded that the bookseller is not only trailing Dupont, but is also being followed himself, he is invited to acknowledge the ironic similarities between the two characters. Here, it would seem that we are not dealing with "disorder" as such, but rather with a new and unsettling brand of order.[14] Troubling patterns, affinities and connections are made between supposedly antithetical categories. As Simpson puts it, "[t]he serial killer as metaphor collapses boundaries between good and evil, Left and Right, male and female, high art and kitsch" (2000, 19–20). Thus Gondol, despite his insistence that "Je ne suis pas flic, moi. J'enquête dans les bouquins. Jamais de réel" (Simsolo 2002, 46), is forced to acknowledge the *rapprochement* of literature and reality as his literary delving draws him deeper into the murder investigation and vice versa.

Similarly, an affinity between Yèble and the reader is suggested via the numerous descriptions of the *commissaire*'s increasingly voracious appetite (and, to some extent, that of Gondol and Iris as well). Gondol and Yèble meet regularly over food and drink "chez *Mario*" to discuss developments in the investigation. Initial, metaphorical references to gastronomy, such as "[le] goût de la vérité" (107), soon give way to descriptions of Yèble's apparently insatiable hunger. He ingests double portions of food (173), multiple bottles of alcohol (111), and is frequently described as speaking "la bouche pleine" (169 and 195). His appetite seems to peak at crucial, suspense-ridden junctures in the investigation and, as such, provides a clear echo of the metaphorical appetite of the avid "consumer" of popular fictions. The following example is a particularly striking one. As Yèble and Gondol wait for the galerie Oudin to open, in order to question the man from whom Dupont bought a photograph left on the body of one of his victims, Yèble devours numerous items of food and drink:

> Il attrapa le gros paquet de biscuits que j'avais entamé en l'attendant et en engloutit tout le contenu.
> –On va y aller ensemble, décréta-t-il après avoir vidé ma bouteille de jus d'orange sanguine.
> [...]
> Rue Quincampoix, la galerie n'était pas encore ouverte et Yèble décida de prendre patience dans un troquet où il dégusta une assiette de charcuterie arrosée d'un muscadet des plus corrects. (205)

As Gondol and Yèble arrive at Dupont's apartment, we see the *commissaire*, much like the serial reader, torn between immediate consumption and the postponement of satisfaction. He orders a sandwich to appease his appetite, and yet is happy to wait for reinforcements before entering Dupont's den, thus delaying the imminent discoveries: "– Attendons les renforts, décida Yèble en commandant un sandwich" (221).

As Simpson explains, drawing on Bakhtin's discussions of orality in carnivalesque folk culture (2000, 5 and 15), biting and eating are also activities frequently associated with the serial killer. Simile is used to suggest the monstrous nature of Yèble's appetite and thus posit a similarity between him and his criminal nemesis: "Il mangea comme un ogre en se léchant les babines et vida deux bouteilles de bourgogne" (111).

A scene towards the end of the novel in which Gondol is struck by the uncanny similarities between the serial killer's endeavours and his own points to the specific function of these surprising conflations of roles:

> J'arrêtai ma lecture, gêné de comprendre que le monstre enquêtait comme moi dans une œuvre littéraire, mais s'en inspirait ensuite pour créer une réalité macabre. (228)

The fact that Gondol interrupts his reading of Dupont's journal to digest this information ("J'arrêtai ma lecture [...]") is crucial. The troubling similarities, between characters and readers and between criminal and detectives, proposed by this novel invite us to adopt a critical distance when reading it. The deliberate blurring of ostensibly clear-cut polar opposites obliges us to pause, just like Gondol, and step back from the novel, so as to fully appreciate its metadiegetic implications.

Conclusion

In *Les Derniers mystères de Paris*, the serial killer narrative is used to explore the complexities inherent to serial form. The novel illustrates Eco's point that "seriality" and "repetition" do not preclude "innovation". On the contrary, we are dealing with an "inseparable scheme-variation knot, where the variation is no longer more appreciable than the scheme" (Eco 1990, 97–98). The reader is invited to adopt a critical stance in relation to the novel, and to recognize that what Eco terms "variation" (I have also used the terms "innovation" and "disorder") are, in fact, integral to "repetition" (or "order"), rather than their polar opposite. In this way, the reader is able to fully appreciate the incongruity of the task the serial killer has set himself. Given that the variations on the Malet theme are potentially infinite, providing a satisfactory conclusion to his work is an impossibility. The message is nowhere better summed up than in the novel's deliciously ambiguous title: these are, of course, not the *last* mysteries of Paris, but merely the *latest* in an ever expanding series.

Notes

[1] Note the distinction Genette makes between the continuation and the sequel (*suite*): "Lorsqu'une œuvre est laissée inachevée du fait de la mort de son auteur, ou de toute autre cause d'abandon définitif, la continuation consiste à l'achever à sa place, et ne peut être que le fait d'un autre. La suite remplit une tout autre fonction, qui est en général d'exploiter le succès d'une œuvre, souvent considérée en son temps comme achevée, en la faisant rebondir sur de nouvelles péripéties" (1982, 223). Genette goes on to argue that the continuation could be better described as an "allographic completion" and the sequel an "autographic prolongation" (1982, 284).

[2] The 2012 film "The Raven", based on a screenplay by Ben Livingston and Hannah Shakespeare, in which Edgar Allen Poe (played by John Cusack) pursues a serial killer whose crimes are based on Poe's work, has a strikingly similar premise. The film does not share the fascinating hypertextual dimension discussed here, however, and provoked largely unfavourable reactions from critics.

[3] Eco also uses the terms "repetition" and "scheme" (1990, 96 and 97).

[4] See also Simpson 2000, 22.

[5] Note the same comparison in the BBC's recent crime drama series "The Fall", in which DS Stella Gibson (Gillian Anderson) mocks the artistic pretensions of elusive serial killer Paul Spector (Jamie Dornan), only for him to voice his mistrust of art and the artificial character of the order it creates:

> GIBSON   How are you free? You're a slave to your desires. You have no control at all. You're weak. Impotent. You think you're some kind of artist, but you're not.
>
> SPECTOR   Art is a lie. Art gives the chaos of the world an order that doesn't exist.
>
> (episode 5/5, broadcast 9.00pm, 10 June 2013)

[6] For two important and insightful reviews of Kermode's seminal study, see Bersani 1967 and Webster 1974.

[7] Dillon explores the fascinating notion of "apocalyptic palimpsesting" with reference to Derrida (1984), who "argues that the possibility of literature is founded on precisely that which both the palimpsest and apocalypse represent - the non-possibility of remainderless destruction" (2007, 80), and Zamora (1988): "As Lois Parkinson Zamora notes, although in contemporary discourse apocalypse has come to be equated with the end of the world, in the biblical tradition apocalyptic narratives predict both the end of the world *and* the coming of a new age" (2007, 79).

[8] Atkine, we are told, is also an actor.

[9] Iris and Gondol's self-conscious play-acting reminds us of Genette's aforementioned "scripte intérieure" (1982, 224). See also Genette's discussion of Virgil's *Aeneid* as "un simple scénario que le travestisseur aurait pour tâche de développer" (1982, 81).

[10] Ponson du Terrail's *Rocambole* series provides what is perhaps the best-known example of such a manoeuvre. Ponson du Terrail's revival of his swashbuckling

hero after a three-year hiatus in *La Résurrection de Rocambole* (1865-66) came in direct response to overwhelming public demand.
[11] We are reminded, once again, of the particular aptness of the theatrical analogy for evoking the tension between repetition (adherence to a script) and variation (interpretation of that script) characteristic of hypertextual transformation.
[12] The project is discussed in some detail by Platten 2011, 203–11.
[13] The Baleine website (http://www.editionsbaleine.fr/9-Pierre-de-Gondol) lists nine other titles featuring the bookseller-detective: Jean-Bernard Pouy's *1280 âmes* (2000), Rémi Schultz's *Sous les pans du bizarre* (2000), Philippe Kerbellec's *La Montre du mède* (2001), Roland Brasseur's *Le Cinquante-quatrième jour* (2001), Jacques Vallet's *Sam suffit* (2001), Cédric Fabre's *La Pente si sage de la vie* (2001), Pierre Brasseur's *Hortense Harar Arthur* (2002), Gekko Hopman's *La Berceuse de Chihuahua* (2002) and Pelé and Prilleux's *La Parabole de la soucoupe* (2002).
[14] As Eco explains, "variability" is linked to "repetition" as much as it is to "innovation" (1990, 96).

Works cited

Bersani, Leo. 1967. "Variations On a Paradigm", *The New York Times* on the web <http://www.nytimes.com/books/00/06/25/specials/kermode-ending1.html> [accessed 25 July 2013].

Borenstein, Eliot. 2007. "To Be Continued: Death and the Art of Serial Storytelling." In *Overkill: Sex and Violence in Contemporary Russian Popular Culture*. Ithaca, NY, USA: Cornell University Press, 98–126.

De Quincey, Thomas. 2004 [1827]. "On Murder, Considered as One of the Fine Arts." In The Project Gutenberg EBook of Miscellaneous Essays, by Thomas de Quincey <http://www.gutenberg.org/files/10708/10708-8.txt> [accessed 25 July 2013].

Derrida, Jacques. 1984. "No apocalypse, not now (full speed ahead, seven missiles, seven missives)." Trans. Catherine Porter and Philip Lewis. *Diacritics* 14.2: 20–31.

Dillon, Sarah. 2007. *The Palimpsest*. London: Continuum.

Dyer, Richard. 1997. "Kill and Kill Again", *Sight and Sound* 7.9 (September 1997): 14–17.

Eco, Umberto. 1990. "Interpreting Serials." In *The Limits of Interpretation*. Indiana: Indiana University Press, 83–100.

Genette, Gérard. 1982. *Palimpsestes : la littérature au second degré*. Paris: Seuil.

Kermode, Frank. 1967. *The Sense of an Ending: Studies in the Theory of Fiction*. London, New York: Oxford University Press.

Malet, Léo. 2006 [1981–84]. *Nestor Burma. Les Nouveaux mystères de Paris (I)*. Paris: Robert Laffont, « Bouquins ».

—. 2006 [1982–84]. *Nestor Burma. Les Nouveaux mystères de Paris (II)*. Paris: Robert Laffont, « Bouquins ».

Nicolaisen, W. F. H. 1989. "Definitional Problems in Oral Narrative." In *The Questing Beast: Perspectives on Contemporary Legend IV*, edited by Gillian Bennett and Paul Smith, 77–89. Sheffield: Sheffield Academic P.

Peckham, Morse. 1965. *Man's Rage for Chaos: Biology, Behavior and the Arts*. U.S.: Schocken Books Inc.

Pierre de Gondol (Éditions Baleine, Le Poulpe) <http://www.editionsbaleine.fr/9-Pierre-de-Gondol> [accessed 25 July 2013].

Platten, David. 2011. *The Pleasures of Crime: Reading Modern French Crime Fiction*. Amsterdam – New York: Rodopi.

Ponson du Terrail, Pierre Alexis de. 1992. *Les Exploits de Rocambole*. Paris: Robert Laffont, « Bouquins ».

—. 1992. *La Résurrection de Rocambole*. Paris: Robert Laffont, « Bouquins ».

Simpson, Philip L. 2000. *Psycho paths: tracking the serial killer through contemporary American film and fiction*. Illinois: Southern Illinois University Press.

Simsolo, Noël. 2002 *Les Derniers mystères de Paris*. Paris: Baleine.

Still, Judith, and Michael Worton, eds. 1990. *Intertextuality: Theories and Practices*. Manchester and New York: Manchester University Press.

Webster, Richard. 1974. "New ends for old: Frank Kermode's The Sense of an Ending", *The Critical Quarterly* 16.4, December 1974: 311–24.

Zamora, Lois Parkinson. 1988. "Apocalyptic visions and visionaries in *The Name of the Rose*." In *Naming the Rose. Essays on Eco's* The Name of the Rose, edited by M. Thomas Inge, 31–47. Jackson and London: University Press of Mississippi.

CONTRIBUTORS

The Editors

Angela Kimyongür is Senior Lecturer in French in the School of Languages, Linguistics and Cultures at the University of Hull. Her research interests lie in the intersections between literature, politics and history. She has published two monographs on the novels of communist writer Louis Aragon: *Socialist Realism in Louis Aragon's* Le Monde réel (University of Hull Press, 1995) and *Politics and Memory: Representations of War in the Work of Louis Aragon* (Wales University Press, 2007). More recently, her interests have refocused on contemporary French crime fiction and the ways in which the genre is used as a vehicle for the exploration of socio-political issues. Recent publications in this area include "Crime in popular fiction: Remembering the Algerian War of Independence in contemporary French crime fiction", *Australasian Journal of Popular Culture* (2014) and "Dominique Manotti and the *roman noir*", *Contemporary Women's Writing* (2013).

Amy Wigelsworth completed her PhD at Durham University in 2013. She is currently Lecturer in French at the Sheffield Business School (Sheffield Hallam University), and also teaches French at the University of York. She has published a number of articles on the nineteenth-century *mystères urbains*, including "*Au seuil des bas-fonds*: Footnotes in the *mystères urbains*", *Dix-Neuf* 16.3: 243–59. Her monograph, entitled *Rewriting* Les Mystères de Paris*: The* Mystères Urbains *and the Palimpsest*, will be published by Legenda in 2015. She works on nineteenth-century French popular fiction and French crime fiction.

Contributors

Adrienne Angelo is Associate Professor of French at Auburn University (USA). She specializes in contemporary women's writing in French literature and theories of life-writing, including autobiography, autofiction and the memoir. She is also interested in cinema, narratives of illness and crime fiction. Her recent publications include: "From Spectacle to Affect: Contextualizing Transgression in French Cinema at the Dawn of the

Twenty-First Century", *Irish Journal of French Studies*; "Wounded Women: Marina de Van's Subjective Cinema", *International Journal of Francophone Studies*; "Crime and Punishment: Calixthe Beyala's Manic Writing of *Femme nue, femme noire*" in *Rebelles, vilaines et criminelles chez les écrivaines d'expression française* edited by Frédérique Chévillot and Colette Trout, Amsterdam: Rodopi, 2013: 183–98; and "Réseau(x) identitaire(s) : La migration et la force 'électrique' dans le parcours littéraire de Nina Bouraoui" in *Frictions et devenirs dans les écritures migrantes au féminin: Enracinements et renégociations*, edited by Névine El-Nossery and Anna Rocca, Paris: Éditions universitaires européennes, 2011: 67–87.

Emma Bielecki is Lecturer in French Studies at Hertford College, Oxford. She is the author of articles on Champfleury, Daudet, and Flaubert, as well as the monograph *The Collector in Nineteenth-Century French Literature: Representation, Identity, Knowledge* (Peter Lang, 2012). Her current research project is on identification in *Belle Époque* crime serials, literary and cinematic, as part of which she has published an article entitled "Fantômas's Shifting Identities: From Books to Screen" in *Studies in French Cinema* 13.1 (March 2013).

Christine Calvet is Chief Administrative Officer of the IRPALL Institute (interdisciplinary research institute devoted to arts, literature and languages) at the University of Toulouse-Le Mirail, where she is also a teaching assistant. Her research area is mainly crime novels and thrillers (with special emphasis on Georges Simenon), along with their televisual and cinematographic adaptations. Her approach rests on contemporary linguistic and stylistic theories, with an intersemiotic perspective. Since 2002 she has also worked as a copy editor of the journal *Champs du Signe* at the Éditions Universitaires du Sud, where she is in charge of a volume entitled "Configurations urbaines et discours des récits policiers" (Éditions Universitaires du Sud, 2013).

Ellen Carter is a PhD student jointly enrolled at the University of Auckland, New Zealand, and the École des Hautes Études en Sciences Sociales in Paris. Her research centres on how cultural outsiders write, translate and read cross-cultural crime fiction.

Claire Gorrara is Professor of French Studies in the School of European Languages, Translation and Politics at Cardiff University. She has published widely in three fields: French women's writing, cultural memories of the Second World War and French crime fiction. Her major publications include *French Women's Writing and Representations of the Occupation in Post-68 France* (Macmillan, 1998), *The Roman Noir in Post-War French Culture: Dark Fictions* (Oxford University Press, 2003) and *French Crime Fiction and the Second World War: Past Crimes, Present Memories* (Manchester University Press, 2012). She is currently working on visual representations of war's end in the cases of the First and Second World Wars and has recently published an article on the war photography of Julia Pirotte and the Liberation of France with Dr Hanna Diamond (2012) "Reframing War: Histories and Memories of the Second World War in the Photography of Julia Pirotte", *Modern and Contemporary France* 20.4: 453–71.

Elise Hugueny-Léger is Lecturer in French at the University of St Andrews. Her main ongoing research interest is in the field of life-writing in twentieth and twenty-first century French literature. Her monograph on Annie Ernaux, entitled *Annie Ernaux, une poétique de la transgression*, was published in 2009. Her current book-length project examines the use and integration of media (especially television, cinema, and digital media) in contemporary autofiction in a corpus of authors including Angot, Beigbeder, Calle, Carrère, Delaume, Nothomb, and Toussaint. Recent publications include chapters and articles on life-writing in Camille Laurens; Annie Ernaux's *Les Années*; and Marguerite Duras's journalistic writings.

Simon Kemp is Tutorial Fellow in French at Somerville College, Oxford. He has written extensively on French crime fiction and its relationship to literary fiction, including a monograph, *Defective Inspectors: Crime Fiction Pastiche in Late-Twentieth-Century French Fiction* (Oxford: Legenda, 2006) and an edited volume with Martin Hurcombe, *Sébastien Japrisot: The Art of Crime* (Amsterdam: Rodopi, 2009). He is currently working on the representation of consciousness in French literature from Proust to Darrieussecq.

David Platten is Professor of French at the University of Leeds and is currently serving as Pro-Dean for Student Education in the Faculty of Arts. His published work reflects a wide range of interests in the sphere of modern and contemporary French fiction and film. His monograph, *The*

Pleasures of Crime: Reading Modern French Crime Fiction, which challenges the dichotomy between the polar and the literary mainstream, was published by Rodopi in 2011. Other single-authored books include *Michel Tournier and the Metaphor of Fiction* (Liverpool University Press, 1999) and *Philippe Djian* (University of Glasgow French and German Publications, 1995). He contributed a chapter on popular French cinema in *Imagining the Popular in Contemporary French Culture*, edited by Diana Holmes and David Looseley (Manchester University Press, 2012). David is currently looking at constructions of literary value and at cultural representations of sport. He is an active member of two research groups: the Leeds-based Popular Cultures Research Network and the Limoges-based Littératures Populaires et Cultures Médiatiques.

Alistair Rolls is Associate Professor of French Studies at the University of Newcastle, Australia. His recent publications in the area of French crime fiction include *Paris and the Fetish: Primal Crime Scenes* (Rodopi, 2013) and, with Deborah Walker, *French and American Noir: Dark Crossings* (Palgrave Macmillan, 2009). He is also the editor of *Mostly French: French (in) Detective Fiction* (Peter Lang, 2009).

Sophie Watt is Lecturer in French at the University of Sheffield. She studied history as an undergraduate at the University of Paris VII and holds a Masters Degree and an interdisciplinary PhD in Modern French History and Literature from the University of Iowa. She joined the Department of French at the University of Sheffield in 2011. Her research interests include the production and writing of history, discourse analysis, post-colonial theories of textuality and neocolonial historical inquiry and her work specifically analyses the construction of minority identities within the broader contours of French national identity and traces ethnic prejudices inherent in republican ideology and language. She is currently working on France's neocolonial practices and language in the French liberal press during French military interventions in former colonies such as Haiti and Mali. Her publications include: "Alexandre Arcady and the re-writing of French Colonial History in Algeria", in *France's Lost Empires: Fragmentation, Nostalgia, and* La Fracture Coloniale (Lexington Books, 2010); "A Comparative Analysis of Three 'Human' Exhibitions: The Semiotic Construction of the Jewish and Colonised subjects", in *The Essence and the Margin: National Identities and Collective Memories in Contemporary European Culture* (Amsterdam: Rodopi, 2009); and "The Discursive Construction of Minority Identities in Third Republic France: The 1937 Madagascar Plan, Exemplification of Republican Racism", in

The European Mind: Narrative and Identity (Malta University Press, 2008).

Andrew Watts is Lecturer in French at the University of Birmingham. His main research interest is in adaptations of nineteenth-century French prose fiction, with special reference to the work of Honoré de Balzac. He is the author of *Preserving the Provinces: Small Town and Countryside in the Work of Honoré de Balzac* (Peter Lang, 2007), and co-author (with Kate Griffiths, Cardiff) of *Adapting Nineteenth-Century France: Literature in Film, Theatre, Television, Radio and Print* (University of Wales Press, 2013). He is the co-editor (with Susan Harrow, Bristol) of *Mapping Memory in French Literature and Culture* (Rodopi, 2012) and (with Loïc Guyon, Limerick) of *Aller(s)-Retour(s): Nineteenth-Century France in Motion* (Cambridge Scholars Publishing, 2013). He has written numerous articles and book chapters on nineteenth-century French literature, and with Michelle Cheyne (University of Massachusetts-Dartmouth) has recently completed a critical translation of Balzac's early play *Le Nègre*, due for publication with Liverpool Online Series in spring 2014.

INDEX